WOMEN, STATE AND REVOLUTION

WOMEN, STATE AND REVOLUTION

Essays on Power and Gender in Europe since 1789

Edited by
SIÂN REYNOLDS

The University of Massachusetts Press
Amherst 1987

First published in the United States of America in 1987
by the University of Massachusetts Press
Box 429   Amherst Ma 01004

© 1986, Siân Reynolds (Introduction and Chapter 6), Irene
Coltman Brown (Chapter 1), Marcia Pointon (Chapter 2),
Michelle Perrot (Chapter 3), Beryl Williams (Chapter 4), Sybil
Oldfield (Chapter 5), Anne Stevens (Chapter 7), Ulrike Hanna
Meinhof (Chapter 8)

Printed in Great Britain

Library of Congress Cataloging-in-Publication Data

Women, state and revolution

   Bibliography: p.
   Includes index.
   1. Women in politics—Europe—History.   2 Women—
Europe—History.   3. Feminism—Europe—History.
I. Reynolds, Siân.
HQ1391.E85W66   1987   320'.088042   86-16074
ISBN 0-87023-552-4
ISBN 0-87023-553-2 (pbk.)   70671

Contents

Illustrations

Contributors

Irene Coltman Brown has taught at the universities of Chicago and Dar-es-Salaam, and was until recently Senior Lecturer at Birkbeck College, London. Her first book, *Private Men and Public Causes* (Faber, London, 1963) has recently been translated into German, and she is completing a history of the European tradition of political persuasion. She now lives in New York with her husband who is working at the United Nations.

Ulrike Hanna Meinhof teaches Applied Linguistics and German at the University of Sussex. Her publications include articles about language in a social context and (with Ruth Rach) a textbook for teaching German, and an edition of a German novel.

Sybil Oldfield teaches Literature and the History of Ideas at the University of Sussex and is the author of *Spinsters of This Parish* (Virago, London, 1984). She is also the grand-daughter of two of Germany's secret resisters.

Michelle Perrot is Professor of History at the University of Paris-VII: she has been closely concerned with the development of women's history in France. The most recent of her many publications is the edited collection, *Une Histoire des femmes est-elle possible?* (Rivages, Marseille, 1985) from which this essay is taken.

Marcia Pointon is Reader in the History of Art at the University of Sussex. She has published widely on nineteenth-century French and British painting, and her most recent book is *The Bonington Circle: English Watercolour and Anglo-*

French Landscape 1790–1855 (Hendon Press, Brighton, 1985).

Siân Reynolds teaches French History and Politics at the University of Sussex and has translated a number of books by French historians.

Anne Stevens has worked in the British Civil Service and now teaches Politics at the University of Sussex. She has published a number of articles and papers on public administration in Britain and France.

Beryl Williams is Reader in European History at the University of Sussex. She is co-editor with C. Abramsky of *Essays in Honour of E.H. Carr* (Macmillan, London, 1974) and is at present working on a book on the Russian Revolution of 1905.

Introduction

I have determined to set out for Paris in the course of a fortnight or three weeks; and I shall not now halt at Dover, I promise you; for I go alone – neck or nothing is the word. During my stay I shall not forget my friends; but I will tell you so when I am really there. Meantime let me beg you not to mix with the shallow herd who throw an odium on immutable principles, because some of the mere instruments of the Revolution were too sharp. – Children of any growth will do mischief when they meddle with edged tools.

The date is 12 November 1792, the writer Mary Wollstonecraft, about to leave for revolutionary Paris (quoted in Holmes, 1985, p. 90). This 'cheerful, daring, strangely modern' voice, as Richard Holmes calls it, came from a single woman in her thirties, intent on seeing for herself the centre of the seismic movement sending shock waves through Europe. Once in Paris, she admitted with characteristic honesty that she sometimes felt very frightened indeed as a woman alone at night in an echoing house. But Virginia Woolf wrote of Mary Wollstonecraft that the Revolution was 'not merely an event that had happened outside her; it was an active agent in her own blood. She had been in revolt all her life – against tyranny, against law, against convention' (Woolf, 1979, p. 98). Although her experience in Paris brought disillusion with the course taken by the Revolution, Mary Wollstonecraft did not abandon her faith in the 'immutable principles' such as reason and republican virtue which she had seen embodied in 1789. She did however regard them as values very largely alien to most women of her time, who had by their upbringing and culture been virtually trained to be the enemy in the city of human rights, as Irene Brown argues in Chapter 1 below.

It is with the historical relations between women and both political principles and political power in the broad sense, that the essays in this collection are concerned. They take the French Revolution as starting point and frequent reference, and their focus is European for deliberate reasons. Much of the best writing in English in the field variously known as women's studies or feminist studies, has been concerned with Britain and the United States. It is not always easy for readers without the appropriate languages to find information about continental European countries. Many of the chapters in this book draw on recent feminist scholarship and research in languages other than English. Even so, the range is necessarily restricted and the countries discussed here are essentially France, Germany, Russia and Britain. We still badly need translations or syntheses of work done in this area in other European countries.

If this collection does not set out to achieve total coverage, that is because its origins were in a set of lectures given at the University of Sussex in Spring 1985 and centred on a specific question: what, in a European context, have been the relations between women and power since 1789? The lectures all had to grapple with the same kind of problem. After almost twenty years of the continuous explosion which feminism has been causing in modes of thought, but when, in Britain and most other European countries at least, women's/feminist studies courses are still not routinely found on university syllabuses, how can one best attempt to re-think, for example, political history, intellectual history, art history, politics, media studies (to mention only the fields from which the contributors speak)? The lectures formally marked the introduction of several new women's studies courses to the European Studies syllabus in one university, but they are neither meant to be specialist nor aimed at a solely university audience. The debate continues, and is changing all the time, about the nature of separate women's/feminist studies courses. (The ambiguity about the term used is symptomatic.) Meanwhile women teaching in 'conventional' disciplines who would like to integrate the theories and findings of feminist research into their work are constantly confronted with the problem of how to do it (or sometimes how not to do it. Irene Brown warns against over-enthusiastic feminist views of Mary Wollstonecraft held by those who have not read what she wrote).

What we did was to take a central notion and to contribute from our different fields of study a number of essays — case studies — which tried to confront the problems in a way that would often not have been possible say, ten or even five years ago. Anyone who has worked in this field will know it changes bewilderingly quickly, not only because of new research but also because even those who think they have 'always' been feminists can find their perceptions shifting. The contributors would all describe themselves as feminists of one kind or another; they write in different tones of voice and with different commitments, but while their feminism is not identical it is broadly compatible. No chapter is written from a thoroughgoing radical feminist perspective for instance, though that is not to say that no one has benefited from the insights of radical feminism. And the contributors are all working teachers who have benefited, often greatly, from discussion with students, as well as with each other. The only chapter which did not originate in a lecture at Sussex was that by Michelle Perrot, which is translated with permission from a collection of essays *Une Histoire des femmes est-elle possible?* (1984) a book which has been at the centre of the debate about women's history in France. It is included for its central insights into the book's theme, and because it also gives English-speaking readers a chance to appreciate writing by a leading women's historian from continental Europe whose work is not widely available yet in translation.

* * * * *

The relation between women and politics — the state, the world of public power — has always been a problematic one. It has posed particular problems for feminism, as Huguette Bouchardeau has pointed out:

(The women's movement) sometimes defines itself as a struggle for equal rights in the political arena, with such striking — and long-lasting — episodes as the struggle for the vote and for the right to hold office; and sometimes as a fundamental challenge to this closed world of masculine ambition, along with a clear perception that access to political equality, as they used to call it, would not change very much in the established disorder . . . In this respect, the women's movement has experienced, and is still experiencing, the same contradictions as the working-class movement, being caught between the desire to alter the democratic system in its favour and the idea of radically transforming it. (Bouchardeau, 1980, p. 42)

It hardly needs saying that it is sometimes easier to maintain a coherent critique of the state and masculine power when women are totally excluded from it than when the state takes a step towards them, or when women apparently reach the corridors of power. Thus the modern women's movement recognises that when women did get the vote in various countries, that effectively demobilised the formidable energies that had been devoted to getting it, and served to mask the reality that women continued to be excluded from power. Similarly, the fact that the British prime minister has for the first time ever been a woman — but one who makes it clear that she has no time for the women's movement — is something of a challenge; feminists have been notably reluctant to write about the Margaret Thatcher phenomenon. The debate among women political scientists as to whether it would change things very much if women were more present in the political arena (from which they continue on the whole to be strikingly absent) is discussed by Anne Stevens in Chapter 7.

Historically, the debate about women and power has often been expressed in terms of public and private, as Michelle Perrot points out in Chapter 3. Lacking public power, women were regarded as exercising a peculiarly potent form of private power within the home. Just as Marie Antoinette was seen by many people, including Mary Wollstonecraft, as literally the power behind the throne, so every wife could be perceived as secret wielder of private power over her husband. Feminist approaches to the history of the family have helped to discredit this over-simple public/private dichotomy: the family was the scene (and still is) of conflict and negotiation between its different members, men, women or children (Jordanova, 1981); and by the same token we may also analyse what is usually regarded as the public sphere and realise for instance that the collective power of supposedly powerless women can be an inseparable part of political history, as Olwen Hufton (1971) has indicated of the French Revolution.

More generally, the post-1970 women's movement has strongly endorsed the view, not exclusively applicable to sexual politics but particularly relevant to it, that 'the personal is political'. 'The result is a redefinition of politics which destroys the barrier between public and private life and therefore opens up questions about what can and cannot be discussed in political terms' (Duchen, 1986, p.44). Some of the particular implications both of this notion and of its converse (that the political may be personal — sometimes revived in reformulations of the 'power behind the throne' argument) are explored by Anne Stevens with reference to contemporary political science in her survey of women's access to power in three present-day European states. And it would be true to say that an understanding of the crucial interrelatedness of the personal and the political is important to all the authors of this book.

It is more usual, however, to find the insights related to this notion being applied to areas previously regarded as less 'political', in order to demonstrate the hidden agenda in sexual politics in say, family life, the statistics of the economy, literature. In history, this has understandably led to a particular concentration by women's/feminist historians on social history in the broad sense, rather than political history, and it is in the former area and in labour history that on the whole feminism has been able to inspire the most fruitful syntheses, altering what Anna Davin (1985) has described as the 'man's or masculinist history' we have often accepted as 'human' history. But much political history (and political science) continues to to be written as if the dichotomy public/private was still in full vigour, uncontaminated by changes in other parts of the field.

Perhaps nowhere is this more true and the near absence of women more striking than in that discussion of state power which still forms the backbone of most 'European history'. Jack Hexter's famous remark that most of the significant institutions and ventures in political history had been 'pretty much stag affairs' (quoted in Carroll, 1976, p.34) has more often been answered (rightly and effectively) by enlarging the agenda of history to encompass other areas of life than by tackling political history head-on. Although we now know a great deal more than we did about the participation of women in, for instance, the French or Russian Revolutions, such knowledge is often either confined to books about women, or referred to in general works as a single index reference, or the odd page devoted to women, masking silence elsewhere.

Well, the reader may correctly point out, this is another

book about women. Quite so. It is still a great deal easier to get at the subject by concentrating on it than by providing the kind of synthesis that is needed. But we hope that the range and character of the topics we have chosen might at least suggest some ways forward to a synthesis. From Beryl Williams' essay on Alexandra Kollontai, for instance, which draws on the large amount of recently published material, it can be seen how closely entangled 'the woman question' was with the entire course of the Russian Revolution, how profoundly challenging and in the end unassimilable was the vision of relations between men and women held by women like Kollontai. Although there were 'events' in the story, the question of relations between the sexes was a structure, rather than an event in the Revolution, and should therefore have its place in any attempt to write its total history. Similarly Sybil Oldfield, while engaged in one of the now classic forms of women's history, that is uncovering the 'hidden from history' in Sheila Rowbotham's phrase, in this case the women who resisted the regime in Nazi Germany, also reminds us that the regime was constructed on a crucial ideological view of the difference between the sexes, something which is not only essential to our understanding of the different forms women's resistance took, but also central to analysing the regime itself. In my chapter on the French Republic, I have tried to see how the maleness of the Republic has been perceived, or not perceived, in historical writing about it, and argued that this makes a difference to the way we read French political history in general.

By placing a special emphasis on revolutions, within the general context of politics and the state, it is also possible to go beyond the exploration of absence and/or oppression of women. For it seems to be a peculiarity of revolutions in Europe – in this period at any rate – that women are often unusually *present*. Visible and active, they are generally welcomed, at least in the early stages of revolution, as proof that 'the people', the real people, including families and children, are involved, thus profoundly legitimising revolutionary action. The women's march on Versailles and the role of women in provoking the February Revolution in Russia are perhaps the best-known examples (both concerned with women's role as mothers and food distributors). Thus during revolutions, women sometimes appear to weigh their full weight as human beings, in a way that they do not under 'normal' political circumstances. Some women's historians have argued, rightly in my view, that this prompts one to construct at the very least a differential chronology of 'progress' for men and women. Whatever one thinks of progress as a historical concept, assumptions are made about progress towards civil/human/political rights which on examination turn out to be gender-determined. Women do not on the whole appear to have benefited collectively in these terms from the revolutions in which they have collectively or individually taken part.

It is possible to go even further and remark on the irony that women often appear to weigh more than their full weight in revolutionary circumstances, that their symbolic and iconographic presence in the imagery and images of revolutions suggest a transcendental and inspirational presence. If La Pasionaria had not existed during the Spanish civil war, would it have been necessary to invent her? And for how many people does her very name (originally adopted by Dolores Ibarruri as a *nom-de-plume* and meaning 'passion flower') carry subliminal echoes of passion and inspiration? Liberty on the Barricades in Delacroix's painting is perhaps the most familiar image of woman in revolution to many people all over the world. Only now is it becoming possible to perceive the many-layered complexity of our response to such a representation. Marcia Pointon in her analysis of the painting in Chapter 2, argues that feminist criticism can take us beyond explanations in allegorical or class terms and lead us to consider the sexual politics and contradictions it contains.

There is an obvious sense in which such a representation of a woman in a violent situation in which she is not a victim disturbs the observer accustomed to associate women culturally with gentleness, acquiescence, non-violence − or alternatively with passive suffering. In our own times, the image of the 'female terrorist' to be found in the contemporary media still holds echoes of this disturbance (contrasting for instance with an increasingly matter-of-fact approach to women soldiers). This representation, in the case of the Red Army Faction in West Germany, is explored by Ulrike Hanna

Meinhof in Chapter 8, using the notion of deviancy from the norm as a concept and relating it to the image of an explicitly non-violent women's peace campaign, that of Greenham Common, with perhaps surprising conclusions.

In her chapter, as in most of the others, 'women', 'state' and 'revolution' are all present in a certain relation to each other, if not exactly in the way one might expect; and perhaps this is the best place to comment on the title of this collection. It is a bit grand, the sceptical reader may think, with its extra-textual reference and highly-charged terms. The sub-title does, I hope, usefully indicate the more precise scope of the contents, but it seemed important both when the title was chosen for the lecture series and when it was kept for the published book, to claim it as a legitimate set of relationships to explore. It does not suggest that some sort of fixed relation between these terms is in any sense discoverable, let alone discovered. It just hopes to hold the door open long enough to suggest the problems and contradictions that can be perceived when these three terms are juxtaposed. One always takes risks when meddling with edged tools, as Mary Wollstonecraft pointed out. Let us at least take the risk: 'neck or nothing is the word'.

Siân Reynolds

ACKNOWLEDGEMENTS

Many people helped in various ways, whether with advice or with typing and word-processing sections of the text. Special thanks to Valerie Blaney, Yvonne Hope, Audrey Coppard, Peter France, Mary Galgani, Rod Kedward, and to Edward Elgar of Wheatsheaf Books.

Michelle Perrot's chapter was translated by Siân Reynolds.

1 Mary Wollstonecraft and The French Revolution or Feminism and The Rights of Men

Irene Coltman Brown

The French Revolution provided the historic background not only for Mary Wollstonecraft's famous *Vindication of the Rights of Woman,* but also for her energetic defence of the rights of men. This essay explores the nature of the connection, in all her major writings, between the value the Enlightenment set on reason and the irrational social relationships between men and women in her time.

Mary Wollstonecraft was born in 1759, the grand-daughter of a respectable manufacturer in the Spitalfields weaving trade, and the daughter of a man whom she later depicted as a domestic tyrant 'simultaneously to be obeyed'. It was after her father had lost most of his inheritance in a series of unfortunate economic ventures, and after she herself had both attempted to run a school and had a humiliating experience as a governess in Ireland that, most unconventionally, Mary Wollstonecraft offered her services to a radical publisher, Joseph Johnson.

He had paid her a 10 guinea copyright on her first manuscript, *Thoughts on the Education of Daughters.* Recognising her intellectual talents (as had also the famous Dissenting minister, Dr Richard Price, who had lived near her school in Newington Green), he commissioned her to write for him, and introduced her to his other friends and authors with whom she became a respected member of London's lively rationalist intelligentsia.

The great national debate on the French Revolution was opened by the publication, late in 1790, of Edmund Burke's *Reflections on the Revolution in France.* Mary Wollstonecraft was one of the first of many reformers to reply to his attack upon the French National Assembly and on the English radicals, particularly Dr Price, for their rejoicing at the events across the Channel. Published anonymously within a month of Burke's essay, Mary Wollstonecraft's *A Vindication of the Rights of Men* was reissued by Johnson under her own name in a slightly enlarged second edition on 18 December 1790. It therefore appeared some two months before her friend Thomas Paine's more popular and similarly titled work. Unlike many later historians, by whom her work on the French Revolution has been varyingly neglected, her contemporaries regarded her defence as one of the most forceful and persuasive contributions to this famous public argument.

It was this work, rather than the notorious *Vindication of the Rights of Woman* that first made her famous, and in which, with her distinctive use of gender language and metaphor, she first attacked Burke's self-indulgent, artificially exaggerated sensibility which she also regarded as the dangerous defect of the unemancipated woman, and the enemy of the rule of reason. Already visible here is her passionate conviction, to be developed in her later work, that the power of reason is the common possession of men and women. Mind, she protested, has no gender but women's reason had been stolen from them. Most were forced by circumstances to live without any freedom for deliberation and even to turn against rational thought by virtue of living under an oppressive yoke. There were many self-satisfied men who believed that women were by nature incapable of logical or abstract thought and that it was destructive of their femininity if they tried, but it was Mary Wollstonecraft's perception that women were not incapable of reason, but denied it.

This denial, she argued, was corrupting to both sexes and to the political order, eroding simultaneously the rational faculties of women and also of men who, she said, were led to misuse their reason in order to justify their inherited prejudices against the other sex. Such a repressive exercise encouraged them to justify oppression in general, and by such oppression both sexual oppressor and oppressed were maimed. As Harriet Taylor and John Stuart Mill would also argue a generation later, men could not retain their full manliness while − like decadent sultans − they guarded as purely masculine the rights and powers that belonged equally to both sexes. As Mary Wollstonecraft wrote in a later work on the Revolution, a whole regime can be diminished in this way, as in Paris during the *ancien régime:* 'a variety of causes have so effeminated reason that the french may be considered a nation of women; and made feeble, probably by the same combination of circumstances as has rendered these insignificant' (Wollstonecraft, 1794, p. 247). Neither the French nor women were born feeble, but despotism had drained the powers of both.

'I war not with an individual', she assured Burke, 'when I contend for the *rights of men* and the liberty of reason' (Wollstonecraft, 1790, p. 2) but, in so far as her argument was directly aimed at him, it attacked the weak and feverish sensibility that she suggested he shared with women impaired by servitude. In his own imaginative book, *The Language of Politics in the Age of Wilkes and Burke,* James Boulton (who is unusual in praising Mary Wollstonecraft's reply to Burke highly − if not uncritically) understood as she had done the instrinsic value of Burke's romantic language to his argument, although giving its purpose a more positive interpretation than she did. Boulton realised that the very strength of Burke's feeling is a salient feature of the case he is arguing; 'the traditional order takes full account of natural feelings; the revolutionists deny them' (Boulton, 1963, p. 121). Boulton rightly concludes that Burke's emotive techniques were often more than persuasive methods: 'they convey the essence of Burke's philosophic position' (ibid.)

Mary Wollstonecraft would have agreed, but she felt that Burke's highly coloured and evocative vocabulary was chosen in order to debar a critical reception of his reasoning. As the rationalist legal reformer Jeremy Bentham also protested, there were great dangers in the dependence of the *ancien regime* on the natural feelings of well-bred gentlemen. Too often, 'a kind of mysterious instinct is *supposed* to reside in the soul, that instantaneously discerns truth, without the tedious labours of ratiocination' (Wollstonecraft, 1790, p. 70). The emotions Burke skilfully excited could overpower reason, and as she put it, 'all your pretty flights arise from your pampered sensibility. . . reflection inflames your imagination, instead of enlightening your understanding' (ibid., p. 6).[1]

His over-heated rhetoric was directed to those, particularly perhaps to women, who in their dislike of the demanding operations of critical thought were, she feared, made enemies of the Enlightenment.

Even the ladies, Sir, (she alleged) may repeat your sprightly sallies and retail in theatrical attitudes many of your sentimental exclamations. Sensibility is the *manie* of the day, and compassion the virtue which is to cover a multitude of vices, whilst justice is left to mourn in sullen silence, and balance truth in vain. (ibid., p. 5)

Burke's exploitation of their emotional response to his passionate oratory had its own oppressive power. It was used (as Boulton suggests) to cow his readers into submission, as the *ancien régime* cowed its subjects; and Mary Wollstonecraft, seeking to liberate captive minds, appeals to Burke in what is the heart of her request to the other sex: 'Quitting now the flowers of rhetoric, let us, Sir, reason together . . . (ibid., p. 6).

In her *A Vindication of the Rights of Men,* Mary Wollstonecraft reasoned that politically the French Revolution was a struggle between the demon of property and the sacred rights of man. Her arguing in this way made use of the same Biblical allusions as Burke, but whereas he used them – as James Boulton has shown – to sanctify tradition as unassailable and therefore to insinuate that to subvert it is both ignoble and sacrilegious, she made the sacredness of man the justification for an assault upon the satanic property relationships that have fettered God's creation. In judging the Revolution, Burke, she claimed, had two great faults: firstly a lack of courage in that for fear of a temporary flood he feared a thaw in a society where social relationships were stiffly frozen into the past; and worse, he had an unjustified antipathy to individual reason.

In his fear of the destructive consequences of critical enquiry, Burke was at one with the counter-revolutionary French court and aristocracy, and spokesman for the unemancipated women who were their dangerous allies. But Burke's sentiments were not as natural as he believed, for like theirs, she alleged, they had been warped by the unnatural manners imposed upon them at the expense of their natural life and morals. The vices of Burke's thinking were in this comparable to the vices of the French court and of the seductive but corrupt courtesan whom Mary Wollstonecraft saw personified in Marie Antoinette, wielding illegitimate power behind the scenes, as courtesans had for centuries. In vindicating the rights of mankind to reclaim their usurped privileges, she felt she spoke for reason and for 'the rational woman' who, she believed and prayed in her work, would as a result of the French Revolution replace the destructive fine lady as the feminine ideal. The consequence of this political crisis could and should be, she believed, a cultural revolution that swept away the courtesan with the prisoner, and made 'women probably act then like mothers' (ibid., p. 52). In the French Revolution she says, 'Reason has at last shown her captivating face' (ibid., p. 19). Reason can be a woman who can win hearts without the harlot's arts and the French Revolution could be interpreted as a rejection of national effeminacy, and the beginning of a new social androgyny.

Burke believed that for government to be obeyed, its ruling class must be the object of habitual devotion and that to be so loved, it must seem beautiful. This was a convention in private as well as public life which enraged Mary Wollstonecraft who believed with Locke – the intellectual ancestor of the Dissenting radical circle of which she was part and which Burke so hated and feared – that the people's unconditional consent did not provide adequate grounds to legitimise a regime. Locke had argued that a government could only claim legitimate allegiance when it had won the consent of the freely reasoning citizen. The magic power of the traditional ruling class to win the support of the people they mistreated was to Mary Wollstonecraft more like the illegitimate wooing of a seducer and the source, as she accused Burke, of 'a spurious sensual beauty that has long debauched your imagination' (Wollstonecraft, 1790, p. 121).

His plea for swords to flash out for the threatened queen was no rational or desirable basis for a just society; it merely showed Burke's susceptibility to such corrupt seduction since he 'could not stand the fascinating glance of a *great* lady's eyes' (ibid., p. 35). His hope, she protested, was that all subjects would be like him and, like all weak characters, love without reason even tyrants and kings. As she lamented, 'They love, they know not why and they will love to the end of the chapter' (ibid., p. 156).[2]

Burke's undisciplined surrender to feeling had caused him to surrender to unprobed sentiment. Without adherence to reason, sentiment can breed its own monsters. Mary Wollstonecraft wrote in her novel *The Wrongs of Woman,* that romance can close the heart, 'and, fostering a sickly sensibility, grows callous to the soft touches of humanity' (Wollstonecraft, 1780, p. 193). Women were encouraged by their masculine masters to suppress their thoughts but to express their feelings with exaggerated displays of sensitivity, often false and misplaced, as she, like Thomas Paine after her, accused Burke of doing, in weeping over Marie Antoinette instead of for France's starving peasants: 'Man preys on man', she wrote furiously, 'and you mourn for the idle tapestry that decorated a gothic pile . . . you mourn for the empty pageant of a name' (Wollstonecraft, 1790, p. 152).

Sentimentality was wrongly interpreted as deep feeling, but as she wrote elsewhere, 'we ought to recollect, that the sex called the tender, commit the most flagrant acts of barbarity when irritated' (Wollstonecraft, 1794, p. 258). With scorn the mother of English feminism asked, 'Where is the dignity, the infallibility of sensibility, in the fair ladies, whom, if the voice of rumour is to be credited, the captive negroes curse in all the agony of bodily pain, for the unheard of tortures they invent?' After complacently seeing their slaves flogged, the colonial wives of West Indies planters could 'compose their ruffled spirits and exercise their tender feelings by the perusal of the last imported novel' (Wollstonecraft, 1790, p. 111). She doubted how true to nature were the tears shed over fictional heroes after such evidence of hardened hearts,[3] but suggested that, encouraged by Burke's adulation of the softly beautiful over the powerful sublime, in his *Philosophical Enquiry* into the origin of these ideas, 'they may have laboured to be pretty, by counterfeiting weakness' (ibid., p. 112).

You may have convinced them (she accused him) that *littleness* and *weakness* are the very essence of beauty; and that the Supreme Being, in giving women beauty in the most supereminent degree, seemed to command them, by the powerful voice of Nature, not to cultivate the moral virtues that might chance to excite respect, and interfere with the pleasing sensations they were created to inspire. Thus confining truth, fortitude, and humanity, within the rigid pale of manly morals, they might justly argue, that to be loved, woman's high end and great distinction!, they should learn to lisp, to totter in their walk, and nick-name 'God's creatures'. Never, they might repeat after you, was any man, much less a woman, rendered amiable by the force of these exalted qualities, fortitude, justice, wisdom, and truth; and thus forewarned of the sacrifice they must make to those austere, unnatural virtues, they would be authorized to turn all their attention to their persons, systematically neglecting morals to secure beauty (ibid., p. 122 ff.)

It was a portrait of women as pampered but captive pets. The only figure to escape from the spacious Burkeian doctrine to which women dependent on masculine favours were particularly susceptible, was, expected Mary Wollstonecraft, 'some rational old woman'. No longer obliged to project herself to the world as *'little, smooth, delicate, fair'*, because she was no longer defined entirely by her femininity, the strong and independent mature woman was for her the exemplar of what was needed to reunite the socially separated qualities of the two sexes and thereby grant to both the common possession of reason. It was necessary for men and women to find 'a beauty in virtue', so that a depraved effeminate sensual taste in men might give way to a more manly one, and melting feelings in women be replaced by rational enquiry. Such a saving reconstruction of gender values could only be produced by the increased liberty of social relations feared by Burke. But Mary Wollstonecraft alleged that in her day, 'This laxity of morals in the female world is certainly more captivating to a libertine imagination than the cold arguments of reason, that give no sex to virtue' (ibid., p. 114). Without subjection to the discipline of a self-questioning critical reason, Burke, she surmised, could slide into an over-reactive extremism – as indeed he later did. His fears of the French Revolution crossing the Channel were believed by some of his former colleagues to have deranged his mind. Desperate, he was to abandon the conservative restraints of precedent and urge instead the extraordinary and unprecedented violent measures that define the counter-revolutionary. It was an outcome which Mary Wollstonecraft brilliantly foresaw when she alleged that 'Reading your *Reflections* warily over, it has continually and forcibly struck me, that had you been a Frenchman, you would have been, in spite of your respect for rank and antiquity, a violent revolutionist . . .' Burke's emotions could be at the disposal of another cause, 'and deceived, as you now probably are by the poisons that cloud your reason, (you would) have termed your romantic enthusiasm an enlightened love of your country, a benevolent respect for the rights of men. Your imagination would have taken fire' (ibid., p. 109).

It was this lack of restraint, this over-eager flood of feeling, that caused Burke, she felt, to esteem revolutionary France too little and conservative Britain too much. Burke had envisioned the French revolutionaries as possessed with a satanic lust for destruction because they had chosen to condemn what could have been reformed, but Mary Wollstonecraft believed that there was much in both countries that was better gone. Burke should have known, she maintained, what an idealistic picture the *Reflections* presented of Great Britain where his own party had at times protested at the corruption of contemporary party politics. As a politician, she protested, 'you have been behind the curtain . . . you must have seen the clogged wheels of corruption . . .' (ibid., p. 42). Indeed 'Our House of Commons has often resembled a bear garden' (ibid., p. 105). Why was it, she demanded, a duty to repair an ancient castle, built in barbarous ages of Gothic materials, when both the English and the French had the means and opportunity to build a light and airy house? It would be necessary for Burke to prove not only that the British Constitution was better than any other, but the very best possible, and that it permitted all the political freedom possible for mankind, if he were to defend himself against the accusation that he was unduly afraid of change. As the less well satisfied Mary Wollstonecraft protested, 'It is, Sir, *possible* to render the poor happier in this world . . .' (ibid., p. 144).

Burke, as she understood, argued that the glaring economic inequalities of eighteenth-century England were justified because the civil liberties of all Englishmen were inherited in the same way as the great lords of the aristocratic ruling class inherited their stately homes. That inherited and long-accepted constitutional rights are more secure than those newly promised in a Bill of Rights or a Declaration of the Rights of Man is a convincing argument, but Mary Wollstonecraft struck at the heart of the connection that Burke made between property and public freedom, by her counter-charge that the poor of England inherited neither property nor secure liberty. Burke's commitment to the British constitution was largely drawn from his belief that it guaranteed every man's safety by making all equal before the law. To Mary Wollstonecraft this was a delusion and the prevailing inequality of property was sustained by the ancient laws Burke wrote to defend: 'Security of property! Behold in a few words the definition of English liberty. And for this selfish principle every nobler one is sacrificed . . . But softly, it's only the property of the rich that is secure' (ibid., p. 24). Like other fortunes, social security was inherited unequally. Fear of the government press gang seizing the man of the family for enforced service in the navy was widespread among the poorer classes of Britain, and became still stronger in the later Napoleonic Wars. The propertyless working man had inherited neither protection against intruders nor the security of his civic freedom when 'the base informer' could reveal the presence of a young man hiding from the press gang in order to remain with a family that depended on his industry for their livelihood. It was characteristic of Mary Wollstonecraft to have noticed that, even when they returned, these unwilling victors of England's glorious naval battles found it hard to settle down again with their families, and to find again the work from which they had been forcibly taken. 'When', she asked, 'is retribution to be made to the miserable who cry day and night for help, and there is no one at hand to help them?' (ibid., p. 30).

Edmund Burke had failed to see this manifest wrong which cast grave doubts upon his acceptance of the justice of the British constitution. He was misled because, she suggested, 'A lively imagination is ever in danger of being betrayed into error' (ibid., p. 138). She warned that without fixed principles even goodness of heart is no security against inconsistency, as sensibility was no defence against evil sentiments. Reason must always be the guardian of the mind and of the just political regime. 'She must hold the rudder', protested this reasoning woman, intent on restoring to reason its sovereignty and its common gender 'or let the wind blow which way it list, the vessel will never advance smoothly to its destined port' (ibid., p. 73).

The strong suggestion that England was not so perfect as to make revolutionary changes in the constitution inherently criminal made her reply to Burke immediately popular with liberal opinion. As William Godwin wrote perceptively in his *Memoirs of Mary Wollstonecraft,* she gained a confidence from her success, which must, he realised, 'stimulate the adventure of any human being', and encouraged her to venture into new intellectual territory (Godwin, 1928, p. 153).

* * * * *

As early as 1787, in her *Thoughts on the Education of Daughters,* Mary Wollstonecraft had begged that women be taught to think, but it was her *Vindication of the Rights of Woman,* published in 1792, that directly linked the fate of women with the fate of the Enlightenment which she saw struggling to be born in the French Revolution. 'You have said many things', she accused Burke, 'merely for the sake of saying them well' (Wollstonecraft, 1790, p. 66); and, still more damagingly, this insincerity, she suggested, was because Burke, like the Roman outsider Cicero, was the defender of an aristocracy which never took him in. Like the woman whose very life might be dependent on being chosen as mistress or wife, he needed above all to please. To do this, he dressed what was drab in furs and diamonds in order to make not only his country and its ruling class but himself lovable: 'I not only tremble for the souls of women (she remarked) but for the good natured man, whom everyone loves' (ibid., p. 115).

It was this need that corrupted the dependent, as she forcefully argued in her second, even more startling and much more renowned work on the French Revolution. In the *Vindication of the Rights of Woman,* she alleged that unemancipated woman was, like Burke, the enemy of the Revolution's ideals. This work was also written quickly – in six weeks – but covers ground far beyond her own thirty years of rage at the injustices endured by women. It is ludicrous to suggest, as has often been done, that this work is a mere reflection of her private grievances. Mary Wollstonecraft did, it is true, grieve over her own life and the hard lives of other

women. In her early novel *Mary,* she uses a phrase that
describes feelings that many women have felt when chained to
a domestic routine for which there seems little at the end to
show, or when obliged to work for others and never for
themselves. Her choice of words well describes their
resentment as 'the waste of murdered time' (Wollstonecraft,
1980, p. 43). One volume of her other unfinished novel asks,
near the beginning, 'Was not the world a vast prison, and
women born slaves?' (ibid., p. 79) and ends, 'Why was I not
born a man, or why was I born at all?' (ibid., p. 139), for she
certainly strained against the constraints upon her sex. She says
of her heroine's brother in that novel, 'what was called spirit
and wit in him, was cruelly repressed as forwardness in me'
(ibid., p. 126). But Mary Wollstonecraft's *Vindication of the
Rights of Woman* was not a shrill scream as Horace Walpole
suggested when he called her a hyena in petticoats. It was a
complex and subtle investigation into the consequences of
social repression, which suggested that the contemporary
revolution in human rights and intellectual enlightenment
would remain incomplete and vulnerable as long as society
continued to create a large class, the class of women, who
would be hostile to both because they had been inculcated since
birth with hostility to reason.

It exposed the same flaws of the soul that Sylvia Plath
explored when she wrote 'Every woman adores a fascist',[4] since
Mary Wollstonecraft wrote, as she said, out of a profound
conviction that the minds of women were not in a healthy
condition and that their unhealthiness had infested the
dominant class of men who had caused this sickness. Her book
was less a description of feminine weakness than of woman
forced to be a whore and exercising what she called women's
illegitimate power. Developing the imagery she had used
against Burke, she insisted that the state of warfare which
existed between the sexes and had made women employ
corrupt wiles to frustrate men's more open designs of force
upon them, had given them the secret power of the slave,
whether fate had placed them in a hovel or a palace. 'When,
therefore, I call women slaves, I mean in a political and civil
sense', she argued, 'for indirectly they obtain too much power,

and are debased by their exertions to obtain illicit sway' (Wollstonecraft, 1975, p. 286).

Women who were refused the independence, because they were refused the education given to men, were excluded from the modern promise that every human creature should become a sovereign power through its reasoning. The kingdom of personal relationships between men and women was as yet a kingdom of unreason that generated a system of mutual hostility and dependence instead of mutual affection and support: 'I do not want to be loved like a goddess', she once wrote to her lover, 'but I wish to be necessary to you' (Woolf, 1935, p. 159). Using perhaps the most potent image of the French Revolution, the storming of the Bastille, in order to describe marriage as it is, Mary Wollstonecraft's fictional heroine Maria would lament that marriage has 'bastilled me for life' (Wollstonecraft, 1980, p. 155), but it could be, she says, as did the French of their storming of the Bastille, the institution 'which fraternizes the world' (ibid., p. 195).

Such a marriage required, in Jane Austen's well-known misspelling, 'Love and Freindship'; and it was, Mary Wollstonecraft believed, the greater recognition in each sex of a more common nature than was presently acceptable that would make this honest reunion of sexuality and comradeship possible. Till then women lived by deception and thus, although women in the later eighteenth century conventionally either concealed or simulated their sexuality in order to please, Mary Wollstonecraft was exceptionally honest about her own. A Swedish friend records that a French woman annoyed her by her insincere refinement in claiming that she had never felt any sexual desire, to which Mary Wollstonecraft retorted 'Tant pis pour vous madame, c'est un défaut de la nature' (So much the worse for you, madam, that is a defect of nature) (Tomalin, 1974, p. 132). She shocked public opinion by saying that making love is only indelicate when the woman is indifferent and that 'we cannot, without depraving our minds, endeavour to please a lover or husband but in proportion as he pleases us' (Wollstonecraft, 1980, p. 153). But although she knew that in her lifetime wedlock for most women was imprisoning and degrading, Mary Wollstonecraft's political feminism was rooted in the conviction that 'Men and women were made for each other' (Wollstonecraft, 1975, p. 296). As Godwin said, 'She set a great value on a mutual affection between persons of an opposite sex. She regarded it as the principal solace of human life' (Godwin, 1928, p. 61).

The Vindication of the Rights of Woman constantly confronts the existing impure relationship between the sexes, especially in marriage, and the pure union between them which would set both men and women free. Modern marriage was a more or less monogamous harem that denied the thrust of modern philosophy and kept women in ignorance under the specious name of innocence. It was the power of women in the seraglio of modern marriage that corrupted them and inhibited their demands for liberation since, within the bonds of marriage, women can exercise that short-lived tyranny which Plato attributed to beauty and are given homage because of the sovereignty of their bodies rather than for their natural rights. For attractive young women, the regal homage they receive is so intoxicating writes Mary Wollstonecraft, 'that until the manners of the times are changed, and formed on more reasonable principles, it may be impossible to convince them that the illegitimate power which they obtain by degrading themselves is a curse, and that they must return to nature and equality' (Wollstonecraft, 1975, p. 103).

Many women, she thought, however civilly and politically oppressed, had developed an attachment to despotism and its rewards which prevented their attachment to the principles of the French Revolution. They were not powerless, but their power was corrupt. 'Women', she insisted, as well as despots, 'have now perhaps more power than they would have if the world were governed by laws deduced from the exercise of reason' (ibid., p. 126). They were hostile to nature, since it was through their artificial graces that they allured. They were hostile to liberty since independence (without economic resources) too often meant for them abandonment, neglect, danger and destitution. They were antipathetic to equality, since they sought to compete against other women to win the hand of the richest and best born and, like many forced into slavery, seized every opportunity to domineer when they could, so that many oppressed wives were tyrants to their children and their servants. They had been made incapable of fraternity as often also of sorority. And it was Mary Wollstonecraft's charge against unequal sexual relationships that they forced husbands to seduce their wives, and women to be mistresses, not the friends of men. As kings and aristocrats placed honour above virtue, so women preferred their good name to good deeds and their code of behaviour was closer to the code of kings than to that of citizens, which she did not find surprising considering that women received much the same scrappy education as royalty. Thus they were turned into allies of the counter-revolutionary forces of Europe. They at last despised the freedom which they could not obtain and it was the emotional attachment to power which their dependence had developed in women that explained why few women had emancipated themselves from the galling yoke of sovereign man.

Women, she saw, sometimes exaggerate their helplessness because they have perceived that men like weakness in others. They especially fear to show their capacity for philosophy and abstract thought because this capacity has been called unfeminine. In this way, they subvert the age of reason and deny their own powers, calling their defects advantages, like the pale skin and delicate health which had become the apparatus of a heroine. In order to pretend that their unnatural and sometimes calculated dependence is their natural state, women, claimed Mary Wollstonecraft, turn to men for protection from the frown of an old cow or a small mouse jumping. They must deny the progressive aspiration towards human perfection implicit in the Enlightenment reformers because they have placed a value upon their imperfections.

Denied the civil existence of public life, the place of women had been confined to those corners of domesticity where men delight in turning from their adult cares and responsibilities. Woman, she complained, 'was created to be the toy of man, his rattle, and it must jingle in his ears whenever, dismissing reason, he chooses to be amused' (ibid., p. 118). As long as she believes unreason is ingratiating, she will not become a citizen or philosopher of the European republic. She was the enemy within the city of human rights so that Mary Wollstonecraft wrote, 'I, therefore, will venture to assert, that, till women are more rationally educated, the progress of human virtue and improvement in knowledge must receive continual checks' (ibid., p. 126).

Mary Wollstonecraft believed that the central thrust of the revolution, however compromised by the Jacobins, was necessary to Europe. 'There must be more equality established in society', she wrote, 'or morality will never gain ground' (ibid., p. 252) but this virtuous equality would never be stable while one half of humanity was undermining it. Her immediate project of reform was a national system of compulsory primary education for all classes and both sexes to be administered by men and women, which would allow women to become economically independent, but the most salutary effects in the long run would follow, she claimed, from a total revolution in female culture. It is her hard lesson, then and now, that 'By allowing women but one way of rising in the world, the fostering the libertinism of men, society makes monsters of them, and then their ignoble vices are brought forward as a proof of inferiority of intellect' (Wollstonecraft, 1980, p. 137). For the time, however, and she said it again even more strongly in the novel she was writing when she died, women were hardly capable of freedom and 'the evils they are subject to endure, degrade them so far below their oppressors as almost to justify their tyranny' (ibid., p. 181).

* * * * *

In 1792, Mary Wollstonecraft fled to France from London to escape the miseries of her drawn-out and unsatisfied love affair with the strange artist, Henry Fuseli. In Paris, she met and fell in love with the American businessman, Gilbert Imlay, and in June of 1793 withdrew from the capital, now fallen under Jacobin sway. In the happy summer spent just outside Paris, secluded in Neuilly where she could be frequently visited by her lover, she began and in 1794 published *An Historical and Moral View of the Origin and Progress of the French Revolution and the effect it has produced in Europe.*

Although it is much longer, over 550 pages, this moral history of the Revolution is less intense than the two brilliant *Vindications* and the argument is looser and less sharply

aimed. Nonetheless, one copy in the London Library shows
that a much earlier reader has recognised that in this narrative
of the political events in France from 1788 to 1793, Mary
Wollstonecraft was still using sexual imagery to contrast
corruption with reason. 'Note Court as she', wrote this reader
in the margin in a fine now faded hand,[5] for the theme of this
history is the replacement of the illegitimate power of a court,
whose representative was Marie Antoinette, by the just power
of the honest woman that is purified, republican France.

The court of Versailles (wrote Mary Wollstonecraft) with power the most
ample, was the most busy and insidious of any in Europe; and the horrors
which she has occasioned, at different periods, were as incalculable as her
ambition was unbounded, and her councils base, unprincipled and
dishonourable. If, then, it were only for abolishing her sway, Europe ought
to be thankful for a change, that by altering the political system of the most
improved quarter of the globe, must ultimately lead to universal freedom,
virtue and happiness. (Wollstonecraft, 1794, p. 490).

When the court was confronted by the state crisis of 1788-89,
its seemingly moderate response is described by this hostile
historian as the deceitful intrigue of an *agent provocateur,*
stirring up popular violence in order to use government force to
suppress it. She accuses Marie Antoinette of entertaining and
flirting with court thugs in order to win their allegiance to a
military initiative to disperse the Assembly and scatter the
crowds milling around Paris. In the traditional mode of courts
and courtesans where illegitimate power rules, Marie
Antoinette pulled the strings of the puppet Louis XVI in a
dangerous and, in the end, lethal dance. It was easy for her to
whisper to him of violent counter-revolution, for kings are
creatures dependent on people who are at home in courts. By
removing the court of France in the name of reason, it was as if
the French Revolution were closing a brothel and opening a
school. It had begun as a project of popular constitutional rule
which Mary Wollstonecraft endorsed fully, but which by 1793
when she was writing, had gone desperately wrong.

Like many modern intellectuals, she wrote in pain of a
revolution flawed, if not betrayed, by other intellectuals. She is
sometimes described as an English Jacobin, but she was a

1. Eugène Delacroix, *Liberty on the Barricades*, (1831) Salon, Paris: Musée du Louvre. Photograph: Réunion des Musées Nationaux.

2. French postage stamps, (1985). Photograph: author.

3. Red Grooms, *Liberty*, (1984) London: Marlborough Fine Art, 1985. Photograph: Marlborough Fine Art.

4. Fred Roe, *Revolution*, (1910–11) Sotheby's, 12 December 1978. Present location unknown. Photograph: Sotheby's.

5. Léopold Robert, *The Arrival of the Harvest Waggon*, (1830)
Paris: Musée du Louvre. Photograph: Réunion des Musées
Nationaux.

6. Jacques Louis David, *The Death of Marat,* (1793) Brussels: Musées Royaux des Beaux-Arts. Photograph: ACL Brussels.

7. Edvard Munch, *The Death of Marat*, (1906) lithograph,
    Sotheby's, 18 November 1969. Photograph: Sotheby's.

8. Eugène Delacroix, *Greece on the Ruins of Missolonghi*, (1826) Bordeaux: Musée et Galérie des Beaux-Arts. Photograph: Alain Danvers.

passionate opponent of the French Jacobins and deplored the extra-parliamentary pressures that the Jacobins brought to bear upon the republic's National Convention through their power in the streets and the revolutionary tribunals. 'My blood runs cold, and I sicken at thoughts of a Revolution which costs so much blood and bitter tears', she wrote on 8 July 1794[6] when Robespierre was wielding power most threateningly but about to fall. For Mary Wollstonecraft the great day of the French Revolution was 4 August 1789, when the aristocrats who had stayed in the National Assembly voluntarily abolished the legal decrees of feudalism. Then, she wrote of France, 'She stood fair as the dawn of her liberty having shaken off the prejudice of ages'.

She rejoiced in what she called 'the universal damp which the revolution in France has given to the courts of Europe' (ibid., p. 415) but the Revolution reached its own corruption in the executions of the Jacobin reign of terror. It was killing itself in the execution of Louis XVI, and even to a lesser degree in the earlier threatening march of the poor market women, made desperate by the food shortages, upon the royal family at Versailles.

To sketch these vicissitudes, she admitted, 'is a task so arduous and melancholy, that, with a heart trembling to the touches of nature, it becomes necessary to ground against the erroneous inferences of sensibility' (ibid, p. vi). Seeking to be less carried away by emotion than Burke, she hoped to give a fairer and more exact description of the wrong path taken by the revolution and yet to reassure her readers that the cause, imperfectly served, had nonetheless been just. She agreed with Burke, at least by 1793, that the victory of political reason in the French Revolution had been marred above all by the influence of Rousseauist Jacobin intellectuals like Robespierre; but Mary Wollstonecraft saw more similarity between Rousseau and Burke than the latter could ever have imagined. In the last days of the old order in France, the Enlightenment was in fashion. The works of Rousseau and Voltaire, she claimed, 'continually slipped off the tongue in numerous sprightly circles' (ibid., p. 10) and Rousseau in particular was admired by many who could not understand him, because his eloquence particularly appealed to minds alive only to emotion. Quite simply, she suggested, Rousseau intoxicated them and they behaved with the same loss of reason as drunkards when 'the writings that had awakened the spirit of these men had a little inebriated their brain' (ibid., p. 89). Patience was a potent quality to Mary Wollstonecraft. The heroines of her novels have to learn it, as she perhaps had had to, but the Jacobins, like many angry young men, were too proud themselves to be patient and they made use of a people 'whose patience had been worn out by injuries and insults' (ibid., p. 68).

They therefore carried with them the French people, whose suffering under the monarchy Mary Wollstonecraft, like her friend Paine, never forgot, nor forgave. Despite the drowning of reason in bloodshed, she still believed in the people and that their voice in enlightened countries is always the voice of reason. But out of vanity, the Jacobins, she complained, went too fast for a people left in brutality and ignorance by despotism for centuries until in the Revolution they were fed on Jacobin ideas.

Without reason, an ignorant people, she said, 'grow romantic like the croisaders, or like women who are commonly idle and restless' (ibid., p. 21). To add to their susceptibility to romantic ideologies as they emerged out of the dark night of complete ignorance, they were overwhelmed by the rage that had simmered within them during their miserable years of slavery and which the Jacobins encouraged them to release. Its origin lay in social and economic inequality, for 'Servility, destroying the natural energy of man, stifles the noblest sentiments of the soul . . . Ought we then to wonder, that this dry substitute for humanity is often burnt up by the scorching flame of revenge?' (ibid., p. 259). Revolutionary violence was a consequence of bitter pain long suffered and endured. As it was in France, so it would always be, she warned, for in a profound phrase she maintained that 'The behaviour of the hardened children of oppression in all countries is the same; whether in the amphitheatre at Rome, or around the lantern post in Paris' (ibid., p. 256). The French had gone overnight from implicitly obeying their sovereigns to becoming sovereigns themselves and mob rule had broken the revolution. When the ignorant market women on their march to Versailles turned on those they thought indifferent to their sufferings as the crowds had turned on the Governor of the stormed Bastille, 'a new cord was fixed to the notorious lamp-iron where the amusement of death was first tolerated' (ibid., p. 427). This terrible pleasure in murder was the price ultimately paid for the legendary amusements of the French court. The vain Jacobins were no more able than the people to let one reform calmly lead on to another, but like them seemed determined to strike at every wrong at once; while the people, she wrote, were rendered ferocious by misery. Every nation seeking to leave behind an absolute despotism and to form a new regime of enlightened freedom would be in danger, she realised, of a similar dangerous alliance of audacity and ignorance, between ambitious intellectuals and the people. Its outcome would be revolutionary tyrannies until, as she put it, the manners and amusements of the people were completely changed.

Only those with civic rights can be secure, but the Jacobins had sought in vain to capture freedom by a too rapid courtship for, as Mary Wollstonecraft concluded, 'Freedom is a solid good that requires to be treated with reverence and respect – But, whilst an effeminate race of heroines are contending for her smiles, with all the blandishments of gallantry, it is to their more vigorous and natural posterity, that she will consign herself with all the mild effulgence of artless charms' (ibid., p. 468). By 1793 in France, 'All Europe saw', she confessed, 'and all good men saw with dread, that the French had undertaken to support a cause, which they had neither purity of heart nor maturity of judgement to conduct with moderation and prudence; whilst malevolence has been gratified by the errours they have committed, attributing that imperfection to the theory they adopted, which was applicable only to the folly of their practice' (ibid., p. 483 f.).

The French Revolution was, she insisted 'a revolution in the minds of men; and only demanded a new system of government to be adopted' (ibid., p. 396). Like Paine, Mary Wollstonecraft saw no reason, in the failure of the French to establish a constitutional republican government on the ruins of the monarchy, to deny that their endeavour was the great cause of the age. It failed through the shortcomings of a revolutionary faction that lacked the purity of heart and maturity of judgement which she believed are both the gift and the safeguard of freedom. Her conclusion on the history of the French Revolution was still that 'the cultivation of the understanding . . . appears to be the only way to tame men, whose restlessness and spirit creates the vicious patterns that lead to tyranny and cruelty' (ibid., p. 21). Once again, sense and sensibility needed to go together to create the conditions of freedom. The pure feelings on which Burke depended would perish without the rational thought which he attacked, and the age of reason in the hands of men and women with unfeeling hearts would be a dance of death.

* * * * *

This volume was intended to be the first of others, but was the only one written and published in a work cut short, as the life of both the French Revolution and Mary Wollstonecraft were to be.

Mary Wollstonecraft had suffered from the perils of love. She was deserted by Imlay, who left her with an illegitimate daughter, who killed herself as a young woman and in a suicide note from which she tore the signature, described herself as 'One whose birth was unfortunate'. Nor did Mary Wollstonecraft marry William Godwin until she was pregnant, so it was easy for critics to confuse the sexual honesty for which she strove with the quite different morality of the sexual libertine. The economic and personal independence of women was in fact, she argued, an alternative to the apparent freedom but complete dependence of the female adventurer whose first need must be to satisfy her clients. But none the less many jeered when, at only 38, she died agonisingly, like many other women of her time, of puerperal fever, after bearing Godwin's child. The disreputable feminist's death was, they felt, a fitting fate and a deserved punishment.

Godwin said rightly that the *Vindication of the Rights of Woman* was written with an 'ardent desire to be found not a flourishing and empty declaimer, but an effectual champion'. In her own life-time the violence of the male and female response to Mary Wollstonecraft was an unwilling tribute to the power of her argument. Godwin realised, not without pride, that she was a symbol of freedom and that 'The pretty‑soft creatures that are so often to be found in the female sex, and that class of men who believe they could not exist without such pretty soft creatures to resort to, were in arms against the author of so heretical and blasphemous a doctrine' (Godwin, 1928, pp. 53-5).

Since then however, she has often been honoured as a passionate feminist as if all she wrote had been a mere declaiming of the virtues of women and a heated protest at their denied rights. The arguments of all three of her main theoretical works have been, on the whole, unread. Admirers have merely assumed what she had most likely written and their false assumptions have circulated unchecked and been handed down second-hand from one generation to the next. Even Virginia Woolf wrote in her short profile of Mary Wollstonecraft that

The outbreak of revolution in France expressed some of her deepest theories and convictions, and she dashed off in the heat of that extraordinary moment those two eloquent and daring books – the *Reply to Burke* and *Vindication of the Rights of Woman,* which are so true that they seem now to contain nothing new in them – their originality has become our commonplace. (Woolf, 1925, p. 158)

a judgement not really true of either of them, and particularly inappropriate to the first whose revealing title Virginia Woolf evades and replaces by an empty one of her own.

If she had written what so many believe she did, her popularity with the feminist movement might be still greater, but Mary Wollstonecraft did not write to please either men or women. In her appeal to Burke – 'Come, Sir, let us reason together', – she showed she wished radicals and conservatives, former enemies, and those exclusively defined as creatures of sense (like men) and of sensibility (like women) to draw more closely to each other. For her, things as they were did not define things as they might be, and the true nature of men and women and their relationships was not yet known. Her love of mankind inspired her conviction that both sexes and the political order suffered from the domestic failure of liberty, equality and fraternity. However, she did not in her critique of the female mind distorted by oppression attack her sex as a misogynist, nor make an early contribution to 'women divided'. She was a good hater, said Godwin, and she hated tyranny the more for what it did to its victims. Her love of women inspired her hatred of what many of them had been forced not only to suffer but to become, and Godwin comments, 'She saw indeed, that they were often attempted to be held in silken fetters, and bribed into the love of slavery; but the disguise and the treachery served only the more fully to confirm her opposition' (Godwin, 1928, p. 54).

She was a loving friend to other women and she tried to look after her sisters and her often mistreated mother. Most of her life she was a night-watcher − a phrase I have borrowed from the night-watchers of Greenham Common (the women's peace camp outside the USAF base) who in order to protect their camp-site are forced to watch it all night and therefore perforce to keep vigil over the monstrous engines of war within the fence. 'The military, (are) a pest in every nation', she declared (Wollstonecraft, 1794, p. 78) and women have often been lonely night-watchers of their pestilence, as they are often the sole observers of the mysteries of the world at night, especially at home watching over crying babies, nursing them in the silence, caring for the sick and keeping watch by the dead. Women stay up late or rise in the dark to write in the early morning before their children are awake, but they also weep through sleepless nights for lost loves, and over the follies and cruelties of the largely male government of mankind.

Despite the historic gains of the French Revolution, the National Convention excluded women from their deliberations. Unlike Paine, Mary Wollstonecraft could take no part in the cause that she defended in her writing and could only lie awake at night to mourn its defeat. As a child, she had lain awake on the landing to protect her mother from her drunken father; and she confessed she spent a terrible and sleepless night after she realised that Imlay had abandoned her;

but she had also spent at least one terrible night in Paris during the Revolution. The night after the storming of the Bastille in July 1789, as she later wrote, 'All Paris was awake . . . All saw the sword (of counter-revolution) suspended over them and over their country − and all feared a morrow still more dreadful' (Wollstonecraft, 1794, p. 200). That fearful morrow did not come on 15 July, but when that unity had gone and people waited at home alone for denunciation and arrest by the self-appointed tribunes of the Revolution, Mary Wollstonecraft deplored first the execution of the aristocracy, then the September massacre of the Revolution's prisoners in the Tuileries, before her own friends, Mme Roland and the other anti-Jacobin Girondins, were sent to the guillotine in 1793. The capital became a place of fear, as the young Wordsworth said, 'unfit for the repose of night'. From an empty house in Paris, Mary Wollstonecraft wrote to Joseph Johnson, her friend, patron and publisher, after she saw Louis XVI going to his trial on 26 December 1792, along the silent streets: 'I wish I had even kept the cat with me! − I want to see something alive; death in so many frightful shapes has taken hold of my fancy − I am going to bed − and, for the first time in my life, I cannot put out the candle' (Tomalin, 1974, p. 124).

She shared this commitment to life with Burke, but in the centuries of conflict that she rightly saw would follow from the assault of reason upon ancient despotisms, she feared Burke's pitting of reason and feeling against each other. What would be needed was in both sexes what she wonderfully described as 'emotions that reason deepens − the feelings of humanity'. After Mary Wollstonecraft had left France, and Robespierre and the Jacobins had been overthrown, she still believed that the popular discussion of political affairs enlarged the heart by extending understanding and that the great popular debates of the French Revolution would have this effect not only in France but upon all Europe.

She wrote angrily of the wrongs of woman, and of their exclusion from this public discourse, but her aim was to negotiate a reconciliation that would enable men and women to be friends and lovers, and allies in the great cause of the French Revolution. Men were not the exclusive property-owners of sense, nor women the exclusive guardians of sensibility. It was for both sexes to reason and feel for each other, together, men with men, women with women, and men and women no longer separated, until they saw neither the dark shadows of the Bastille nor of the guillotine but, as she said, unable to resist claiming a special affinity of freedom with her sex, 'liberty, with maternal wing . . . promising to shelter all mankind'.

2 Liberty on the Barricades: Woman, Politics and Sexuality in Delacroix

Marcia Pointon

Delacroix's painting *Liberty Guiding the People,* more popularly known as *Liberty on the Barricades,* is one of Europe's most familiar images.[1] (Plate 1) The picture, and especially its central figure, has effectively never been out of sight. To state what the picture represents is to imply that everyone sees the same thing. For Hobsbawm it shows 'a bare-breasted girl in Phrygian bonnet, stepping over the fallen, followed by armed men in characteristic costume' (Hobsbawm, 1978, p. 122). For Clark however, 'in Delacroix's *Liberty* it is the worker and the street-urchin who predominate. The National Guard lies dead in the foreground, his tunic torn and his helmet off: the cocked hat and the immaculate jacket of the Polytechnicien are glimpsed in the background, over the young bourgeois' shoulder to the right. And around Liberty cluster the student and the mob; there are five figures close to us and four of them are the *canaille,* the rabble' (Clark, 1973, p. 19). It is significant that Clark emphasises only living figures, ignoring the recently dead in the immediate foreground, closest to the viewer. I shall return to these figures later.

   In so far as it is possible to be precise about the circumstances surrounding the picture, they are as follows. The July Revolution broke out after publication of Polignac's four notorious ordinances, signed on 25 July 1830. In three days, Charles X's ultra monarchy was overthrown by a spontaneous uprising of the Paris workers led by former soldiers, national guardsmen and students of the Ecole Polytechnique. Delacroix himself was not present, though Alexandre Dumas tried hard to identify him with the figure of the top-hatted bourgeois in the foreground now generally agreed to be

Etienne Arago, director of the Théâtre de Vaudeville (Johnson, 1891, no. 144). Delacroix's own political alignment was Bonapartist, but in 1830, as opposed to 1848, Bonapartism and republican sentiments were confused and not incompatible. His intention to paint the picture is first recorded in a letter of 12 October, which makes clear his lack of actual involvement. 'I have undertaken a modern subject, *A Barricade* . . . and if I didn't fight for my country, at least I will paint for her.'[2] He completed the picture by December and it was accepted by the Salon jury on 13 April 1831.[3] By the time the exhibition opened on 1 May, Louis-Philippe was well installed and republican views were judged subversive. Finally Louis-Philippe purchased it in order to placate republican opinion. But despite efforts to put it out of sight, the picture was acclaimed in 1848 in a way it never had been in 1831. It was engraved in 1848, shown with the Emperor's permission at the 1855 Exposition Universelle where it again created a stir, and engraved again in 1870 (Adhémar, 1954).

The figure of Liberty, usually wrested from her context, has appeared on the sleeves of record albums and the covers of books, on German, Russian and Spanish revolutionary posters, in protests against the building of the Centre Pompidou, on bank notes, stamps and wall-paper advertisements.[4] (Plate 2) Writing in *Encounter* in 1972 about the trial of a Baader-Meinhof terrorist, Melvin J. Lasky headed his piece 'Lady on the Barricades' and declared: 'Her full right breast exposed, as in Delacroix, Marianne angrily climbs on to the barricades. For 30-year-old Margit Czenki the barricade at the moment happened to be the cashier's grille in the Bavarian *Hypotheken und Wechselbank.*'[5]. John Heartfield's photo-montage *Liberty Fights in their Ranks, Madrid 1936* takes up the theme, while Alexander Moffat's portrait of a group of contemporary Scottish poets, *Poets' Pub* (1980) features a depiction of 'Liberty' on the wall surface behind.[6] Most recently, at Marlborough Fine Art, we have seen the American pop artist, Red Grooms's *Liberty* of 1982 which both replicates Delacroix's image and interrogates its currency. (Plate 3) The bland face and simpering smile derive from media stereotypes of the feminine visage, the breasts (constructed of cardboard) project into the viewers' space and

Liberty's freedom-fighters are reduced to two token male faces barely visible over her shoulder.[7] For a picture that was received with marked lack of enthusiasm at the time of its exhibition, *Liberty on the Barricades* has attained an extraordinarily privileged status within cultural history.[8]

The reader may ask why, if Delacroix's painting has been so prominent in discourses verbal and visual, is there need for yet another article dealing with the image. In particular Hadjinicolaou (1979) has done a very thorough job and more recently Marina Warner (1985) has addressed the role of the allegorical woman in a specifically feminist text. My reply would be that Warner contributes nothing new to an analysis of this particular painting, fails to address the question of gender on anything but a very overt narrative level, and presents the imagery as an essentially unproblematic expression of the artist's political 'disquiet' and the 'clash of cynicism and optimism in his feelings' (Warner, p. 271). Hadjinicolaou, in a generally excellent analysis replete with a massive amount of empirical evidence, does not consider gender either and only addresses sexuality as a materialist issue around class as communicated through the isolated figure of Liberty.

The prime object of this paper is neither to chart the role of Delacroix's *Liberty on the Barricades* in cultural history nor to offer new light on the painting as an object produced within any art-historically identified tradition. I have no new evidence to adduce on the specific relationship between the production of the painting and the events of 1830. And I have no new information on Delacroix, the artist. *Liberty on the Barricades* is 'the most enduring image of the July revolution' (Johnson, no. 144) yet at the time of its execution its meanings were surrounded with uncertainty and have been disputed ever since. Paradoxically the very visibility of Delacroix's painting, and especially the visibility of the central figure, has rendered the painting virtually invisible. In so far as I refer to the literature of social and cultural history and of art history, it is to demonstrate how the complex and contradictory relationship between allegory, actuality, politics and the erotic is never confronted but always negotiated or side-stepped. My object is to address the question: what happens when you introduce the figure of a woman into a painting?

During the British miners' strike of 1984, a *Guardian* correspondent reported seeing a naked woman posing on top of a taxi holding an NUM strike poster (*Guardian,* 16 April 1984). This incident – in which an anonymous naked female posed on a public vehicle – demonstrates the abiding power of woman as a symbol in revolutionary politics. The fact that for the participants at the male rally a naked female on a taxi holding a strike banner probably constituted at best entertainment (a living manifestation of their page 3 fantasies) and at worst an example of bad taste, does not alter the fact that the presentation of female nudity or near-nudity in the context of a call to arms has an exceedingly long pedigree. We are not always aware of why we pick on stereotypes at particular moments; the explanation lies embedded in the general cultural consciousness. The *Guardian* reporter found it 'bizarre' but in fact this woman raised to a height above a crowd and bearing the insignia of the insurgents was a twentieth-century version of a living allegory, signifying an alliance of the erotic and the political, which would have been readily recognised in nineteenth-century France. Whether or not she, as an individual, had any connection with the NUM was immaterial; her role was symbolic. While absence of clothing may at one level signify eroticism, at another level – especially when accompanied by a banner or a flag into which the identity of the bearer is subsumed – nakedness signifies Truth. And the well-recognised tradition of representations of Truth in western culture bears this out. The anonymous woman on the taxi as well as named women who participated in picket-line activity were particular and individual women. But they are valorised in discourse and in history not for who they are but as aspects of womanhood culturally constructed.[9]

Now the process whereby actual characters participating in historical events are mythicised is common to women and men. Napoleon, Boadicea, King Alfred, Mussolini, Margaret Thatcher have all been in one sense transposed into the arena of the symbolic. It is a characteristic of powerful rulers to collude in this process. What we are considering here is rather different because we are not concerned with powerful rulers but with individuals who, if they ever did exist and possess an identity in actuality, have altogether lost that identity in the process of mythicisation.

Liberty on the Barricades may originate in an actual event within the historical specificity of the 1830 July Revolution. It has been suggested that Delacroix was inspired by an anonymous pamphlet of 1831 headed 'An unknown event of July 1830' describing the heroic action of a poor laundry-girl Anne-Charlotte D. who dressed only in her petticoat ('jupon')[10] went in search of her young brother, Antoine, an apprentice gilder who was fighting on the streets on 27 July. At length she found his naked corpse, so the story goes. Counting ten bullets she swore to kill as many Swiss. She shot nine and was killed herself just as she was about to shoot the tenth (Johnson, no. 144). Whether or not this is a true account does not matter; the notion of a 'real woman' behind Liberty is amply reinforced in contemporary and subsequent commentary on the painting.[11] Liberty was perceived to be an allegory who retained her womanhood. Like the naked woman on the taxi, Liberty is simultaneously real woman and allegorical female. My concern is to examine the invisible seam where the one shades into the other and to consider what implication the ambiguities arising from that shading have for the painting's meanings. What cultural meanings are generated in the shifts, uncertainties and ambiguities between the axes of Real and Allegorical? They are ambiguities more readily manifest in visual than in literary forms. The matrix upon which this study depends is thus constituted of complementary and opposing relationships and can be summed up as follows:

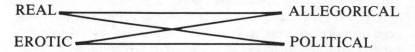

REAL ——————————————— ALLEGORICAL

EROTIC ——————————————— POLITICAL

To begin with we must ask why *Liberty on the Barricades* cannot adequately be explained by recourse to traditional art-historical procedures. Although a study of convention, of iconography and of reception is essential to any serious examination of the painting, it leaves unacknowledged and unexplained the central ambiguities of the work. Why, for a start, is the painting not straightforwardly an allegory? There has always been a tradition for introducing allegorical figures into actual historical situations, most notably in Rubens's work. The cycle of pictures relating to the Life of Marie de Medici, itself a programme with an overtly political aim, would have been very familiar to Delacroix as it was located in the Palais de Luxembourg.[12] Allegory, when she appears in a real context like this, can be said to constitute quite simply the visual manifestation of an idea in someone's head. Thus art historians may argue over whether the figure of Liberty derives from the winged Victory of Samothrace or the Aprodite of Melos, both in the Louvre, and how far Géricault's *The Raft of the Medusa* contributed to the foreground figures. But the overall view would be that Delacroix's Liberty is essentially an unproblematic embodiment of a communal idea that drives these men onwards towards the opposing forces defending the Hotel de Ville. The fact that, unlike the Aphrodite or the Winged Victory, she has hair under her arms and the fact that she was widely repudiated by contemporary critics can be set aside. 'La femme est ignoble.' Her skin is dirty, she has only one leg, her figure is gross, wrote the critics.[13] But we with hindsight, the argument would go, recognise the convention for the representation of allegorical females in actual situations, and that is what matters. The picture is thus part of a tradition within which the relationship between real and ideal is explored in French nineteenth-century painting. Thus its successor is Manet's *Dejeuner sur L'Herbe* which presents the locus of contemporaneity and realism (which is male) in a setting redolent of allegory (which is female) but stripped of any evident iconographical meaning.

Art history, focusing on Delacroix's Liberty, can produce arguments of interest to feminist history *and* help to locate Liberty within a different tradition. We might point out that there is a tradition for the representation of humble and often unnamed women engaged in heroic acts of warfare. They constitute a form of symbolic sexual inversion that serves to reinforce the existing order for, as Davis remarks, a world turned upside down can only be righted not changed (Davis, p. 184). Many of these Amazons acquire or are endowed with the attributes of great figures of the past like the Biblical Judith or Joan of Arc. The Napoleonic Wars produced memorable modern versions of this brand of female heroism by Wilkie and

Goya and the motif remained a crucial piece of encoding in the class conflict of the Russian Revolution as viewed from Europe. Fred Roe's *Revolution* (1910 – 11) depicts a buxom, red-lipped woman whose bared breasts, straw-stuffed clogs and courageous stance are enhanced by the genteel clothing and evident terror of the woman who clings to her.[14] (Plate 4)

Delacroix's Liberty certainly belongs to this lineage and also generates a great progeny especially after 1848 when, as Clark has demonstrated, many testified to the presence of individual women on the barricades (Clark, 1973, p. 25). Millet's drawing of a fierce woman trampling on men and dragging a woman by the hair is the best known.[15] In the most famous of these descriptions of 1848 we hear how 'a young woman, beautiful, dishevelled, terrible appeared on the barricade. This woman, who was a whore, lifted her dress to her waist and shouted to the National Guard: "Fire, you cowards, if you dare, on the belly of a woman!" A volley of shots knocked the wretched woman to the ground. She fell, letting forth a great cry' (quoted Clark 1973, pp. 25-6). Clark defines this reporting as travesty which is part deliberate invention. 'The image of the whore and the tricolour was not simply a lie or a piece of propaganda . . .', he says. 'It was an attempt to match . . . the horror of events' (ibid.). Women, as Agulhon tells us, became standard-bearers, living allegories (Agulhon, 1981, p. 65). Nevertheless the motif remained an inversion, however fixed in social consciousness, and when Courbet adapted Delacroix's composition for the cover of Baudelaire's radical journal *Le Salut Public* in 1848, he subsumed female Liberty into the male fighter with the silk top hat.

Reception aesthetics has remarked on a considerable disturbance around the exhibition of Delacroix's *Liberty on the Barricades*. Explanations for this disturbance are offered by reference to the current political circumstances within which the painting was produced. Bellos has drawn attention to the wobble over the date in the title of the picture – Delacroix gives 29 juillet and the official Salon catalogue gives 28 juillet which, given the speed of events, does make quite a difference. He also points out that the title varies between *La Barricade* and *La Liberté guidant le peuple,* with or without the date, and *La Liberté*. The curious wobble between the two dates — whether or not its cause or origin lies in a printing or scribal error — is a wobble between two different historical interpretations of the canvas and also between two different interpretations of history.[16]

The contradictory stances of critics around the issue of dirt in the painting are less readily explained by reference to the confused politics of 1830. Several commentators remarked on the muddy tones of the painting; 'a dirty and shameless woman of the streets', 'the most shameless prostitute of the dirtiest streets of Paris' are among the phrases used to describe the figure of Liberty.[17] Five of the critics identified by Bellos actually quote the well-known poem by Auguste Barbier which is generally accepted as providing a correlative for viewers of Delacroix's painting at the Salon:

> The truth is that Liberty is not a countess
> From the noble Faubourg Saint-Germain,
> A woman who swoons away at the slightest cry
> And who wears powder and rouge
> She is a strong woman with thrusting breasts
> A harsh voice and a hard charm
> Who with her bronzed skin and her flashing eyes
> Walks agile with great strides
> Delights in the shouts of the people, in the bloody
>   melée
> In the long drum rolls
> In the smell of powder, in the far-off pealing
> Of church bells and the rumble of canons
> Who takes her lovers only from among the people
> Who lends her wide flanks only
> To people who are strong like her, and who want to
>   embrace her
> With arms soaked in gore.[18]

Hadjinicolaou regards the accusation of dirt as deriving from the colour of Liberty's flesh. This, like the suggestion of hair under the arm, ruptured the conventions of the Salon nude (Hadjinicolaou, 1979, p. 25) and had, as Clark has recently established in his study of Manet's *Olympia,* profound political connotations (Clark, 1985, Ch. 2). Bellos rightly points out that the identification of the goddess as whore comes from a wide political spectrum. He puts forward an argument which, without reference to gender or sex, explains the issue of dirt by reference to the political uncertainty of the context and the issue of class. Thus the goddess is seen as a 'common prostitute'; her role on the barricade can be seen as confirming the aristocratic–legitimist opinion of the reign of Louis-Philippe, brought to power by the rabble; *and* her role can also be seen, within the same general vision, as supporting the left-wing liberal view, namely that Louis-Philippe had betrayed a genuinely *popular* uprising (Bellos, forthcoming).

Persuasive though this is as a class analysis, it leaves unopened the question of why a 'dirty' woman, if that is what she is (rather than simply a proletarian), should be a symbol that is so widely recognised. As Mary Douglas says: 'Dirt. . . is never a unique, isolated event. Where there is dirt there is system' (Douglas, 1984, p. 35). Moreover, this analysis presupposes one single meaning (and two opposing interpretations) inscribed in the image of the woman as Liberty, the evacuation of all other meanings and the isolation of the main figure from its pictorial context.

The iconographers, chief among whom are Agulhon and Hobsbawm, have also concentrated on the figure of Liberty removed from the pictorial construction of which she forms a part. They examine her role as bearer of meanings relative to gender. For Hobsbawm she is 'an active emancipated girl' (Hobsbawm, 1978, p. 124). For him as for Heinrich Heine, whose response to the painting (which he saw in the Salon of 1831) has been examined by Margaret Rose in her recent book *Marx's Lost Aesthetic* (1984), Liberty is a Venus of the streets, her semi-nudity a sign for Saint-Simonian sexual and social emancipation. With astonishing facility Hobsbawm discards Liberty's function as allegory. The figure's 'concreteness removes it from the usual allegorical role of females', he says. 'She does not inspire or represent; she *acts*.' This is the cue for Hobsbawm to ask why, in the imagery of the labour movement, women become images of suffering (as in the figures of Käthe Kollwitz) while the clothed male appears to begin to replace the unclothed or semi-clothed female as image of the heroic proletarian (Hobsbawm, 1978, p. 127).

Hobsbawm deservedly gets severely reprimanded by both feminist historians and by the French historian Agulhon. The former point out that Hobsbawm is guilty of comparing images and emblems with 'the social realities of the period' as if we were unquestionably in possession of a full and accurate knowledge of what these realities were (Alexander et al., 1979). Agulhon in turn gives a detailed account of the genesis of the figure of Liberty, of her assimilation into the personification of the Republic in official iconography after 1792 and establishes the importance of convention in the dissemination of this particular image, a question wholly ignored by Hobsbawm. Thus in 1792, we learn, it was decreed that the Republic should be represented by a seal which was 'to bear the image of France in the guise of a woman dressed in the style of Antiquity, standing upright, her right hand holding a pike surmounted by a Phrygian cap or cap of Liberty, her left resting upon a sheaf or fasces; at her feet a tiller and as an inscription, the words: in the name of the French Republic (Alughon, 1981, p. 18).

Agulhon's work establishes the frequency of images of Liberty and the process whereby Liberty appropriates the traditional role of the Virgin Mary in popular cults. Whether Liberty is a saint or a new goddess on the one hand or a trollop on the other depends upon how you view the politics of liberation. Agulhon distinguishes between the alluring Liberty who is a child of nature and therefore semi-naked, and the nourishing life-giving Liberty who suckles her children (as in Daumier's celebrated image of the Republic).

On the question of nudity Agulhon states that a chastely clad Liberty represents the politics of moderation and that the exposing of parts of the body has a fundamental democratic significance. We must not, says Agulhon, equate nudity with sexuality, otherwise all allegory is sexual. If Hobsbawm makes misguided assumptions about the relations between art and society, Agulhon is in danger of assuming that there are no such relations. The account in his book *Marianne into Battle,* essential though it be to any student of the subject, does not explain the transition from the chaste and emblematic representations of Liberty that were a commonplace of the period to Delacroix's arresting figure.[19] Agulhon's argument excludes multiple meanings or metonymic connections. Whilst nudity does not *necessarily* imply sexuality it is absurd to insist that it never does so. And allegory need not, *per se,* render imagery immune from representations of sexuality.

Now here we come to the main focus of my concern: how if at all, are questions of gender and sexuality a part of this image's complex and many layered communication? Hobsbawm recognises the latent eroticism but accounts for it in terms of class. Hadjinicolaou, too, separates Liberty from her surroundings and reads her sexuality represented through the recognised medium of dirt as a sign for class: 'From all points of view, this dirty woman can only be a *woman of the people, Liberty guiding the People* is no more than a woman of the people guiding the people' (Hadjinicolaou, 1979, p. 25). Clark, evidently profoundly uncomfortable with the notion of sexuality, says: 'It is not, of course, that the final Liberty is sexless, far from it. But her sexuality is a public one: her nakedness is not one with which Delacroix was endlessly familiar: her breasts and shoulders are those of Marie Deschamps' (a working woman on whom tracts and pamphlets had been published) (Clark, 1973, p. 18). Clark turns back to the artist and sees, by looking at sketches, how this figure has grown from the habitual private fantasy, a fantasy that can be pictorially related to female figures in Delacroix's execution of non-contemporary themes, into public image. He sees the sketch as privately erotic and the painting as publicly sexual. The implication is that if female sexuality is made public it becomes as a consequence politically identifiable with a position on the left. Agulhon refuses the question of sexuality altogether by insisting that nakedness is exclusively a convention and, as such, cannot carry other meanings beside those that belong in tradition with the convention.

Without rejecting the historical appropriateness of the various political readings of the painting that have been proposed, I would like to suggest that there is a further hitherto unexplored level of meaning within this picture, a level which centres on the politics of sexuality and the recognition of gender power relations. The central paradox of Liberty as a concept (Freedom is good but Licence is bad) is represented through the visual paradox of the exposed body in which nakedness equals Truth but nudity equals Eroticism. The relationship of women's bodies to history is, as Brown and Adams have pointed out (1979, p. 35), complex and, as yet, unfathomed. They speak of the 'ambiguity which allows the body to be ever present and hence a witness to history and yet never *implicated* in that history and always there only in a repressed form'. We might add, in relation to a discussion of *visual* representation, in a conventionalised form. 'We cannot know in advance the precise intersection (if any) of questions of sexuality with questions of the body with respect to any particular issue' (ibid., p. 35). In the issue of revolutionary struggle it would seem that the presence of woman is requisite to representation as a symbol of the irreconcilable duality of the feminine (hearth and home in opposition to war and the picket line) and the erotic as socially constructed (naked women with banners, whores with dirty skins). It may well be that this duality is an essential component in the psychology of aggression. Sexuality is a powerful agent in political discourse (we only have to look at the imagery of Fascism to recognise that).[20] What I want to suggest here is that it *does* matter beyond the considerations of convention and its operation that Liberty is a woman, that her function in the picture is more than the simple embodiment of an idea in people's heads, that she cannot be explained as an unproblematic cypher for proletarian struggle. We must ask what happens when you introduce the figure of a woman into the picture. There is a discourse of sexuality in the picture such as cannot be adequately explained by the iconography of republican or proletarian imagery. In other words, the recognition of sexuality in the figure of Liberty, a recognition that historically has been mediated through her identification with prostitutes and dirt, cannot simply be assimilated into an argument about republican or anti-republican sentiment.

In opposition to the usual practice of looking for sources for particular motifs (comparing Liberty with the sun images of Delacroix's teacher, Guérin, for instance).[21] I want to look at the imagery in terms of its deviancy. There are, at the very least, three manifestly deviant points in *Liberty on the Barricades*. Call them negative comparisons if you like. In the first place we might ask not what the source is for the figure of Liberty but where in the canon we find the figure of a woman singled out and surmounting a pile of bodies. In military scenes it is normally a male function;[22] the female equivalent is the harvest waggon. Here wholesome images depict a buxom woman surmounting an energised mass of humanity. (Plate 5) Delacroix, probably unconsciously, calls up this image and in an unnatural alliance fuses notions of military conquest, forging a connection between what is male and what is female. Liberty, for all her fine, wholesome, thrusting breasts, surmounts a pile of debris and bodies − male bodies. She is a powerful woman striding towards the viewer over the bodies of dead men.

Liberty's allegorical status does not protect her from direct association with violence and death. Indeed, as Bellos points out, the overt message of a picture featuring both Liberty *and* a barricade has to be either that violence is necessary to the attainment of liberty or that liberty can only be achieved by violence (Bellos, p. 3). Earlier representations keep Liberty, in her allegorical role, clean of violence; she enters the stage at the final point in the narration, as a divine witness to the goal having been attained.[23] In pictorial imagery, once a woman is associated with violent confrontation even if she is symbolic or token rather than individual or participatory, the accusation of prostitution is frequently levelled at her. And this is true of life as of art. The accounts from the coalfields of women observers during the 1984-85 miners' strike being told: 'Get back home, you whore, you prostitute' by the police, are legion. The perturbation over the question of dirt in this image is a direct consequence of the deviation which substitutes a harvest of death (of whatever side is not important at this level) for a harvest of corn. The filth is metonymically transferred from the barricade to the woman in the minds of the viewers just as class and political hatred are focused on sexuality when the police allegedly abuse the miners' wives.

The concreteness of the figure of Liberty (the hair under the arm, the hand grasping a contemporary fire-arm) is not only a feature that can be interpreted as an image of emancipation and enthusiasm on the part of the proletariat. It is rendering visible that which should remain implicit and which, having been made visible, is extremely threatening. Nakedness in its guise as Truth has the power to inspire. Eroticism harnessed to the cause (whether it be the commercial selling of motor cars or the solidarity of the miners) and controlled, depersonalised and managed may have a comparable function. But sexuality is inherently dangerous. It is the recognition of sexuality that leads to the naming of Liberty as a whore.

Historians of sexuality have drawn attention to the construction of 'woman' both in terms of gender contrast and around the polarity virgin/whore. 'The bourgeois lady's (a)sexuality was defined against not only the prostitute but also a sexuality imputed to working-class women in general' (Cherry and Pollock, 1984, p. 223). It is also significant that one of the 1831 critics described Liberty as 'une pensionnaire de Bicêtre' (an inmate of one of the Paris lunatic asylums) and that Du Camp in 1855 suggested that she had escaped from St Lazare.[24] These identifications of Liberty with lunacy suggest that she may well have been apprehended as precisely the type of the hysterical woman whom Foucault names as a privileged object of knowledge and also as a target and anchorage point for ventures of knowledge in the construction of sexuality (Foucault, 1978). The line between inspiration and fear is a very narrow one. The eroticism of the partially clothed can give way to terror before the totally exposed as an anonymous East European cartoon with its nexus of sex, danger and power indicates. The woman soldier here exposes herself above the dug-out and the men run away clutching their grenades.[25] The sexuality of Liberty is, as Clark points out, very public. I would draw attention to the disjuncture between the profile cameo head and the three-dimensional body with breast as the composition's centre. But it is a mistake to locate sexuality in the picture exclusively within the figure of Liberty, for all that it is upon her that the critics' attention focused and continues to focus. Sexuality is constructed within the picture as a whole by a complex concatenation of images. The whole painting becomes the site for the construction of sexuality within imagery *and* within history. And here I want to move on to the second of the three deviant points I identified.

Recent work on the gaze of the spectator by Mulvey, Bryson and others, taking up a proposition originally made by John Berger, posits that men watch and women watch themselves being watched. *The Oath of the Horatii*, Bryson suggests, divides male activity from female passivity. In *The Intervention of the Sabine Women* female activity merely constitutes a screen between us the viewers and the world of male violence (Bryson, 1984, Ch. 3). In Delacroix's painting (which Bryson omits from his discussion of tradition and desire) Liberty in full-bodied vigour strides towards us; we are separated from her predominantly by the corpses of two men. Both are sexually suggestive and the one at the left is manifestly erotic with his finely featured head flung back, his abundant dark hair falling away, his shirt open to reveal one nipple, his naked legs arranged to reveal his pubic hair (though not his penis) and one sock suggesting the *déshabille* of the boudoir as much as the spoliation of the battle-ground.[26]

It may be said that in so describing this figure I am guilty of precisely the same subjective defining of the erotic that feminists have rejected in male discourse. As the well-known photograph of the man posing on the roof of the car demonstrates,[27] we are culturally conditioned in a society in which heterosexuality dominates image-making, to recognise the erotic via images of women. Leo Steinberg's recent work (1983) has, moreover, shown how we can be culturally conditioned to be oblivious to parts of images that disrupt a dominant received notion. In this case the received notion is that the figure of Liberty constitutes the image and she, in isolation, is the site for the sexual or political discourse. Contemporaries noticed the corpse in the foreground and attention is drawn to it by the gaze of the terrified young freedom-fighter at the left which passes directly over this body in its confrontation with the enemy; it is a body which, in its exposed finesse of limb, is as deviant from its source among the emaciated corpses in Géricault's *The Raft of the Medusa* as it is dependent. The tension between the exposed flesh of the living Liberty and the deceased flesh of the man is striking. The phallic gun of the *sans-culotte* to the left explicitly reinforces the theme, making visible what, on the corpse, is hidden. The complex metonymic structure of Delacroix's picture can, perhaps, most clearly be apprehended if we set it alongside the celebrated documentation of 1851 and 1870 by Meissonier and Manet from which this tension is absent.[28]

It is significant that posterity has frequently lifted the figure of Liberty away from her barricade. The picture, taken as a whole, is poised uncomfortably on the threshold where subtext becomes text. In attempting to examine this seam or juncture, it is worth noting two facts from Delacroix's life. First, his diaries contain many accounts which suggest a fundamental fear of women. He longed for women, was very disturbed by them, but needed their presence. He was often impotent. Baudelaire says of Delacroix: 'Long before his death, he had expelled women from his life . . . In this question as in many others, Oriental ideas got the upper hand in him in vivid and despotic fashion. He considered woman as an *objet d'art,* delightful and suitable for exciting the mind but a disobedient and disturbing *objet d'art.* If permitted to cross the threshold of one's heart, she would ravenously devour one's time and strength.'[29] In the second place we should remember that Delacroix himself regarded the whole enterprise of *Liberty on the Barricades* as a sublimation for his own non-participation in the actual violence: 'If I didn't fight for my country, at least I will paint for her.' So that the visual image itself constitutes, for Delacroix, a kind of vicarious involvement with life.

Delacroix has allowed into his picture an implicit alliance between the erotic and the political which transgresses in so far as it begins to transform into an imagery of sexuality that is, by its nature, essentially an imagery of power. And here I come to the third example of deviancy from the expected or anticipated. In David's famous picture *Marat Assassiné*[30] (Plate 6) the murderess, Charlotte Corday, is expelled from the narrative. Only her handwriting − neutralised as a fact of history − remains. Marat's murdered body is sanctified, purified, desexualised. It is in striking contrast, for example, to the corpse in the foreground of Delacroix's painting. In fact we know that Marat had a very elaborate fancy bathroom and was stabbed by a young woman. Munch's lithograph *Marat Assassiné* (Plate 7) restores to the narrative the explicitly sexual motif that David carefully evacuated. The events surrounding the death of Marat must have had profoundly disturbing sexual implications: an unknown woman enters the famous man's bathroom and stabs him while he sits in the bath. David recognised the need to neutralise those implications if the painting were to be about anything but sex. The option of neutrality is not one chosen by Delacroix; on the contrary he chooses to play upon precisely that conjunction of violence, sexuality and death that David avoids. Given that the naming of woman as whore constitutes recognition of sexuality inscribed in imagery, the indecision among critics about whether Delacroix's Liberty is a whore or a heroine is a response not only to political uncertainty but also to ambiguity in the construction of sexuality within the picture, and by implication within history. The same ambiguity is apparent in Delacroix's earlier painting, *Greece on the Ruins of Missolonghi.*[31] (Plate 8) The image is, like that of Liberty, essentially contradictory. Is she a personification of Greece or is she a Greek woman who symbolises her country? Her half-open lips, heavy-lidded eyes and clothing which reveals most of her breasts and falls in suggestive folds between her legs make her an erotic and desirable image. Her gesture is one of surrender, or one of appeal. The connotations may be sexual and/or political. In the distance a Turkish warrior stands guard but it is Greece who occupies the painting's space and kneels with her weight upon a great boulder from beneath which appears the hand of a dead man. The lower foreground contains, at rhythmically defined intervals from left to right: the artist's signature (his presence in the picture), a splash of blood and a disembodied human hand very like the hand at the bottom right of *Liberty*. The severed right hand functions on a symbolic level in association with the artist's signature whose position it matches on the paint surface. It represents the artist's creative effectivity and, imaged thus, has powerful connotations of castration. It is the sign on a simple pictorial level for the castration anxiety that is expressed metaphorically in *Liberty on the Barricades*.

To ask whether the painting is sexual or political is to ask the wrong question because it is a painting in which — in a much less complex manner than in *Liberty* — the political in the sense of the war between the Greeks and the Turks is communicated via the intensely personal exploration of the ambiguous relationship between sex and power. In this relationship the vanquished possesses power, female sexuality is both bloody and inviting, and male individuality is reduced to a limp token hand under a stone.

It is significant that for most of its life this picture has been deprived of its correct title. It was not possible to describe Greece as dirty or as a whore; Greece was the beautiful cradle of western civilisation, the home of Antiquity, raped by the Turks. But it was possible to mis-recognise her. When the picture was exhibited in 1829 it bore the title *La Grèce (Allégorie)*. 'She is represented with the appearance of a woman weeping on the ruins'. Until very recently, however, the picture has habitually been known as *Greece Expiring on the Ruins of Missolonghi* (Johnson, no. 98). The process whereby a strong woman, powerfully pleading, is recognised as a woman at her last gasp, expiring, is curious indeed.

Delacroix's own political displacement in 1830 finds expression not only through a narrative which celebrates an alliance between the bourgeoisie and the proletariat but also — and on a profoundly disturbing level — through the visual exploration of his own ambivalence towards sex and power. The partially clothed, naked woman introduced into the discourse of contemporary politics can never be exclusively allegorical *or* exclusively real. Sex is a metaphor for confrontation and violence is a means of exploring sexuality. Violence is, as we have seen, inextricably connected with Liberty in Delacroix's depiction of 1830. In *The Death of Sardanapalus* and many other paintings Delacroix depicts violent acts perpetrated on women by men. In *Greece* and *Liberty,* however, powerful women hold sway in a world of male violence. They do not intervene like the Sabine women, they are not vague shadowy figures seen in the distance like emblems of the feminine as in Millet's 1848 *Liberty*. They reign triumphant. And the visual statement of *Greece* is thus in contradiction with the narrative. She cannot logically be both defeated and dominant. But this is the central paradox of the Real — Allegorical — Political — Erotic relationship. Both Greece and Liberty are sexually dominant in a world of male carnage. Misrecognitions of Liberty as a prostitute or of Greece as expiring are in no sense 'incorrect' since the powerfully affective central paradox of both pictures demands a contradictory response. In both pictures the artist has asserted his authorship — and thereby his involvement — not by a signature outside of the picture's main space, in a vacuum, but by inscribing his name on the rocks, the material substance on which the weight of Greece bears down and on a spar of wood which makes up the barricades over which Liberty strides.

3 Women, Power and History: The Case of Nineteenth-Century France

Michelle Perrot

The word 'power' in French is polysemic: in the singular (*le pouvoir*) it has political connotations and refers primarily to the central, cardinal power of the state, generally recognised as being male. In the plural, it breaks up into a number of fragments, equivalent to those diffuse and peripheral 'influences' in which women have a large share.[1] While women do not have power, it is said, they do have powers (*des pouvoirs*). In the contemporary western world, they have taken over private life, the family, even perhaps social life and civil society. They reign over men's imaginary world, peopling their nights and their dreams. 'We are more than half of you; we are the life you spend in your sleep', declares the heroine of a novel in the century – the nineteenth – which, more than any other, celebrated woman as 'Muse and Madonna' (Michaud, 1985, n. 1).

AN AMBIGUOUS THEME OF OUR TIMES

Representations of the power of women could easily be the subject of an immense historical and anthropological study. Such representations are numerous and have a long history, but are often repetitive. They are variations on the original theme in Genesis of the seductive powers of the eternal Eve. Woman, fount of evil and misfortune, nocturnal force, power of darkness, queen of the night – as opposed to Man, the representative of order and reason in the full light of day – has been a major romantic theme, most notably in opera, from Mozart to Wagner. In *Parsifal,* the quest for 'salvation consists of exorcising the threat posed by woman, so that the order of men shall triumph' (Michaud, 1985).

In nineteenth-century French society, the image prevails of a tentacular power, circulating within the tissue of society, an occult, hidden power, the secret driving force of the world. According to an English traveller in 1908, 'though legally women occupy a much inferior status to men, in practice they constitute the superior sex. They are "the power behind the throne", and both in the family and in business relations undoubtedly enjoy greater consideration than English women' (Zeldin, 1972, p. 346). This is a prosaic version of the frequently-held notion that women pull strings behind the scenes, while poor men, like puppets, gesticulate on the public stage. Like Lady Macbeth, prompting a political decision often made in the bedroom, woman, though rarely a criminal herself, is seen as the real instigator of the crime. 'Cherchez la femme', chorus the great criminologists of the nineteenth century, Lombroso and Joly.

But women are not only seen as a force for evil, it must be said. They can also be a civilising power, another very old theme revived in the nineteenth century by insistence on the educational influence surrounding the newly valued child. Mothers hold 'the destinies of the human race' in their hands, as Louis-Aimé Martin wrote in a book with the significant title *On the Education of Mothers, or the Civilisation of the Human Race by Women* (1834). The obsessive image of the mother tends to absorb all other possibilities.

But does this not mean that women *in practice* possess the real power? 'There is a sex, known as the weaker one which nevertheless exerts over both family and society, a sort of omnipotence, for good as well as for ill', preached Father Mercier, whose arguments have been penetratingly analysed by Marcel Bernos.

This view of the reversed roles of men and women has an oddly contemporary ring. It is an approach encouraged by the increased importance nowadays accorded to civil society and its actors, to the private dimension of life. In a period of growing privatisation, to borrow Hirschman's expression, the feminine pole of society comes to take precedence.[2]

The notion has become a commonplace of which echoes can be found in the mouths of politicians of every colour. Thus we find the former French President, Giscard d'Estaing, saying in the 1970s: 'it is women who will change the world' — a remark which revives the old myth of woman as man's salvation. From this starting point stem both the new level of responsibility to be assumed by women — a formidable one — and the notion of women defeating men and taking over the world which underlies many texts by contemporary male authors and is rendered explicit in works like Fellini's *City of Women,* or Philippe Sollers' novel, *Femmes.*

From another perspective, recent feminist research has also at times contributed to this new evaluation of women's power. In their concern to go beyond the language of oppression, to subvert the notion of the domination of women by men, feminists have sought to portray women as present and active, to demonstrate the richness of the parts they play, the coherence of their specific 'culture' and the real existence of their powers. This was during what might be termed the heyday of matriarchy as a key concept, particularly noticeable at a certain stage in feminist anthropology in America, and represented in France by Françoise d'Eaubonne's *Amazons* and Pierre Samuel's *Guerrières et Gaillardes* (1975) — a passionate and committed demonstration of women's physical strength.

Certain works of social anthropology, themselves of major importance, have contributed to this change of direction: for example, Martine Segalen's very striking studies and to some extent those of Yvonne Verdier. Rightly wishing to reject the false vision of woman in rural society as a victim, an image constructed out of the preconceptions of nineteenth-century folklorists like Abel Hugo, Martine Segalen tends to depict a society without conflict, based on a balanced division of roles, tasks and spaces, complementary rather than competing. This balance, the product of many centuries of accumulated habits, was only disturbed, she argues, by modern economic developments, which, with the coming of the banking system, strengthened the impact of masculine business management. It is a thesis developed far more systematically by Ivan Illich in his book *Gender* (1983) in which he contrasts the complementarity of recognised and organised differences in traditional societies with the 'single-sex economics' of industrial societies and their disastrous consequences for women.

Two anthropological studies by Susan Rogers (1975, 1977) illustrate both this concern to demonstrate women's alternative powers and an awareness of the ultimate limitations of this thesis and its variable applicability. In her earlier monograph on a village in north-east France, Rogers laid much emphasis on the informal powers of the women who in practice controlled the greater part of resources and decision making; in such circumstances, the perpetuation of the 'myth' of male power served the interests of both sexes; behind the fiction of male power, the women were free to develop their own strategies. In a later study, this time in the Aveyron in south-west France, Susan Rogers was compelled to modify her conclusions quite considerably. Here, the women had far fewer powers, even of an informal kind. The explanation was chiefly to be found in the more dispersed pattern of habitat (which made it more difficult for women to communicate with each other) and also in different inheritance patterns. So it is difficult to claim that there is a single general model for all rural societies and the author concludes that more refined models, with several variables, need to be developed. This also prompts one to be cautious about universalist evaluations of societies of the past.

A similar wish to overturn conventional historical perspectives, to show the reality of women's presence in the most everyday forms of history, has also been behind the endeavours of women's history in recent years. Let three examples stand for the rest. Two recent, much discussed books by Jeanne Bourin (1981) and Régine Pernoud (1984) have suggested that women may have enjoyed comparatively privileged status in the Middle Ages. Georges Duby has however argued against a view he regards as over-idyllic. In *The Knight, the Lady and the Priest* (1983), he stresses on the contrary the extent to which women remained an object of male power, a counter in matrimonial exchange and, when all is said and done, a very silent group. 'A lot is talked about them. But what do we really know about them?', he asks at the end of his book.

A second example is the study of 'the bourgeoises of northern France in the nineteenth century', by Bonnie Smith (1981) who uncovers the multivalent activities of the 'ladies of the leisured class', elbowed out of their original position in the family firms but attempting to build what she describes as a sort of domestic feminism based on the household and religion. And thirdly, the same spirit can be traced in the book *L'Histoire sans qualités* (Dufrancatel *et al.*, 1979) in which in my contribution, I wished to replace the prevalent image of the housewife as perpetual victim, neglected and negligible, beaten and humiliated, with the figure of the 'rebellious woman of the people', actively resisting oppression, standing guard over the food supply, managing the family budget, occupying the central place in urban society.

All three examples display a similar approach. They proceed by inversion, turning the world upside down. Black becomes white (or red if preferred). They stress division rather than conflict, insisting on the existence of a separate sphere, a 'world of women', characterised by its own forms of sociability, forms of expression, in short, its own 'culture'. This type of approach was undoubtedly the product of a euphoric phase in the re-evaluation of women's history, along with the discovery of the pleasures of all-women conviviality.

But it carries with it its own dangers and weaknesses. It is too systematic and too dichotomic. It reinforces the view of women's 'social power' held by those who have every intention of keeping it that way. Since women have this kind of power, what more do they want?

So it must be realised that the analysis of women's power can itself be a stake in the power game.

THE QUESTION OF WOMEN'S POWER IN THE
NINETEENTH CENTURY

By taking the example of the nineteenth century, I should like to demonstrate the links between the formulation of a question and the type of society that produces it, in particular the type of relationship between the sexes which structures it. It should be made clear that this is not a search for origins. The nineteenth century did not invent anything in this respect; it merely reformulated an extremely old — indeed an age-old — question, appropriating it for itself. It could be said perhaps to have added some extra emphasis, to the extent that the construction of the western democracies was accompanied by – indeed based on – a stricter definition of the public and private spheres and the roles of the sexes.

In fact it would be interesting to compare the nineteenth-century experience with others. In some societies, the exclusion of women from political power was taken for granted; in others it was accompanied by justifications or compensations; in others again it admitted of degrees of exclusion. Both theories and practices could well be examined and compared. Women and politics is a field where our joint efforts of reflexion are still needed (cf. Chapters 6 and 7).

History and women's power in the nineteenth century: the case of Michelet

'Les femmes! Quelle puissance!', wrote Michelet. Both as individual and as historian, he was haunted by the question. Michelet had a profoundly sexualised notion of history as Thérèse Moreau has shown (1982). According to Michelet, the opposition between man = culture and woman = nature has dominated the history of societies and dictated the pulse of events. Deeply ambivalent, the female principle was to be held in respect – the more so since female nature had two poles – one maternal and beneficial, the other magical, red as blood, black as the devil and the bearer of evil. As mothers, women did good – thus on 5 and 6 October 1789 they were fulfilling their traditional role as housewives. 'Women were in the vanguard of our revolution. There is no reason to wonder at this: their suffering was greater' (Michelet, 1939, I, p. 254). Similarly, during the festival of the Federation, they cemented the union of citizens by contributing family spirit to patriotism, combining public and private.

Whether bidden or unbidden, they took a most energetic part in the feast of the Federation. In one village, the men had met together alone in a great building to compose an address to the National Assembly. The women approached and listened, then entered the building with tears in their eyes and wanted to join in. The address was read out to them; and they associated themselves with it with all their hearts. This profound union of family and fatherland penetrated all hearts with a sentiment hitherto unknown. (ibid., pp. 408-9)

But if they were to depart from this role, and usurp male power − like Catherine de Medici, the incarnation of evil and misfortune − if they were to unleash the violence, bloodthirstiness and nocturnal passions contained within them, Michelet warned, history like a torrent bursting its banks would destroy everything in its path.

The course of public events depended, as did the happiness and tranquillity of households, on the proper balance of power between the sexes. Michelet demonstrates this in his account of the different phases of the history of France and in particular of the Revolution. The fourteenth century, dominated by patriarchal rule and royal authority, seemed to him to be an age of progress precisely because of the exclusion of women. In the fifteenth century, the confusion of the law, the mingling of the sexes led to disorder in the mind, like the madness of Charles VI followed by that of the kingdom. That perfect embodiment of maleness, François I, restored order, but after his death, Catherine de Medici's rule ushered in a long period of role-reversal and sexual deviance. Thus woman 'perverted history for a hundred years'.

The feminisation of the monarchy at the end of the eighteenth century was also a sign of decadence. By education and by nature, women were counter-revolutionary; they preferred the anarchy of the spoken word to the order of the written. Naturally 'aristocrats', they were hostile to equality. 'The sacred word of the New Age − Fraternity − is one that woman is learning to spell but cannot yet read' (quoted Moreau, 1982, p. 170). It was woman who provoked outbursts of violence − the September massacres were a bloody witches' sabbath, an orgy shot through with women's desire. And the men responsible for the Terror − Marat, Couthon, Robespierre − were 'men-women'. Marat especially 'was by temperament a woman and more than a woman, nervous and sanguine'; his house, like his skin disease, were effeminate. Only Danton was 'first and foremost a male' and thereby able to impress both women and the people − itself feminine − and perhaps the only man capable of saving the Revolution (cf. Moreau, 1982, pp. 201-39).

Sex roles have probably never been defined with such normative and explanatory single-mindedness. For Michelet, political power was an attribute of men – and of virile men. What was more, the patriarchal order should everywhere prevail: both in the family and in the state. It was the law of historical equilibrium.

Matriarchy: a myth about origins

The question of matriarchy was at the centre of anthropological debates in the nineteenth century. Françoise Picq[3] has shown that there was a broad measure of consensus about it. For Bachofen, Morgan, Engels or Briffault, it was self-evident that women promoted the idea and had established it as a barrier to protect themselves from the lubricity of men (Bachofen). But most writers considered this a primitive and barbaric stage. Maternal law was one step in the establishment of a law in which patrilinear descent marked the decisive progress. For Bachofen, paternal Roman law was a leap forward for civilisation. Engels alone underlined 'the historic defeat of the female sex' which accompanied the consolidation of private property and saw in monogamy and its modern form – bourgeois marriage – the key to women's oppression. Unlike Morgan, to whom he otherwise owed so much, Engels considered that this evolution could not be called progress. In a sense, the golden age was in the past. But by the same token, Engels lastingly subordinated women's liberation, in socialist theory and action, to the collectivisation of property.

This is too familiar to be dwelt on here. But on the subject of women's power, several interesting features are embedded in the dominant ideas of the nineteenth century. First there is the civilising power vested in the mother; Briffault in particular develops the theme of sedentarity and agriculture. Then there is the dominating figure of the paterfamilias, the ultimate goal of this teleological progress, whose achievements by the end of the century were numberless and could be justified in the name of the general interest, public and private. Finally, there is the location within the historical progress of relations between the sexes: they are not rooted in some natural fixed order, but are the end-result of a development. The subjection of women is therefore the result of a process which could easily be regarded as reversible.

It is easy to understand then the passionate interest shown in these theories by feminists. In 1902, a 'French feminist study group' put the question on its agenda and published a brochure about it. But it was above all in Germany, in Heidelberg and Munich, in the progressive intellectual circles so well represented by the Von Richthofen sisters with their connections with Gross, Max Weber and Lawrence, that the question of matriarchy was submitted to intense discussion, along with sexual relations, madness and free love (Green, 1974).

It is easy too to understand the appeal such authors held a few years ago for feminist anthropologists facing the sexless logic of structuralism. But matriarchy has turned out after all to be a dead end. Even the Trobriand islanders have lost something of their appeal. On the other hand, as a representation of the power of women and the relations between the sexes, these texts still retain something of their savour.

PUBLIC, PRIVATE, AND WOMEN'S POWER IN THE NINETEENTH CENTURY

The frontiers between the public and the private have not always been fixed. They have changed over time. Their evolution, the fragility of their equilibrium, the overall trend towards privatisation, with alternating phases when first public then private predominate, have been one of the major themes of contemporary thought, as the writings notably of J. Habermas, Richard Sennett and A.L. Hirschman have shown. Nineteenth-century liberalism in this respect marks a high point, even if the notion of civil society (somewhere between the private individual and the state) remains, in France at any rate, a rather imprecise notion.

What interests me most here is the way the political arena was constituted, an arena virtually coterminous with the 'public' sphere and one from which two groups were excluded: proletarians and women. In France, the Fourth Estate was more successful in promoting its rights than the Second Sex. Proletarian men, after 1848, willingly concurred in the bourgeois veto on recognising the political capacity of women.

This exclusion of women sat uneasily with the Declaration of the Rights of Man, which had proclaimed the equality of all individuals. Were women not 'individuals'? The question was an embarrassing one, as many thinkers − Condorcet for example − had realised. The only justification could be to argue that the sexes were different. That is why, in the nineteenth century, the old arguments were given renewed vigour, drawing upon the discoveries of medicine and biology (Gould, 1981). A naturalist discourse was revived, insisting on the existence of two 'species' with very different aptitudes and attributes: men were credited with a brain (much more important than a penis) intelligence, clear-sighted reason, the capacity to take decisions; women were identified with the heart, sensibility and feelings.

Are these just stale, old stereotypes revived by the bitter enemies of feminism? No doubt to some extent they are, as a recent thesis by Anne-Lise Maugue has shown.[4] But they are also the principles of political organisation as pronounced by some of the most serious of philosophers. Thus Fichte: 'Her femininity bestows upon woman an increased capacity for practical aptitude, but in no way one for speculative aptitude.' As a consequence, 'women cannot hold public office.' Hegel speaks of the 'natural vocation' of the two sexes. 'Man has his real and substantial life in the State, science and other activity of the same kind − let us say in general in combat and work, which pit him against the external world and against himself.' Woman, on the other hand, is intended for piety and domesticity. 'If women are placed at the head of the government, the State is in danger. For they do not act according to the requirements of the collectivity but according to the whims of their own preferences and thoughts' (quoted Michaud, 1985). Auguste Comte goes even further since he speaks of the 'radical inaptitude of the female sex for leadership, even of the family', on account of the 'sort of state of continuous childhood' which characterises the female sex. Even domestic affairs cannot be handed over to them without supervision. But most of these writers agreed that within limits, women could be entrusted with the family and the household, the cornerstone of the private sphere.

The nineteenth century underlined the harmonious

rationality of this sexual division. Each sex had its function, its role, its tasks and its sphere of influence – its place, predetermined, down to the smallest details. There is an equivalent discourse in the world of skilled trades, which makes the language of labour the most sex-loaded of all. 'Wood and metal are man's work, family and fabrics are woman's', as a worker delegate to the Paris exhibition of 1867 put it.

Political economy reinforced this view of the world by making distinctions between production, reproduction and consumption. Man was responsible for the first, woman for the third, and they cooperated in the second. The notion of a female domestic economy can be seen appearing in the treatises of the late eighteenth and early nineteenth centuries. Madame Gacon-Dufour, for instance, in her famous treatise on household economy, addresses it to the housewife, the manageress of the household, whereas the equivalent books of the seventeenth and eighteenth centuries had spoken of the 'householder' as the proper head of a rural business.[5] This language of the household as economic unit, of 'domestic science' and of the housewife as 'the mistress of domestic affairs' was developing elsewhere as well in the nineteenth century, in England as well as in France.[6] Control of the budget was the key to this new branch of political economy. In the twentieth century, with the coming of electricity and household gadgets, the lady of the house would become a sort of technical overseer, controlling the machines of the new mechanised kitchen.

But this power also spilled over into the city. In the newly autonomised sphere of purchasing, the housewife, whether bourgeois or working class, would reign supreme, deciding what was to be bought, acting as the arbiter of taste, the dictator of fashion, the driving force behind the crucial textile industry, the queen of consumption. Symbolically, the language of advertising was addressed primarily to women; and the big department stores were to become a female space *par excellence,* truly a woman's realm (Williams, 1982).

Wife and mother, 'divinity of the domestic sanctuary' as Chaumette put it in 1793 (quoted Michaud, 1985) woman was also invested with immense social power, for better or worse.[7]

Such at any rate was the theory. Such was intended to be the norm. But the flood of words on the subject, embellished with reciprocal fantasies, cannot tell us what went on in practice – something much more difficult, perhaps impossible, to find out. What was the real nature and extent of the power or powers exercised by women in the nineteenth century? How was decision-making shared between the two sexes? What open or hidden conflicts went on? Only an exhaustive study, looking into the detailed workings of the family, the local community and the state could tell us this.

A triple movement can be seen during the nineteenth century: the comparative withdrawal of women from the public arena; the constitution of a private, female-dominated family sphere; and a huge investment of masculine imagination and symbolism in the representation of women, Some nuances must be added. In the first place, the whole of the public world was not accounted for by politics: the public world was not exclusively masculine. The presence of women – so noticeable in the streets in the eighteenth century – continued in the towns and cities of the nineteenth century, where they held on to their chosen places of circulation, moved into mixed areas or created their own all-women areas (Farge, 1979; Perrot, 1980). Secondly, the private sphere was not exclusively female. Inside the family, the highest power continued to be the paterfamilias, both in law and in practice. Recent political studies have even shown that the penetration of the French countryside by the republican order led to an actual strengthening of the power of the father – the only full citizen – over wife and children.[8] The Republic triumphant had a Roman flavour (Nicolet, 1982). Inside the household were to be found both public rooms (the bourgeois drawing-room) and the serious masculine workplace (the master's study) which wife and children could only enter on tiptoe. The frontier between private and public was a shifting, sinuous one and even ran through the micro-world of the home.

Nevertheless, the tripartite division holds as a general indication of the major domains of power. The activity of women in the nineteenth century consisted above all of organising the private, family and maternal power assigned to them. Bonnie Smith has shown how the bourgeois ladies of northern France, eliminated after about 1860 from the management of the family businesses with which they had until then been closely associated, banished to their great houses and no longer living next door to the factory, administered their households, their large families and their domestic staff by constructing a coherent domestic morality that gave a meaning to their slightest doings. Faith as opposed to reason, charity as opposed to capitalism, reproduction as the major justification for their existence, were the pillars of this morality. These wives of the textile barons were highly self-conscious: they were not merely resigned or passive, on the contrary they were determined to set up their world-view as an overall judgement. This 'Christian feminism', as the author describes it, was expressed by novelists like Mathilde Bourdon, Julia Bécour or Joséphine de Gaulle, who created a sort of composite domestic epic in which good confronted evil, women confronted men. Men with their thirst for power and money caused chaos and death. The domestic heroines, through their suffering, sacrifice and virtue, restored the harmony of the household and peace to the family fold. They had the power − and the duty − to do good.

In working-class urban households, the greater prominence of the mother − in the absence of the father who was increasingly taken up with his work − is attested by most surviving autobiographies, as well as by the series of monographs on the urban family produced by Le Play. It was the mother who controlled the father's pay-packet − a female victory which certainly implies increased power but also increased responsibility and in times of hardship, personal privation. And yet the survival of this 'budgetary matriarchy' continues in our own times as a reality to which housewives remain attached (Michel, 1974). Women of the people had other kinds of knowledge and power as well, notably medical, religious and even cultural. Their role in the early education of their children including the first steps in reading was considerable. Literacy among women made rapid strides in the towns in the nineteenth century and private reading of novels and newspapers furnished their imaginary worlds.[9] The development of institutions like hospitals or schools generally took place within women's sphere of experience and knowledge, hence the sense of dispossession they sometimes felt.

Outside the home, women were active in public life and a list of their interventions, formal or informal, sporadic or regular, would take up much space. Bourgeois ladies − women of the world − were increasingly called upon to leave their firesides and devote themselves to charity or philanthropy, as did Bonnie Smith's northern ladies. But this also marked the limits of their influence. Encouraged when they were helping to manage society, their 'good works' were criticised and even attacked by the northern factory-owners who, faced with the violence of the labour movement, opted for the secular republican administration deemed more appropriate to the circumstances, and labelled their own wives and mothers reactionary.

Criticism of the supposedly reactionary character of women was indeed a major theme of the times. It was taken as the basis for the call for a new education for girls, already being expressed at the end of the Second Empire by republicans, in particular by Protestants. Already in 1867 the Church and the Republic were meeting head on, in the persons of Mgr Dupanloup and the Ferrys, Favres and Legouvés, the creators of secondary education for girls.[10] The extent and the violence of this conflict indicates how high the stakes were: the extension of women's social power, but at the same time its lack of autonomy.

Non-existent on the political level, considerable but contained within the family, the place of women in nineteenth-century France found most extravagant expression in imaginary worlds, both public and private, whether these were political, religious or poetic. The Catholic Church celebrated the cult of the Virgin Mary, and great pilgrimages were inaugurated to sites where she had been seen in visions. The Saint-Simonians dreamed of salvation through the Goddess-Mother from the East. The Republic was represented by the female figure of Marianne. Poets and painters celebrated women as enthusiastically as in their daily lives they practised misogyny. Baudelaire is perhaps the classic case − dominated by his mother, the terrible and pathetic Madame Aupick, but scornful of the stupidity of the women of his age and exalting the 'Muse and the Madonna'.[11]

The mother was the point on which all these various cults converged: they ended by creating intolerable overload and nourished men's age-old fear of women, in particular of the power of the Mother. Darien, Mauriac and André Breton are the modern interpreters of this atavistic terror. 'Mothers! We rediscover Faust's panic, we are like him possessed by an electric shock at the very sound of these syllables in which lie concealed the most powerful goddesses escaping from time and place', as the last-named wrote (quoted Michaud, 1985).

Nevertheless, this was not the only source of the new anti-feminism of the beginning of the twentieth century; that was also fuelled by women's victories, by the first, very timid, steps towards the reversal of roles by the 'emancipated woman' who claimed equality of political and civil rights and admission to the intellectual professions and refused, precisely, to be confined to her maternal 'vocation'. This 'new Eve' (as Jules Dubois called her in 1896) aroused the enthusiasm of those few men who dreamed of free and cultivated companions, but provoked far more fear among those who feared dispossession and saw in the threat of female power a risk of degeneration of the race and decadence of morals.

The case of Otto Weininger, recently analysed by Jacques Le Rider (1982) reveals the scope of the anti-feminist reaction around 1900 and the nature of its arguments.[12] This was the source of the vibrant appeals from all sides for the restoration of the father-figure and virile values, among them Marinetti's Futurist Manifesto of 1909: 'We seek to glorify war − the only hygiene in the world − militarism, patriotism, the destructive act of the anarchist, the mighty ideas that kill − and scorn for women. We want to tear down museums and libraries, to fight against moralism, feminism and all the opportunist and utilitarian forms of cowardice.' War would soon dramatically put each sex 'back in its place', since the effect of war on relations between the sexes is usually conservative if not retrograde.

Finally, we might ask about the attitudes of women themselves, especially towards political power − the one that really causes the problem. In France did their attitude not to some extent embody a certain inhibition and acceptance of the patriarchal society? Was feminism in France more a social than a political phenomenon? The idea that politics was not for women, that they were not at home in the political world, remained until very recently embedded in the minds of both sexes. Women themselves have tended to accord higher value to social or informal than to political activity, thus internalising traditional norms. Once again, the whole question of consent is raised. Both in the past and in the present, power remains central to relations between men and women.

4 Kollontai and After: Women in the Russian Revolution

Beryl Williams

Alexandra Kollontai, controversial, flamboyant, aristocratic, and above all independent, dominated Bolshevik theory and practice about 'the woman question' from 1906 to 1922. Inevitably it is on her and her ideas that most attention has been focused, by her contemporaries and by later historians, when considering the relationship between women and the state in the Russian Revolution. In the West the feminist movement has recently revived interest in Kollontai's life and especially her ideas on sexuality and the family. In the Soviet Union, after falling into disfavour in the Stalin period, Kollontai has undergone a mild and selective rehabilitation as part of a new concern with women's issues. The Soviet interest is quite distinct from a western feminist one, and recent western and Soviet writers have looked to her for very different purposes and been interested in different sides of her career and her writings. However the result of this dual concern has been that a Soviet biography of Kollontai went into a second edition in 1970 and three major western biographies have now been published.[1]

BOLSHEVIK WOMEN

All this attention has perhaps obscured the fact that Alexandra Kollontai was highly untypical of Bolshevik women. Only Angelica Balabanova, another ex-aristocrat, rivalled her in independence and importance. After a career in the Italian socialist movement Balabanova became Secretary to the Comintern and briefly Foreign Minister in the Bolshevik government in the Ukraine, before leaving Russia for good in

1921 (Balabanoff, 1938, 1964). But Balabanova was not a theorist, as Kollontai was, and she also kept well away from the woman question seeing it as of only marginal importance. Kollontai was unique in being both a feminist and a Bolshevik theorist and politician. In 1917 she was on both the Central Committee of the Bolshevik Party and on the Central Executive Committee of the Petrograd Soviet. She became Commissar of Social Welfare in October 1917, the only woman in the new government, but held the post only until the following March, resigning in protest against the Treaty of Brest-Litovsk. After Inessa Armand's death in 1920, Kollontai succeeded her as head of the women's section of the party (*Zhenskii otdel;* hereafter *Zhenotdel*) but as a result of her involvement in the Workers' Opposition this post was taken from her and she ended her career in diplomatic exile and in unhappy subservience to Stalin. She was the only Bolshevik on the Central Committee to vote with Lenin for the April Theses in 1917 and was to be, after his death, the only member of that Central Committee besides Stalin to survive the purges of the 1930s, dying in Moscow in 1952.

Most Bolshevik women were not of her stature, or her notoriety. In fact the Russian Marxist movement has a poor reputation compared with the nineteenth-century Populists for the use to which it put its women members. Populist women were leaders of the movement; they were significant in the Chaikovsky circle and the Going to the People movement and were active terrorists.[2] There were Bolshevik women in the top echelons of the party but they were rarely important politically. Elena Stasova was the party's secretary in emigration. When the new government moved to Moscow early in 1918 she was left in Petrograd, and a man, Sverdlov, took over the job. Nadezhda Krupskaya was an important educationalist in her own right and, like Inessa Armand, was important in the pressure within the party for work with women and supported a women's section when it was finally formed. Krupskaya had written a pamphlet on *The Woman Worker* as early as 1900 (Stites, 1978, p. 239) but like Armand, was too completely loyal to Lenin to oppose him on any issue or to act with real independence.

Other party women gravitated, or were pushed, into jobs

regarded as suitable for the female sex — in education or propaganda fields, or in the *Zhenotdel* itself. A few, like Balabanova, resisted this fate. Others came to identify with it, arguing, as did Kollontai, that if women themselves did not work for women's issues, no one else would. One ex-partisan fighter in the civil war, who had been a guerrilla leader and who was, as a woman, told to work with the *Zhenotdel* after the war was over, described her reaction to the assignment as follows: 'When peace came they requisitioned me to work amongst women. Everybody laughed. They didn't think of me as a "baba" at all. I didn't think much of the idea myself at first. I was so used to chasing around like a man . . .'[3]

This highlights the persistent problem that women in the party faced — that of male suspicion of women's issues. It had dual roots in Russian masculine chauvinism and in Marxist theoretical dislike of any separatist activity which could be interpreted as weakening the class struggle and proletarian unity. After Kollontai's removal from the *Zhenotdel* its leadership was considerably weakened. Its later directors, Sofia Smidovich and those who followed her, were lesser figures in the party and carried less weight in party decisions. The women's department itself was finally abolished — its work having been 'completed' as the offical pronouncement put it — in 1930. But it is also true that the *Zhenotdel* fought a continuous and ultimately losing battle with male prejudice and indifference within the party throughout the entire period of its existence. Stalin's closure of it was merely the final victory in a long-standing battle with the party apparatus. The *Zhenotdel* survived as long as it did — indeed, was founded in the first place — because of support from important patrons, among them Lenin, Sverdlov and Trotsky. By 1927 all three were lost to it.

The ironic name for the department within the party — 'Tsentrobaba' — testifies to male attitudes. As one woman delegate complained, her activist party husband forbade her to take part in public life:

And in those very meetings which he forbids me to attend because he is afraid I will become a real person — what he needs is a cook and mistress wife — in those very meetings where I have to slip in secretly, he makes thunderous speeches about the role of women in the revolution, calls women to a more active role. (quoted in Geiger, 1968, p. 59)

At the ninth party congress in 1920, a woman delegate upbraided the conference: 'When I raise this question at this serious party congress it brings a smile to your faces' (quoted in Hayden, 1976, p. 162). It was not only smiles that women had to deal with. There are many reports in the 1920s of women being attacked or beaten by their husbands for becoming involved in party or women work, not all of them from 'backward' areas like Central Asia or from rural Russia.

Some Bolshevik leaders recognised and deplored the situation. Lenin was only too willing to admit that 'unfortunately it is still true to say of many of our comrades "Scratch a communist and find a philistine". Of course you must scratch their sensitive spot, their mentality as regards women' (Zetkin, 1929, p. 68). Trotsky in his 1923 articles, 'Problems of Everyday Life', pointed to the same problem:

An old family — husband is a good worker, devoted to family — wife lives also for the home . . . But just by chance she comes in touch with a communist women's organisation. A new world opens before her eyes. The family is neglected, the husband irritated, the wife is hurt in her newly awakened civic consciousness. The family is broken up . . . (Trotsky, 1973, p. 40)

Russian literature in the 1920s is full of similar examples. Gladkov's novel *Cement* (1925) relates the return of a civil war hero to his village to find his wife an activist, his house neglected and his child in a children's home where she dies. The fear of the new woman, prepared to sacrifice family, home and sometimes children for the cause, was widespread. Sometimes the guilt and the conflicts of the woman herself were portrayed too. Kollontai's own fiction shows the preservation of possessiveness and jealousy in the new society — the loneliness of the new woman, and also frequently the failure of her man to support her in the new life. If a choice had to be made, in Kollontai's stories as in her life, work came first but the isolation and insecurity of the new woman in 'the transition period' made the search for the collective and its support more urgent.

It was not going to be easy to emancipate non-party women if party women had such problems from their own party husbands; and indeed if, with the exception of certain top party leaders, the average party official remained at best indifferent and at worst hostile. Kollontai's successor as head of the *Zhenotdel,* Sofia Smidovich, issued an ultimatum to the party leadership saying that the work either had to be taken seriously and given resources or the department might just as well be closed down (Stites, 1978, p. 343). This particular *cri de coeur* was caused by an attempt to merge local branches of the *Zhenotdel* with the *agit-prop* departments. The *Zhenotdel* was then reprieved but the enthusiasm with which many party bosses in the regions tried to abolish the department was symptomatic of the problem. The influence of the women in the party declined steadily after 1922. The ninth and tenth party congresses in 1920 and 1921 had had only 5 per cent of their voting delegates as women. At the eleventh congress in 1922 it was 2 per cent — 9 women out of 513. At that date 7½ per cent of party membership was female — a mere 40,000 (Farnsworth, 1980, pp. 316-17; Hayden, 1976, p. 166).

WOMEN AND PARTY POLICY

But it was not just male prejudice. The root problem for the women was one which many of them shared — the suspicion of the sin of separatism within the class struggle. Kollontai was urging the need for a women's section within the party as early as 1906 but it was not until 1919 that it was achieved and then with misgivings and as a result not of a change in theory but of practical necessity. Some women involved were reluctant from the beginning to abandon proletarian solidarity for sectional interest. Nikolaeva in an opening speech to a Bolshevik women's conference declared: 'We, conscious women workers, know that we have no special interests, that there should be no separate women's organisations. We are strong only so long as we are organised together into one fraternal proletarian family with all workers in the struggle for socialism' (Hayden, 1976, p. 156).

Kollontai's initiation into the women's cause came with the revolution of 1905 and was developed in direct conflict with the 'bourgeois feminist' movement. She was later to say that her interest in feminism had brought her to socialism, but that is not strictly true. Certainly, her own personal desire for fulfilment as a person and not just as a wife and mother caused her to leave her own marriage and go to Europe to study, but her early concerns as a Marxist (and she was a Menshevik until the First World War) were not directly with women. Her first major work was on Finland and her early writings are economic in character. It was her experiences in 1905, when she was present on Bloody Sunday, and her realisation in the course of the year that working women were in danger of being won over by the feminist movement, that brought her attention to the issue. By 1905 there were at least three active feminist groups on the Russian political scene of varying degrees of radicalism but all connected with the liberal movement: the Mutual Philanthropic Society, which dated from the 1890s and was concerned primarily with equal educational opportunities for women and with traditional philanthropic and charity work; the Kadet-based All Russian Union for Women's Equality which concentrated on the suffrage issue; and a smaller Women's Progressive Society, perhaps the most feminist of all.

The suffrage campaign failed in getting female suffrage for the First Duma, and had considerable difficulty in getting the Kadet leadership to adopt the cause; but the more radical members of the Union for Women's Equality had surprising success in campaigning among working women and thus came into direct conflict with the Social Democratic groups. It is not often realised how radical the Union for Women's Equality, like other 'liberal' groups, became in the course of 1905. This was far from being a suffragette movement but campaigned for changes in the marriage law and had widespread appeal. In practice Kollontai and her helpers soon began to organise working women against the feminist threat. The All Russian Congress of Women in 1908, organised by the feminist groups, became the forum in which the arguments were fought out as Kollontai and a small group of Social Democratic women mobilised to attack the feminist arguments that women had specific interests which bound them together across class lines. For the feminists, women were to be mobilised for the vote and to attain equal legal and educational rights. Kollontai accused bourgeois women of being content to throw off their legal shackles, while continuing to exploit working women, and especially their own servants. The Social Democratic group effectively exposed the lives of factory women — the unsafe machinery, the long hours, low pay and lack of insurance. It was the economic fight, the fight for a 'crust of bread', that Kollontai, as a good Marxist, was to highlight. The argument raised the real issue between the two groups: were women united by their lack of rights or divided by their economic circumstances?[4]

Kollontai, like all Marxists, believed the second. But it was not enough, as many of her colleagues believed, to say that women had to wait for the revolution, when all would be solved. For Kollontai believed that women were doubly exploited — by the economic system of capitalism and also by the men in their own families. Certainly, under capitalism the family was bound to be affected by bourgeois attitudes of property and inheritance, but this might not be automatically changed when capitalism collapsed unless the party took the issue seriously. Although both wings of the Social Democratic movement opposed Kollontai's call for separate women's groups within the party in 1906, by 1917 both Bolshevik and Menshevik newspapers directed specifically at women were launched (in the Bolshevik case the shortlived *Rabotnitsa,* first founded in 1914, was re-established) and the Socialist Revolutionaries and the Kadets also started working independently to gain women's support. The Bolsheviks now recognised that they were competing for the women's constituency not only with the bourgeois feminists but with the other socialists as well. In practice the editorial board of the journal *Rabotnitsa,* which included Kollontai, Armand and Krupskaya, became a *de facto* women's section. Throughout 1917 they convened women's meetings, tried to mobilise women to support Bolshevik candidates in elections, and participated in women's strikes and protests against the war and against rising prices.

The women's conference in November 1918 in Petrograd, which they organised, was a far greater success than anyone had anticipated, but it was not until the following year that the *Zhenotdel,* or the women's department of the party, was at last created. In his conversation with Zetkin, Lenin showed the contradictions in the Bolshevik position. It was, he declared, an ideological principle that there should be no special organisations for women. 'A woman communist is a member of the party just as a man communist. With equal rights and duties.' Nevertheless it was necessary to work among women and to win them for the proletarian class struggle, and appropriate bodies were therefore needed. 'That is not feminism', he said, 'that is practical revolutionary expediency' (Zetkin, 1929, p. 63). Thus women were too important in the labour force to be ignored by the Bolsheviks and the revolution could not be won without them. *Pravda* announced the creation of the *Zhenotdel* with a banner headline about the mobilisation of women for the Red Front. Nevertheless there was a clear contradiction in creating a separate women's section of the party in order to persuade women that they had no separate interests, and some Bolsheviks were aware of this as a potential problem.

Women had been important in the industrial labour force in the nineteenth century. In 1897 two out of every five textile workers were women. After 1906, when Stolypin's land reforms loosened the powers of the village commune, women flocked to industries or joined their menfolk in the towns, where it quickly became apparent that a woman's wage was going to be necessary if the family was going to be able to stay together. The 1905 revolution had led to improved wages and conditions of labour for men. The industrialists responded by employing women. According to one estimate 88 per cent of the total increase in the industrial labour force between 1901 and 1910 were women. Women were cheaper, earning little more than half the male salary. The female illiteracy rate was higher and with almost no child-care facilities available and with a family to feed, the women left it to their men to attend political meetings, and took what unskilled jobs were available at any wages, undercutting men's gains in 1905.

The First World War, as in all countries involved, brought women into the labour force in vast numbers. By 1917 they were 43 per cent of industrial workers. By February 1917 one-third of Petrograd factory workers were women. In the Central Agricultural region it was half. All the political parties despaired of what they called 'women's backwardness'. Nevertheless, as Anne Bobroff has shown, female radicalism was noticeable from 1910 and came to the surface suddenly and dramatically in Petrograd in February 1917.[5] One unsympathetic observer remarked that the February revolution was led 'by hungry women demanding bread and herrings'.[6] Certainly women were prominent in the events which culminated in the fall of the monarchy; events which were a combination of a bread riot, a strike movement and International Women's Day. The women's demands were political as well as economic however, and they called for an end to the war and the regime as well as for bread. But if radical, and to some extent politicised, the women were not controlled by any political party. They ignored Bolshevik warnings about premature action in February [7] and once they had been given the vote by the Provisional Government all political parties, including the Bolsheviks, ran campaigns to gain their support.

However Lenin was a staunch supporter of women's emancipation, especially from the 'stultifying and crushing drudgery' of housework and cooking, on which subject he could wax eloquent. He looked forward to the transformation of an individual household economy into a large-scale socialist, collective one. Elsewhere he added, significantly, that women's backwardness pulled men back from building the new society, 'like little worms which, unseen, slowly but surely rot and corrode' (Zetkin, 1929, p. 68). His purpose, echoing Kollontai's 'crust of bread', was the removal of women's dependence on men and thus, he thought, bringing about the end of their inequality and freeing them to participate in production – the ultimate goal.

In order to achieve the complete emancipation of women and to make them really equal with men, we must have a social economy and the participation of women in general productive labour. Then women will occupy the same position as men.[8]

Lenin's essential message has remained the same until today. Economic participation in the labour force plus socialisation of domestic duties equals female emancipation.

KOLLONTAI AS THEORIST

Kollontai accepted both these elements, but her emphasis was different and her thoughts on women's liberation went much further. It was this difference in emphasis and this widening of range which was to bring her into conflict with the party majority and with Lenin, and it is to Kollontai's ideas as the Revolution brought her the opportunity to implement them that we must now turn. It is instructive to look at Kollontai's views on women's emancipation in the context of the two movements that shaped her ideas – the radical feminism of the 1860s and 70s, and the particular brand of Marxist socialism she adopted as her own.

We have shown the Bolshevik reaction to the 'Women Question' as it evolved between 1905 and 1917 in the context of the liberal feminism of these years. But Kollontai's feminist inspiration, like that of most of her generation, came from the populist movement. Her heroine was not a suffragette but Vera Pavlovna. the heroine of Chernyshevsky's novel, *What is to be Done?*, written in 1862. Lenin was to take the title of Chernyshevsky's book for his 1902 pamphlet on party organisation. Kollontai was to take its content as her inspiration, both for women's liberation and for a cooperative, collectivist vision of society. The liberated, radical woman of the 1860s, to the horror of the police and society, wore blue stockings, had cropped hair and lived in civil matrimony (or a fictitious, arranged marriage to enable her to leave her parents' house) in a commune. Contrary to scandalous rumours, that commune was not a place of licentious sexual activity. It was more likely to practise complete sexual abstinence and to subordinate personal life to the good of the cause. But the commune would often be, as in Chernyshevsky's novel, a cooperative workshop where labour and profits were equally shared, or a student commune where all tasks, books and money were pooled and eating and living were communal. Some of the earliest circles were all-women but by the 1870s women joined men's circles, deciding that feminist separatism did not help the wider social issues of poverty and development with which they were primarily concerned. Feminism took second place to radical politics. The needs of women were thus subordinated to those of the working class. This vision of radical socialism was, of course, not unique to Russia. The communal life-style was a common goal of much of what is loosely known as Utopian Socialism.

Kollontai, however, became a Marxist and she combined this radical, collectivist vision of society with a faith in spontaneous proletarian action and world revolution — a combination that reminds one strongly of Rosa Luxemburg. Indeed, Kollontai had many contacts during her years as a Menshevik with the German Social Democratic world. She joined the Bolsheviks during the First World War in horrified reaction to the failure of Social Democracy to stop that war and despite the fact that she herself, unlike Lenin, was a pacifist. Her emphasis on mass action and spontaneity put her with Shlyapnikov on the left wing of the party, and her resignation from the Commissariat of Social Welfare in 1918 over the Treaty of Brest Litovsk also put her in the forefront of the Left Communists. With visions of armed revolution spreading to Europe she was (in unacknowledged contradiction to her earlier pacifism) prepared to risk the survival of the revolution in Russia if necessary. 'If our Soviet republic is to fail', she declared, 'others will pick up the banner' (quoted Farnsworth, 1980, p. 112).

But it was the Workers' Opposition, for which she wrote the programme, that showed her ideas most clearly, and finally ruined her career in Russia. It showed that even in 1920 her faith in the proletariat was undiminished. The new society must be created from below. She wrote of 'the healthy class call of the broad working masses . . . the creative powers of the rising class'. Trade unions must be preferred to the party bureaucracy; the party should return to the ideals of 1917. Trade unions, soviets and other elected workers' organisations should be trusted to run industry and create socialism themselves, through the medium of an All Russian Congress of Producers. She even proposed (a good Maoist idea) that every party member should be required to live and work for three months of every year as an ordinary worker or peasant.[9]

As the end of the civil war revealed widespread economic chaos and famine, this was openly attacked as utopianism.

Lenin reacted swiftly. At the tenth party congress he attacked Kollontai with every weapon he could lay his hands on. He linked the Workers' Opposition with the Kronstadt revolt – an unfair charge as Kollontai's belief in the masses running their own affairs did not extend to the right to do so against the party, and the Workers' Opposition group had supported the suppression of Kronstadt. Secondly, he accused her pamphlet of containing syndicalist and anarchist ideas, one of the worst crimes in the Leninist book. And thirdly, he attacked her private life. Insinuating that her relationship with her ex-lover, Shlyapnikov, was more than a political collaboration, when she was still married to the sailor Dybenko, Lenin was not above a blatant and sexist appeal to the gallery (Farnsworth, 1980, p. 247; Balabanoff, 1938, p. 252). Shlyapnikov remained on the Central Committee. Kollontai was sacked from the *Zhenotdel.*

Kollontai's ideas as they emerge from a reading of her pamphlet *The Workers' Opposition,* however, merely reflect what she had always believed. As early as 1906 she talked of the society which would follow what at that stage was still seen as the imminent bourgeois revolution. This was to be a republic in which state power would be located entirely in the hands of the people who would run it through elected local organisations and a popular armed militia. In 1912 she talked of the worker as wiser than the party agitator (Clements, 1973, pp. 326, 330). Her belief in the wisdom of the proletariat and her notion of revolution as a spontaneous movement from below has been linked with both Rosa Luxemburg and the early Trotsky. We should, however, be careful to point out that she was not voicing Luxemburg's wider criticisms of Bolshevik policies in 1921, and *The Workers' Opposition* is a very different document from Rosa's pamphlet on the Russian Revolution. As many of her critics in 1921 would have recognised, it also had a strong resemblance to parts of Lenin's *State and Revolution.* In 1921, unlike both Lenin and Trotsky, Kollontai still believed this approach was possible – indeed had to be possible if socialism were to be achieved. As Commissar for Social Welfare she had practised what she preached and had run her commissariat through a system of direct participatory democracy with meetings of all workers, including the cleaners and doormen, deciding policy (Clements, 1979, p. 127).

Kollontai's view of women's liberation is intimately bound up with her view of socialism as a mass movement fashioning a new world, or a new society, from below. Women must liberate themselves and help fashion a new way of life — a collective society. Lenin and Trotsky believed that economic and political change would precede the cultural transformation of society. Kollontai, with many on the left of the party, stressed the pre-eminence of a cultural revolution. Women, for Kollontai, could spearhead the building of a new, collective society in the process of achieving their own emancipation. It was not necessary, indeed it was impossible, to wait until socialism was announced before starting to change life styles and attitudes. 'All the experience of history teaches us' she wrote, 'that a social group works out its ideology, and consequently its sexual morality in the process of its struggle with hostile social forces' (Clements, 1973, p. 332).

The differences within the party were partly over timing and partly over method. Was socialism going to be achieved from above or below? Kollontai held longer than most to the idea that a new life style could be achieved swiftly from below, simultaneously with, or even before, the establishment of political and economic control. Women would transform life styles while men concerned themselves with military and political problems — a good example of her unconscious sexual stereotyping. In terms of women and the family the differences were clear. For Lenin women were to be emancipated from housework and enabled to join the workforce by state-provided amenities, but the family would survive into the foreseeable future. For Kollontai the family could wither away now; or perhaps more accurately, be transformed into something new and unrecognisable.

Specifically, what was to become of sexual and marital relations? For Kollontai socialism was to lead not to 'free love' in the sense her detractors defined it — i.e. promiscuity. It was to lead to a new form of love freed from the economic dependency of bourgeois marriage and freed also from the tasks of housework and childcare. The first was to be removed by the right — indeed the duty — of women to enter the labour force and to work for the new society; the second was to be removed by the provision of a network of alternative services.

Her vision of the new society was one which had much in common with Chernyshevsky's. She envisaged a network of communes or collectives made up of a group of people working and living cooperatively together. Kitchens, dining rooms, laundries and childcare would be provided by the state.

In the hygienic, morally pure atmosphere of the nurseries and kindergartens, under professionally trained teachers, the child will be saved from the grim conditions in which proletarian children are now raised. These will be in the custody, not of charity organisations (run by people of a different class), but in that of whatever collectives the future will organise. In these the new generation will, from the earliest years learn to value the beauties of solidarity and sociability and become accustomed to looking at the world through the prism of the collective and not through its own selfish eyes.[10]

Certainly enthusiasts to the left of Kollontai talked of forcibly removing children from the harmful influence of their parents to be brought up by the state, of the abolition of marriage, of free love;[11] Kollontai did not, or at least did so with caution. The new marriage would be based on love, not on economic considerations or purely on sex, and would be unhindered by inequality, dependence or family ties. It need be neither monogamous nor long-lasting, but it would be a true love relationship – the 'winged Eros' she writes about in her much misunderstood *Letter to Soviet Youth* (Holt, 1977, pp. 276-92). Like Lenin she disapproved of the casual sexuality of Soviet youth in the 1920s, what she called the 'wingless Eros', although unlike Lenin she was tolerant towards it, seeing it as an inevitable transition phase towards the new love and the new family.

She lectured the young on both unnatural sexual abstinence in the revolutionary cause (a common civil war phenomenon) and its parallel development of easy sexual relations with no love behind them, the glass of water theory with which she is often, erroneously, associated. Sex was natural and healthy, she argued, but it must be part of a love relationship and subordinate to the collective's interests.

Motherhood remained important to her. Kollontai sanctioned abortion with reluctance, as necessary in the conditions of revolution and civil war, but the modern feminist idea that a woman has the right to control her own fertility was not part of her beliefs. The state needed socialist citizens and if the mother did not want her babies it was only too willing to rear them in socialist ideas for her. Motherhood was a duty, it ought not to be a burden. In the new collective society she assumed that exclusive mother love, like exclusive erotic love, would decline. Children, once weaned, would be the joint possession of the collective and possessiveness towards children, as towards a sexual partner, would end. Children would be 'ours' in the common care of the collective or the state. It was the logical result of this to pass legislation in 1918 to make adoption illegal.

THEORY AND PRACTICE AFTER 1917

How much was Kollontai able to fulfil her dreams? The early months of the revolution saw some real achievements and many paper hopes. As People's Commissar for Social Welfare, Kollontai got through the early labour legislation which gave an eight-hour day, social insurance, pregnancy leave for two months before and after birth, time at work to breast-feed, and prohibition of child labour and night work for women. She envisaged and tried to start a network of mother and baby homes. A Commission for the Protection of Mothers and Infants was headed by a revolutionary doctor, Vera Lebedeva, and plans were drawn up for maternity clinics, milk points and nurseries.

The early months also saw legislation to bring in equality between husband and wife, civil registration of marriage, easy divorce, abolition of illegitimacy and the ending of the wife's obligation to take her husband's name and share his domicile. Students and intellectuals threw themselves with energy and enthusiasm into communal experiments. There were 2000 agricultural communes by 1919; even some all-women peasant communes were reported. The most famous, the Artyukhina commune of day-labourers, survived until the end of the 1920s when it had 168 members, of whom only 16 were men. It had a communal kitchen, dining room, clubhouse, bakery and laundry and the children lived and ate separately. It even had its own orchestra and ran a journal. But this was a showpiece.[12] Student communes pooled all grants, books, even underclothes, and one in Moscow University forbade individual friendships.

The *Zhenotdel* undoubtedly achieved much in the decades of its existence. Inessa Armand started a scheme of elected women delegates from factories or institutions who would serve for two or three months on local soviets or commissariats as apprentices or in doing social welfare work, before returning to their units. *Zhenotdel* members toured factories trying to ensure the new laws protecting woman were enforced. They started campaigns to stop prostitution, to carry the Bolshevik message into Central Asia, where they organised mass unveilings of Muslim women (a very dangerous enterprise) and ran literacy classes. They mobilised support for the Red Army, organised medical support for the wounded and helped war widows. During the civil war women ran armoured trains, led guerrilla partisan bands and fought in jack-boots and greatcoats alongside men. A woman headed the Petrograd branch of the *Cheka*. Under Kollontai's directorship in particular the *Zhenotdel* did not see itself just as an agency to get women to support the party but as a force to represent women's interests in the party and to transform society.

As early as 1923, the differences between the ideal and the reality were only too apparent, even to Kollontai, and hopes of a rapid transformation of society were fading. As one observer said,

In principle we separated marriage from economics, in principle we destroyed the family hearth, but we carried out the resolution on marriage in such a manner that only the man benefited from it . . . the woman remains tied with chains to the destroyed family hearth. The man happily whistling, can leave it, abandoning the woman and children. (quoted in Geiger, 1968, pp. 70-1)

The reality of war, revolution and civil war vitiated many of the hopes from the start. The new state did not have the resources, even it had had the will, to transfer domestic chores and childcare outside the home. It is true that public feeding was of major importance during the civil war, but that was more out of necessity than choice. In Petrograd in 1919 – 20, 90 per cent of the population was fed communally and 12 million urban workers used laundries – but that was partially due to the lack of food and fuel. Communal living was often a by-product of the housing shortage. Creches were dirty and understaffed. There were complaints that public laundries tore and stole more than they washed. The cost of an extensive system of state care would have been phenomenal. One estimate in 1922 was that 7 million helpers would be needed for 20 million people (cooks, cleaners, etc.) at a cost of over 1000 million roubles each year.[13]

Once the civil war was over, the poor quality of the food and services, and personal inclination, drove people back to their individual kitchens. New housing did not in practice include communal facilities. The number of childcare establishments was tiny compared with demand. Only 200,000 children were in state care in 1928. The reality of Russia was not a network of socialist kindergartens but gangs of orphans – several millions of them by 1921 – living by crime and hooliganism on the streets. Makarenko's military-style orphanages were probably the most conspicuous example of collective childcare in the 1920s. Easy divorce and the assumption that the state would provide led to women being abandoned on pregnancy. Mixed dormitories for Komsomols and students and the pressures of the new morality on girls led to what a party wit described as 'liberty, equality and maternity'. Kollontai was increasingly associated with the corruption of Soviet youth rather than the liberation of Soviet women.[14]

But it was the New Economic Policy which had a catastrophic effect on Kollontai's plans. It was perhaps as well that she was not in Russia for much of the 1920s. With the return to a private sector and a money economy, state factories had to be seen to be paying their way. A new age of financial austerity crept in and the implementation of laws protecting women in private enterprises proved impossible. To make matters worse demobilisation of the Red Army led to the return of men into the economy and women were pushed aside – from skilled to unskilled work, from heavy industry to the consumer and service sectors, from employment to unemployment. Prostitution returned and a new class of *Nepkas* benefited from a new semi-bourgeois life style.

By 1925 the party had recognised the problem. Kollontai, home on leave from her embassy in Scandinavia, argued furiously for an insurance scheme to cover women whose relationships would not qualify as a *de facto* marriage. Although she recognised that some reliance on men would be necessary, her emphasis was on state care rather than alimony. The party's decision went the other way. The 1926 marriage code looked radical from outside the USSR. Divorce was still easy, marriage was merely a declaration of living together. But in the context of Kollontai's ideas it marked the beginning of the Great Retreat that was to culminate in Stalin's marriage law of 1944. It enshrined women as the weaker sex needing to be looked after by men. It revived alimony and it accepted that childcare was the duty of parents. As one woman activist declared in 1928, 'In the family life of women the old way of life is retained in all its totality. All the burdens of the organisation of domestic life in the present period lie completely, fully and exclusively on women.[15] Kollontai had said almost the same thing in 1919.

But one thing had changed and was soon to change even more radically — women were now firmly in the labour force and expected to be so. In the years of the First Five Year Plan and the Second World War, they were recruited in huge numbers, including into heavy and dangerous jobs which they had been barred from as dangerous to their health in the early years of the Revolution. The First Five Year Plan initially saw a revival in plans for collective living. Socialist cities and agro-towns were designed with such schemes in mind. Some theorists again advocated children being separated from their parents at birth, by force if necessary, and educated by the state. There was much talk of the family withering away and civil war enthusiasms were rekindled. But by 1936 what had been achieved was merely an official revival of the family, the banning of abortion and the making of divorce a costly and difficult proceeding. By the mid-1930s, female virtues and large families were returning to favour and the ideal new socialist woman was one who could juggle the demands of work, home and family and remain a traditional and feminine wife and mother whilst also labouring for Soviet power.

This cannot be blamed on Stalin alone. It must also be seen as a reflection of the survival of traditional Russian attitudes in Soviet society. Male party leaders pushed 'women's questions' into the orbit of a small and second-rank department of the party and marginalised them. Moreover as the party assumed that female emancipation would automatically come with socialism, so Kollontai assumed that male attitudes would change naturally from the new roles that women would take. Even Kollontai took for granted that the communal childcare, cooking, etc. would still be done by women — either hired or those of the collective. Lenin, in his letters to Zetkin, talked of men helping with the housework until collective functions could take over (Zetkin, 1929, p. 68) but this side of the new life was not pushed with any determination.

In 1922 Kollontai had commented that the Soviet state was run by men: women were deputies in all fields. That did not change and still has not. The *Zhenotdel* got more women into political life, as party members and especially into the Soviets, but with very rare exceptions they remained in secondary positions and at low levels. Kollontai's thought contained unresolved contradictions. Were women's needs and the needs of the new government in fact identical or reconcilable? She never faced this problem any more than she faced the question of whether women would want to be forced to work in male jobs, to give up their children to the collective, or indeed to have children for the state at all. There is an authoritarian streak in Kollontai for all her beliefs in spontaneity and mass action. In January 1920 she welcomed Trotsky's compulsory labour law; compelling women into the labour force would alter their view of themselves more quickly (Farnsworth, 1980, p. 187). The dislike of abortion, the lack of any attention to birth control, are part of the same assumption that women would embrace the definition of liberation she had developed.

*   *   *   *   *

In the last decade, Soviet women have begun to question their lot. After Stalin's death, legal rights to abortion and easy divorce were restored to them. The 1961 party programme echoed that of 1919 in its theoretical commitment to improve public catering, creches, day schools and pioneer camps. But once again, as in the 1920s, the Soviet economy failed to deliver. The falling birth rates of the 1960s and 1970s led to a spate of sociological surveys and reports on family life styles. The hard-pressed activists of the *Zhenotdel* would have recognised their findings. In the 1970s, in 87 per cent of urban families women did all the housework chores alone. A questionnaire given to three and four year olds in 1977 produced statements like 'Mummy does the laundry, cooks and washes dishes. Daddy eats, watches films on TV and reads the paper.'[16] Women have less time than men for leisure, for study and gaining qualifications. Thus women as a whole still work in lower-status occupations. Natalia Baranskaya's novel, *A Week Like Any Other,* produced eloquent testimony to the problems of women and to the lack of support they get from the state, and from their men.[17] But a feminist movement in the western sense has been slow to emerge and what did emerge was in *samizdat* and is now in emigration.

The editor of one illegal feminist journal who is now in the West shows, in her references to her, how selective has been Kollontai's rehabilitation. Whilst listing many 'wonderful women' of the Revolution in her preface, Mamonova seems to know Kollontai only as an ambassador of the Soviet Union (Mamonova, 1984, p. xvii). This underlines the fact that recent Soviet sources stress Kollontai's diplomatic career and her significance as an early example of Bolshevik encouragement of women to participate in public life. Itkina's biography and recent Soviet editions of some of her writings largely ignore her views on erotic love, on the family and on Soviet democracy and her disagreements with Lenin. It is merely stated by Soviet writers that Lenin and Krupskaya were in favour of the continuation of the nuclear family and Kollontai is awarded a mention for recognising the need for relations based on psycho-sexual attraction.[18]

Kollontai's hopes for the transformation of the bourgeois family into a new, communal life style and for women's liberation within the context of an egalitarian, collectivist society remain unfulfilled and largely unknown in the Soviet Union today. Equally the western feminist movement, which has done so much to resurrect her ideas, contains many elements of which she would have disapproved. Nevertheless she remains a significant figure in the history of both feminist and Marxist thought, evolving radical solutions to the challenges faced by the 'new woman' in a revolutionary society. More than anyone else in the Russian revolutionary movement she thought about and tried to solve the problems posed by the title of one of her own pamphlets: *The Family and the Communist State.*

ACKNOWLEDGEMENTS

I would like to thank Alix Holt for her comments on a first draft of this chapter.

5 German Women in the Resistance to Hitler
Sybil Oldfield

'German women inaugurated the march of women up the calvary of resistance against Nazism' (Vera Laska, 1983)

The extent of German resistance to Nazism and the suffering it endured are still not general public knowledge — not even in the two Germanies, let alone abroad. And even less is known of the resistance put up by German women. The very fact that there are two Germanies means that there has been a division in the writing of German history: in East Germany the history of the German Resistance has been almost exclusively that of the Communist German Resistance, whereas until very recently West German historians have 'foregrounded' that of the non-communists. In any event most German historians have focused on resistance by institution or organisation — the churches, the trades unions, the banned political parties — the leadership of all of which was exclusively male. And most English historians of the German Resistance have concentrated on the 20 July 1944 'Generals' Plot', an attempted *putsch* from above in which again, very few women could be directly involved. For all these reasons the women in the rank and file of the German Resistance have remained largely nameless and invisible[1] — invisible that is to us, but not to the Nazis who hunted them down. The very recent German history of resistance by women that has emerged is largely a combination of prison statistics and personal anecdote.[2] A systematic coverage of women's resistance in Germany still has to wait until all the local studies, some of which are already under way, are completed. This essay, therefore, can only be an interim report, the first to my knowledge in English, and will cover the period from 1928 until 1945.

THE POSITION OF GERMAN WOMEN BEFORE THE RISE OF NAZISM

Prussia, like the rest of the world, had long cherished the belief that politics — matters of state — are essentially the business of men. The influential Heinrich von Treitschke, Professor of History at the University of Berlin, had thundered every year between 1874 and 1895 that:

The features of history are virile, unsuited to sentimental or feminine natures . . . It may be said roughly that the normal woman obtains an insight into justice and government through men's eyes, just as the normal man has no natural aptitude for petty questions of household management. *Politics*, 1916, Book I, *The Idea of the State).*

Against Treitschke's view of the state as being essentially the nation-in-arms and therefore excluding women, the German women's suffrage movement had had a hard struggle. Nevertheless there had been an organised women's movement in Germany at least since 1894,[3] and during the First World War German women had been enrolled as essential contributors both to the national war effort and the administration of the state just like their counterparts in Britain. In 1919, during Germany's abortive revolution in the wake of her defeat, all German women over 21 were granted the vote. The ensuing decade, however, was a roller-coaster ride into chaos, although some aspects of the Weimar period were actually liberalising and liberating for women. By 1931, for instance, there were 19,000 women students at German universities and women comprised one-third of all teachers. The number of women doctors had multiplied 13-fold since the war, and women made up most of the nursing and social work professions. There were also women film stars, actresses, dancers and even 60 women politicians, all of whom were much in the public eye.[4] But also under Weimar there was recurrent near-starvation, total economic insecurity and mass unemployment, none of which was liberating either for German women or for German men. One ominous sign of the times was the 'revolutionary' National Socialist Party which had as its programme not only the exclusion of Jews from German national life, but also the exclusion of German women from any positions of economic or political power. Already in 1921 the Nazi Party conference had unanimously declared that 'a woman could not be accepted for a leadership position in the Party'. And the party's ideologue, Alfred Rosenberg, declared that the first task of the next Nazi generation of women would be to 'clear up the mess and emancipate women from women's emancipation . . . One thing must be made clear: *Man* must be and must remain Judge, Soldier and Statesman' (Elling, 1981, p. 11). Thus those German women who could see beyond the struggle for basic survival during the 1920s were already alerted to the threat presented by militaristic, anti-feminist Nazism to all those women who wanted not only *Kinder, Küche und Kirche,* but education, work, a place in the *polis* and peace in the world as well.

THE FIRST PHASE OF ANTI-NAZI RESISTANCE BY GERMAN WOMEN, 1928 – 33

German resistance to Hitler began several years before economic catastrophe and political chaos finally enabled the Nazis to seize power. This resistance, however, was fatally weakened by the official (Stalinist), Communist Party policy of identifying the Social Democrats rather than the Nazis as their chief political enemy – a hostility that was duly returned. The German left would only learn to make common cause in the struggle against the Nazis once it was too late. It was principally, therefore, left-wing, pacifist (but not Communist Party) women and men who took the Nazi threat seriously as early as 1928 and who worked to rally a political alternative that would not alienate a German electorate already battered by defeat, attempted revolution, foreign occupation and grotesque currency inflation:

By 1928 four large federations of women's organizations had coalesced, joining millions of women to form Germany's largest, most powerful bloc of voters . . . In the 1928 elections, (Martha Kearns argues) this coalition helped to rally twenty-nine million voters to the Social Democratic Party, to the numerous middle-class parties, and to the Catholic Centre Party. As a result the Nazi Party, with less than a million votes, was soundly defeated. (Kearns, 1976, p. 196)

But the October 1929 Wall Street crash changed all that. Unexampled mass unemployment in Germany (over 6 million unemployed out of a labour force of 20 million) and a halving of the standard of living in real terms over the next three years caused an all too understandable polarisation in politics. The Brownshirts profited most from the ensuing violence on the streets and left-wing pacifist women now found themselves waging a more and more despairing struggle against not a tide but an avalanche. In October 1930, Käthe Kollwitz produced her drawing, *Demonstration,* as her protest against the brutal suppression by the Nazis of a workers' rally. In January 1931, the pacifist, Constanze Hallgarten, founded the German League of Mothers as a counterpart to the French *Ligue Internationale des Mères et des Educatrices pour la Paix.* Within 18 months it had over 10,000 members all over Germany, mostly educated, middle-class women in the large towns and cities. In 1932, 1500 women attended an overflow women's peace conference in Munich, including Catholic, Social Democrat and radical pacifist women, chaired by Erika Mann. The Nazis tried to break up the conference without success and their newspaper reported it nationally with the scare headlines: 'Pacifist Scandal in Munich. Women Traitors!' (Brändle-Zeile, 1983, pp. 45-50). On 13 June 1932, Emmy Ender, addressing the *Bund Deutscher Frauen,* won majority backing for her declaration: 'National Socialism has grown big in its fight against Jews and women. It will not give up this fight. Today I am for struggle' (Evans, 1976, p. 255). But 'today' was too late. In December 1932 and January 1933, the last meetings of the German branches of the Women's International League for Peace and Freedom (again with a largely middle-class, educated, left-wing membership, and labelled 'Jewish/Marxist' by the Nazis) took place in Stuttgart, Hamburg and Frankfurt. At their Munich meeting in January 1933, the veteran German feminist and pacifist, Lida Gustava Heymann, aged 65, had to stand guard at the door of the hall:

So imposing was her carriage and expression that several of the Brownshirts shrank back. Her last appeal to the blind German people rushing towards their fate went: 'Hitler means war. Protect your children, don't let yourselves be fooled by words, — behind these words hide the most brutal, strong-arm tactics which you yourselves will be made to feel on your own flesh!' (Hoppstock-Huth, 1948, p. 14)

THE IMPACT ON GERMAN WOMEN OF THE NAZIS' ACCESSION TO POWER

When Hitler seized power in February 1933, he could exploit a specifically German (or rather Prussian) tradition that women *qua* women were unfit to take part in matters of state, but he could also rely on a gut assumption that always resurfaces in times of economic depression, and which is far from peculiar to Germany, that a woman's rightful place is in the home. But Hitler also knew from the outset that he would be confronted by opposition from certain sections of German women within the professional middle class and/or on the left, who would have to be driven out or eliminated. Therefore, he used every means available, ranging from changes in the law and state propaganda to arbitrary mass arrests, imprisonment without trial and even murder in order to neutralise all opposition including that of women. It is generally assumed that revolutions occur in opposition to the state power and that, at least in their early days, they will have a left-wing, democratic, egalitarian and humanely reforming political orientation. But in Hitler's Germany an extreme right-wing revolution was swiftly put through *by* the state machine itself, manipulating enthusiastic popular support for Hitler and the Nazi Party. In addition to the now Nazi-dominated armed police and secret police, backed by a network of informers in every city street, the law itself was swiftly changed, converting all political opponents into 'Illegalen'. Agents-provocateurs and spies were now paid or blackmailed into betraying their former comrades.

Before any politically-aware German men or women could *begin* to resist, therefore, the Nazis got in first. Even as the Reichstag was, unbeknowst to her, still burning, the communist Lina Haag was arrested in Stuttgart – she being just one among hundreds of left-wing German women immediately picked up for 'questioning' and taken into 'protective custody'. Women were included in political persecution from the first day. Already in March 1933, the Social Democrat MP Minna Cammens 'disappeared' and her ashes were sent to her husband in a cigar box a few days later with orders to keep quiet about her death. The Jewish Social

Democrat MP Toni Sender, was warned only just in time of the Nazis' plans to murder her and she escaped to America. Women writers who refused to write what one of them called *Blut-und-Boden-Quatsch,* were placed under *Schreibverbot* and denied access to publication. Veteran German feminists, including Helene Stöcker,[5] Lida Gustava Heymann[6] and Anita Augspurg[7] were placed on the first Nazi proscription lists and fled into exile where they died. The pacifists Constanze Hallgarten and Professor Dr Anna Siemsen also went into exile in 1933 but survived. The communist writer Anna Seghers was arrested but escaped with her children to France and then to Mexico. The actresses Erika Mann, Therese Giese and Helene Weigel all had to become political exiles. Othe women, like the Social Democrat MP and leading German feminist, Toni Pfülpf, so despaired over what was happening in Germany, that they killed themselves.

Many of the new Nazi laws specifically targeted women in Hitler's attempt to create a new Germany. Women were dismissed from factories, offices and administrative posts under the campaign against 'double-earners'. Women were paid to marry and leave the workforce in order to bear children for Germany. 'For (the woman's) world is her husband, her family, her children and her home', as Hitler said at the Nuremberg Party Rally in September 1934. Girls were not allowed to take up more than 10 per cent of the places in higher education and pressure was placed on women to resign from the professions of law and medicine.[8]

But the women who braced themselves to resist Hitler as the 1930s 'progressed', did not do so out of outraged feminism. Nazi anti-feminism was subsumed in Nazi anti-humanism, including its militarism and racism, and it was on humanist grounds that the women who resisted Hitler defied him. They scorned his pseudo-scientific classification of the species into a hierarchy of Aryan, Slav, Negro and Jew, and they rejected his reduction of men to mere fighting animals as passionately as they rejected his reduction of women to mere breeding animals.

Many of the women who resisted Hitler were to be accused of being 'enemies of the state'.[9] They defied this new totalitarian, militarist Germany, because they were convinced that its vaunted 'National Socialist Revolution' violated every humane moral law. The fact that psychopaths were now in power did not make them sane and just. On the contrary. Lina Haag spoke for all the German women who were to resist Hitler on the grounds of humanism when she asked defiantly:

What is the authority of the state, the power of this state? Terror. The storm-trooper and the policeman who may beat you and arrest you. The SS man and Gestapo official and the concentration camp . . . (The) horror and fear of that state are its power and authority. It is true that I stood out against that power and authority. (Haag, 1948, pp. 101-2)

Or, as Joanna Jacob put it: 'Every woman (in prison) came from a different group or party, but we all wanted the same thing, to prevent another war and to fight injustice' (Szepansky, 1983, p. 215).

THE SECOND PHASE OF ANTI-NAZI RESISTANCE BY GERMAN WOMEN, 1933 – 39

As we have seen, many of Germany's most eminent women intellectuals and leading feminists were immediately driven into exile early in 1933; those few who remained in Germany were left with scarcely any way of expressing their anti-Nazism. For example, Germany's greatest woman writer, Ricarda Huch, publicly resigned from the Prussian Academy of Arts in order to register her angry protest against the expulsion of the brothers Mann, Döblin, Wasserman and Werfel, and Goebbels publicly retaliated by insulting her on the occasion of her seventieth birthday. Sometimes, however, women managed to write in code as when Gertrud von le Fort published her essay, *Die ewige Frau* in 1934 on the necessity for women to act as the humane conscience of society in order to counteract the brutality of male power-politics.[10] In 1935 the artist and sculptor Käthe Kollwitz, (who had already been expelled from the Prussian Academy of Arts in March 1933), defiantly attended the funeral of the Jewish painter Max Liebermann. In July 1936 the Gestapo came for her, then aged sixty-eight, interrogated her and threatened her with concentration camp. Thereafter she and her husband always carried poison on them lest the Gestapo came to take them away. In 1937, an outstanding woman resister among the intellectuals, the Catholic university lecturer, Dr Margarethe Adam, was arrested for high treason. She had written to army officers (i.e. seven years *before* the overdue 20 July Officers' Plot) urging them to overthrow Hitler before he ruined Germany. She was sentenced to nine years' penal servitude, the effects of which killed her (Hochmuth and Meyer, 1969, pp. 271-3).

The German woman resisters found themselves at this time in a situation of ever-increasing isolation as they watched their Satan being hailed as the Messiah. That Hitler was Germany's saviour was now being taught in schools, on newsreels, over the radio, and in the pulpit. Christa Wolf has reconstructed the feelings of her own five-year-old, Nazi self in 1934:

The Führer was a sweet pressure in the stomach area and a sweet lump in the throat, which she had to clear to call out for him, the Führer, in a loud voice, in unison with all the others, according to the urgings of a patrolling sound truck . . . Although it frightened her a little, she was at the same time longing to hear the roar, to be a part of it. (Wolf, 1980, p. 45)

Nevertheless, Hitler still found it necessary to set up more and more prisons, including concentration camps, designed specifically for women, *before* September 1939 in order to punish all those German women who would not shout 'Heil'. Already in 1933, Gotteszell in Baden-Württemberg, Stadelheim in Bavaria, Barnimstrasse in Berlin and Moringen in Lower Saxony were designated as new women's prisons. Moringen became the first women's concentration camp, then Lichtenburg and, in spring 1939, Ravensbrück. Weisenborn,[11] using German prison statistics, estimates that *c*. 225,000 German men and women had passed through the courts on political charges by September 1939. A surviving Gestapo report for 10 April 1939, states that on that date alone there were 27,369 prisoners in custody awaiting sentence for political offences and 112,432 convicted political prisoners actually serving sentences. Henri Bernard (Brussels, 1976) estimates that 'without counting Jews, 302,000 Germans were imprisoned . . . for political reasons before the war'. We cannot as yet be certain what percentage of these prisoners were women. Hanna Elling's estimate of 20 per cent is possibly too high. But even 10 per cent would mean over 30,000 German women imprisoned, and just 5 per cent would mean 15,000. What is certain therefore is that there were many thousands of German women who resisted Nazism in one way or another before 1939 and whose struggle is still far too little known. Who were these women?

The women who suffered even worse than did the intellectuals from the Nazis' accession to power were, indubitably, the active socialists and communists. Among the hundreds, if not thousands, of women arrested in Berlin, Hamburg, Leipzig, Bremen, Hanover, Wupperthal, Essen, Frankfurt, Munich, Mannheim, Dortmund and Stuttgart during the first years of Nazi power were the socialists Herta Brünen-Niederhellmann and Anna Stiegler and the communists Maria Zeh, Trude Gessmann, Hanna Melzer, Erika Buchmann, Lina Haag, Gertrud Meyer, Lina Knappe, Gertrud Schlotterbeck, Maria Deeg, Katherina Jacob, Berta Karg, Charlotte Gross, Dr Doris Maase, Anne Bohne-Lucko, Käthe Popall and Centa Herker-Beimler.[12] The charges against them included typing, duplicating and distributing illegal leaflets (which often pathetically and unrealistically called for a 'mass uprising against the Fascist war-mongers!'); trying to form a now illegal trade union; giving aid to the families of political prisoners ('Rote Hilfe'); spreading 'atrocity stories' about the Nazis abroad ('Greuel im Ausland'); attempting to help re-organise the banned Social Democrat or Communist Parties; harbouring wanted left-wingers in their own homes; and even just putting flowers on Rosa Luxemburg's grave (Elling, 1981, pp. 47-8). It is clear from many of these charges that most of the women played a characteristically subordinate and supportive role in the political resistance but it was none the less a role that was both essential and dangerous. As one woman resister pointed out:

How could the active men and women comrades who had been outlawed do their work at all without the many women who afforded them secret refuge? . . . These women had to know the precise details of their neighbours' habits – when they departed for and returned from work, when the housewives swept the apartment-block stairs, when they went shopping and so on, in order that the hidden resistance-worker could leave the house and return without being seen. Above all the *Quartiermütter* had to know the political attitude of every one of their fellow-tenants. Every day there would be some cause for panic and all too often things would go terribly wrong (Käthe Popall, interviewed in Elling, 1981, p. 151)

Once arrested, women might be held for months and even years without trial and subjected to repeated brutal interrogation. Indeed the real motive for their arrest would often seem to have been the Gestapo's assumption that they would break under continuous cross-examination and betray the names and whereabouts of a whole network of 'wanted', much more important, left-wing *men* – their fathers, brothers, husbands, lovers or sons. Thus the women's resistance had to continue within prison as they refused to name other people, no matter what was done to them. As a punishment for their non-cooperation they were sentenced to quite disproportionately long terms of penal servitude or solitary confinement, and even after their sentences had been served they were still not released. Instead, these women 'politicals' were moved to concentration camps, and so became some of the first to endure Nazi torture, the grey-cloaked women guards with their dogs and whips, and the punishment cells underground where women were beaten to death. As Lina Haag wrote:

I always thought that after my two years of solitary confinement there was nothing left in this world that could frighten me, but I was mistaken. I had a terrible fear of the whippings, of the dark cells in which women died so quickly, of the dreaded rooms in which the prisoners were interrogated by the Gestapo . . . The fear alone was martyrdom enough, martyrdom enough the certainty that these things would happen to us. (Haag, 1948, p. 135)

On Easter Sunday 1938, at Lichtenburg, she had to watch the communist Steffi Kunke of Vienna, who had been arrested for helping her Jewish communist lover escape across the frontier, be stripped naked, tied to a post and whipped to death. The Nazis' sadism, towards both men and women, could now flourish at will in the new, isolated camps, with their specially recruited staff. And on 23 June 1938, the first German woman was legally executed in Berlin because of her political resistance to Hitler. She was 27-year-old Liselotte Herrmann, a former student of chemistry and biology, who had been expelled from University in 1933 for signing a students' anti-war petition. She had made contact with the banned Communist Party in Stuttgart, and, on discovering during her work in a South German aircraft factory in 1935 that Hitler was definitely rearming for war, she had got word out to friends in Switzerland to rouse public opinion abroad using her technical and industrial evidence. In December 1935 she was arrested for treason; in 1937 she was sentenced to death and in June 1938 she was beheaded. Several prominent Englishwomen, including Lady Violet Bonham-Carter, Eleanor Rathbone MP, Sybil Thorndike, Viscountess Rhondda and Ellen Wilkinson MP, had cabled Hitler petitioning for a reprieve, in vain.

One large group of women resisters whom the left-wing 'politicals' had never expected to find as fellow sufferers in the concentration camps were the Jehovah's Witnesses. They constituted the first, and for a long time the only, religious group openly to defy Hitler, as Lina Haag testified:

They were among the few people in Germany who said what they thought to the all-powerful party and Gestapo demi-gods. They said that they were against war, and that the quasi-divinity which Hitler assumed was blasphemous and criminal . . . They held fast to their faith, and endured imprisonment and death for it. They refused . . . any work that served armaments;. . . They accepted all maltreatment and every insult without complaint, as a trial imposed by Jehovah; or they replied calmly and soberly with prophecies of woe. Their attitude was more than admirable, it was most moving, but it was 'not of this world' . . . it belonged to Old Testament times. (Haag, 1948, p. 120)[13]

Meanwhile, in the rest of Germany, away from the hideous prisons and camps, the persecution of German Jews was on the increase and reached its pre-war climax on Kristallnacht, 9 November 1938. Hundreds of synagogues and shops were set on fire, at least a thousand Jews were arrested and about a hundred killed. H.D. Leuner (1978) cites many instances of individual Germans, most often women (and including servants, nursemaids, governesses, and the Gentile wives of Jews) who stood by the stigmatised German Jews before 1939. Even though they did not, as yet, risk imprisonment or death for their loyalty they did risk being pilloried in the Nazi press as 'Judenfreunde' and even dismissal from their work, quite sufficient sanctions to make many women hesitate before going out of their way on behalf of the Jews.[14]

All in all, the political resistance of German women between 1933 and 1939 was essentially a resistance grounded in moral revulsion at the Nazis' brutality, their militarism and racism, and it was often reinforced by the women's loyalty towards their men who were already political prisoners or in hiding. The women would often practise hidden resistance as they refused to work in the armaments industries or secretly committed themselves to sustaining the families of the racially persecuted or the politically outlawed. As yet it was only if they could be convicted of complicity in some *overtly* politcal activity that they would be savagely punished. Mere human fellowship or the expression of anti-Nazi views were not yet crimes. But that would change.

THE IMPACT OF WAR ON GERMAN WOMEN RESISTERS

Once Hitler initiated the Second World War the situation of anti-Nazi women in Germany became infinitely more difficult. Whatever slight foreign support they had hitherto received was now cut off. Any aid they now gave to Jews gradually became criminally punishable. Brutal new measures were now swiftly brought in for the elimination of 'useless eaters' including schizophrenics, epileptics, the senile, the paralysed, the mentally handicapped, the long-stay mentally ill and those suffering from Huntingdon's or other neurological diseases (and, in addition all patients of mixed Jewish, negro or gipsy blood also had to be 'reported' for extermination). It was generally women, most often nuns, who were committed to caring for these afflicted people and who were soon faced with a horrific choice. In addition, new categories of untouchable people were being herded into Germany – foreign prisoners of war and slave-workers: Poles, Frenchmen and Russians, and with them came new crimes and new penalties, many of which targeted characteristically 'womanly' acts of fellowship and affection. Any girl or woman discovered to be having a love affair with a slave-worker or prisoner of war could now be sent to a concentration camp for 'Rassenschande'. It was now an offence to bake a cake for a foreigner, or to speak in French to a French prisoner, or to invite a Pole to a birthday party, or even to mend a prisoner's socks.[15] Any help such as food or ration coupons seen to be given to a foreign slave was made a criminal offence. Whereas under Weimar only three offences carried the death penalty, under Nazi law, *forty-six* different 'crimes' were punishable with death (Meyer, 1971, p. 227). For example to hide a Jew or to help a Jew escape was now made a capital offence. Listening to a foreign radio station was made a capital offence. Uttering anti-Nazi, or anti-war 'defeatist' remarks was a capital offence. And informers were everywhere.

Clearly it is far more difficult for a woman to resist her own government and country in war-time than it is to do so in peace-time or than it is to resist a foreign occupation force. What had been dissidence now seems to be treason, not merely to those in power but also to all one's neighbours, and even perhaps to oneself. How can you try to sabotage a war-effort in which your own and your friends' menfolk are being killed? 'Even to appear to differ from those she loves in the hour of their affliction has ever been the supreme test of a woman's conscience', as Jane Addams wrote of those women who had publicly opposed the Great War of 1914-18. Moreover, German women were not only tempted to try to alleviate the suffering of their men, and to ensure their victory, by supplying them with every sort of material and psychological support; they were also being asked to welcome the pain of being bombed and of ever-increasing hardship all for the sake of the Fatherland. Goebbels evolved a Nazi version of the theology of suffering especially addressed to German girls and women. As Christa Wolf bitterly remembers in her *Model Childhood,* all the idealism and self-immolation of her adolescence were harnessed to the Nazis' war-effort between the ages of 12 and 16; she was desperate to be thought worthy to become a leader of Hitler's *Jungmädel,* she worshipped the dedication to duty of her beloved Nazi history mistress, eager to emulate her in all the women's tasks of war-service — potato-harvesting, fire-watching, billeting and tending the wounded and evacuees, seduced by her own very innocence into believing that evil was good, convinced that her Führer really meant what he said about collective self-sacrifice for the good of the suffering Heimat. The worse things became for herself and for Germany the more loyal she would be until at 16 she was grieving bitterly for her worst enemy — the dead Hitler (Wolf, 1980, Chs. 8, 10 and 15).

But German women had still more internal barriers to overcome, besides terror for themselves or a misplaced idealistic masochism, before they could resist Hitler and Hitler's war. Women have a special area of vulnerability because of the existence of those totally dependent upon them. It is not unnatural that women should feel that their first duty must be to those who would be helpless without them — their babies and small children, their sick and their elderly. Bacon remarked that he who has wife and children has hostages to fortune; from 1939 to 1945 she who had helpless dependants had hostages to Hitler. If a woman were caught, her relatives would be arrested also under 'Sippenhaft' and her children could be taken away from her altogether to be brought up as good Nazis. It is not surprising that of the 280 women listed by Hanna Elling as executed for political reasons the majority were single women. A few were pregnant with their first child when arrested; they gave birth in prison, were allowed to breastfeed for a few weeks and were then beheaded. Nevertheless, despite all these horrors, there still were thousands of German women, even including some married women with children, who risked resisting both the Nazis and their war.

This resistance took one of two contrasting forms. Either it would be waged in maximum isolation and with complete secrecy in order to be effective, or it would attempt to gain maximum exposure, reaching as many key people as possible. An example of the first, 'secret' resistance, was the hiding of fugitive Jews or of handicapped young people on the death-lists; an example of the second was the leafleting of university lecture theatres, factories, army barracks or railway stations, giving the truth about the war news. Secret resistance was not directly political in that it did not work to overthrow Nazi power; nevertheless it was still resistance, since it aimed at frustrating and undermining Nazi policies. Erna Lugebiel, who was sent to Ravensbrück for helping to hide Jews, said she did not regard what she did as resistance; it was just a matter of acting according to one's human feelings (Szepansky, 1983, p. 155). But she was wrong. To act like a feeling human being in a society which forbids humanity *is* to wage resistancè against that society, and to do so when the penalty for discovery is torture or death is to be a heroine.

THE THIRD PHASE OF ANTI-NAZI RESISTANCE BY GERMAN WOMEN: SEPTEMBER 1939 – MAY 1945

Among the Germans who risked their lives for Jews before 1945, says H.D. Leuner, women considerably outnumbered men. He cites Frau Angermeier, the caretaker of the Jewish cemetery in Munich, Countess Bullestrem-Solf and her daughter who forged visas, hid Jews and led them secretly across the frontier, and the concert singer Lydia Borelli who said later: 'I was ashamed to be a German; to keep my self-respect I had to share the fate of the persecuted Jews. I had to make it my own.' So she sheltered two Jewish women 'for the duration'. The 'Onkel Emil' group in Berlin consisting of about 24 professional people including the actresses Karin Friedrich and Ruth Andreas, forged identity papers for refugees. They also tore down Nazi propaganda slogans, spread foreign news, looked after the families of political prisoners and secretly fed foreign slave-workers. Martha Beicht took her first two Jews into her flat when she was only eighteen; twenty-three Germans, most of them women, were needed to save just one Jewish couple and their little girl by taking it in turn to hide them. The retired teacher, Elisabeth Abegg, used her home constantly as a hiding-place. And for every helper and fugitive alike every waking minute had to be lived in fear. (Elisabeth Langgässer has written the best imaginative account of what it meant for women to hide and to be hidden in her story *In Hiding*.) In Königsberg, five German village women – Frau Klieger, Frau Schmiedel, Frau Metzger, Frau Krantz and Frau Seifert – were sentenced to six years' penal servitude for having taken in eight children of deported Jews and for having brought them up as their own. In Berlin,

.two women teachers of an illegal school for Jewish children were killed by the Gestapo. Two Protestant women who then continued to run the school were arrested and sent to Ravensbrück, as was the Catholic Gertrud Lucker who had tried to help Jews through Caritas. The young nurse, Gertrud Seele, was executed in Plötzensee for helping Jews. Perhaps the most eminent of all German women who suffered for this kind of resistance to the Nazis' race mania was the Protestant educationist and former headmistress of an outstanding girls' School, Elisabeth von Thadden. With her hands manacled behind her back she dictated her last words in the death cell to the prison chaplain: 'We wanted to be good Samaritans.'

Simultaneously, those German nuns who cared for the sick, the handicapped and the incurable were having to risk concentration camp or even death as they tried to save at least some of their charges. They falsified the official returns about the inmates of their hospices, they sent patients away without authority back to the greater safety of their families, they warned these families of the imminent danger that the afflicted ones were in, they did not surrender the patients demanded of them, they tried to obstruct the death-transports, and in each case they were risking a charge of sabotage or anti-state activity. Onc Franciscan nun, Sister Oswenda, managed to get a spastic boy adopted just in time; another, Sister Gislaria, hid a boy with a skin disease who was on the death-list in her bread kitchen during a search; a third, Sister Paulilla, took twenty mentally handicapped boys out into the fields with her every day where they weeded and picked stones and so were saved from the fatal 'useless eater' label. All in all the nuns saved nearly 1500 of the sick and handicapped from being killed like defective cattle. Those they could not save were a lifelong torment to remember (Kempner, 1979).

Never before have so many of the kindest people, the least selfish, the most capable of pity and generosity and moral courage, had to risk a hideous death *because* they were decent human beings. There was the communist, Lore Diener, for instance, who was punished by the SS with death in Auschwitz merely for having allowed the Polish women prisoners in her block in Ravensbrück to pray aloud together and sing their folk-songs (Szepansky, p. 179); there was the Catholic, Marie

Terwiel, executed for distributing Bishop von Galen's sermons and for forging passports for Jews (Leber, 1957, pp. 123-6); there were the Jehovah's Witnesses Margaret Baalhorn, Helene Gotthold and Mathilde Hengeveld, executed for giving asylum to young men who would not kill for Hitler (Elling, 1981, p. 182); and there was the irrepressible Countess Erika von Brockdorff, convicted of having a radio set in her flat which was used for making contact with the Russians. Her Nazi judge threatened that she would soon stop laughing. 'Not while I can still see you', she retorted; and Hitler personally insisted on the death sentence for her (Weisenborn, 1974, p. 257). More than 300 women's names have so far been found on the Gestapo execution records, and the list is still not complete.

By far the largest group of *detected* anti-Nazi resisters were communists. That they were detected was directly related to the openness of their mode of resistance − leafleting, fly-posting, sabotage, contacting prisoners of war, radioing military intelligence to Russia, and urging German soldiers to desert. Some of these women, like 75-year-old Ottilie Pfühl, had been active communists long before Hitler's time. Others, like the graphic artist Elisabeth Schumacher, the film researcher Libertas Schulze-Boysen, the secretary Hilde Coppi, the tailoress Lisbeth Rose and the housewife Anneliese Hoevel had worked with their communist husbands in illegal political activity after 1933 and were all executed with them in the early 1940s.[16]

The Nazis liked to label all their opponents 'Bolsheviks' and to assert that such people were simply traitors to Germany in the pay of the Kremlin. And to some extent this 'Red' reputation has stuck in the West − some post-war western commentators seeming to feel that the Nazis did have a point in executing people who listened in to Russian news bulletins and radioed military information back (though how the Nazis could have been defeated as swiftly as possible *without* Russian knowledge of Hitler's war strategy they do not say).[17] It is not possible to interrogate the dead about their degree of ideological independence, but the last letters written by communist women resisters before their execution certainly do not sound like messages from people inspired just by narrow political sectarianism. The resistance courier, and kindergarten teacher, Rose Schlösinger, for instance wrote to her small daughter:

My dear little big Marianne,
. . . think of our evenings of discussion in bed, about all the important things of life − I trying to answer your questions. And think of our beautiful three weeks at the seashore − of the sunrise and when we walked barefoot along the beach from Bansin to Urkeritz, and when I pushed you before me on the rubber float, and when we read books together . . . (Gollwitzer, Kuhn and Schneider, 1962, pp. 190-1)

One other group of women resisters who should not be forgotten consisted of girls who had received all their education under the Nazis but who nevertheless risked their lives to testify that Nazism was evil. Twenty-year-old Liane Berkowitz and Cato Bonties van Beek, for instance, who typed and duplicated resistance materials for the Schulze-Boysen Harnack organisation in Berlin; Eva Buch who translated their illegal leaflet 'Inner Front' into French to circulate among French prisoners of war; Margarethe Rothe of the Hamburg 'White Rose' group which published the illegal radio wavelength of the *Deutsche Freiheitssender* calling for the overthrow of the Nazis;[18] 21-year-old Sophie Scholl in Munich. Sophie Scholl has, up till now, been the best known, if not indeed the only known, example of political resistance by a German girl.[19] Her independent mind and passionate conscience ring out in the leaflets that she helped her brother and his friends to write, duplicate and distribute in cities all over southern Germany as well as in Hamburg, Vienna and Berlin.

Their first leaflet quoted Schiller to support their stand against the totalitarian Nazi state:

Anything may be sacrificed to the good of the State except that end for which the State serves as a means. The State is never an end in itself; it is important only as a condition under which the purpose of humanity can be attained . . . In Sparta a political system was set up at the price of all moral feeling . . .

Their second pamphlet spelt out the slaughter of the Jews in Poland: 'Here we see the most frightful crime against human dignity, a crime unparalleled in the whole of history. For Jews, too, are human beings.' Their third leaflet declared: 'our present "state" is the dictatorship of evil.' Their fourth:

Every word that comes from Hitler's mouth is a lie. When he says peace he means war, and when he blasphemously uses the name of the Almighty, he means . . . Satan . . . We will not be silent. We are your bad conscience. The White Rose will not leave you in peace!

Their last leaflets, January/February 1943, called on the Germans to commit sabotage and to dissociate themselves from the Nazi gangsters before it was too late:

Are we to be forever the nation which is hated and rejected by all mankind? . . . Do not believe that National Socialist propaganda which has driven the fear of Bolshevism into your bones . . . The name of Germany is dishonoured for all time if German youth does not finally rise, take revenge, and atone, smash its tormentors, and set up a new Europe of the spirit (Inge Scholl, 1970, pp. 73-93)

Sophie Scholl was always quite clear how her open resistance must end. Two days before her arrest she had said to a friend: 'So many people have died *for* this regime, it is time that someone dies for being *against* it.' In their defence during interrogation the brother and sister simply said that they had wanted to save hundreds of thousands of lives by building up opposition to the continued waging of the war and that they believed that the sacrifice of their own lives for that cause was not in vain. At 5.00pm on 22 February 1943, Sophie Scholl was manacled to two assistant executioners and beheaded. The announcement of the execution of the Scholls at Munich University was greeted with roars of approval.

Finally, there were all those individual German women who belonged to no resistance group at all but who had to express their abhorrence of the Nazi barbarism even if it were only by 'talking out of turn'. Elfriede Scholz, for example, the sister of Erich Maria Remarque, was denounced by one of her dressmaking customers for saying:

Will this idiot let every one of our towns be smashed flat before he agrees to make peace? All the men marched off to the front are nothing but cattle going to the slaughter. If Germans are hated all over the world, then that is their own fault − foreigners are much better people than we are always being told. (Weisenborn, 1974, pp. 315-16)

She was convicted of 'defeatism and shameless betrayal of her own German blood' and executed. Another such stubborn individual was the distinguished Munich actress, Hanne

Mertens, once famous for her Electra and her Hedda Gabler. She too spoke out against the war-mania and dared to mock Goebbels himself. Arrested and held for months without trial in a Hamburg concentration camp, even starvation in the freezing punishment cell could not silence her – she still could be heard singing or reciting Goethe, Heine, Theodor Storm or the Shakespeare sonnet 'Full many a glorious morning have I seen/Flatter the mountain-tops with sovereign eye'. The letters NN, Nacht und Nebel, had been put against her name, signifying that she was to be got rid of without anyone ever knowing what happened to her. What did happen was that ten days before the end of the war the SS came for her and for twelve other women prisoners (and 58 men) all of whom thought they were about to be released; they were stripped naked instead, and hanged (Zorn and Meyer, 1974, pp. 74-90).

It was not granted to them to save Germany; only to die for her; luck was not with them but with Hitler. Nevertheless, they did not die in vain. Just as we need air in order to breathe, light in order to see, so also do we need noble human beings in order to live. They are the element in which the spirit grows and the heart can become pure. They tear us out of the morass of the mundane; they fire us to struggle against evil; they nourish our faith in the divine in humans . . . *Meine Helden, Geliebte* . . .
(Ricarda Huch aged 82, in 1946, appealing to Germany to remember all those Germans who had been killed for their anti-Nazi resistance, quoted in Weisenborn, 1974, pp. 11, 401)

Why have we remained so long in ignorance of the resistance by German women? The Nazis themselves of course destroyed a lot of the evidence and the Allies at first wanted to suppress the facts about any German resistance since they needed the collective guilt of all Germans to justify their call for unconditional surrender. (And not even during the Nuremberg trials were any surviving German resisters called to testify, although they were a living proof that it had been possible not to obey orders.) Then the swift resumption of the Cold War between the erstwhile Allies caused communist historians only to acknowledge the authenticity of the communist resistance and western historians only that of the non-communists. And the thousands of women typists, couriers, 'Quartiermütter' and rescuers of the persecuted within the German resistance remained largely invisible on both sides of the political divide because they were never the leaders of their groups, only the enablers. For that reason alone it is worth recording that there *were* women in the German resistance who pitted themselves against a totalitarian state fused with a populist revolution, and who overcame all the barriers specific to the female condition (physical, social and psychological) in order to do life-sustaining work, in spite of its being forbidden, and *because* it was forbidden. The women resisters did not overthrow Hitler but they did save thousands of his victims, for the personal has never been more political than it was in Germany then. Whether communist or non-communist, hundreds of these women ended up side by side, manacled, naked, hanging from the same gallows or beheaded by the same guillotine, united in their humanist resistance to the Nazi policies of 'the elimination of the inhuman' and 'total war'.

Liselotte Herrmann, Lina Haag, Rose Schlösinger, Erika von Brockdorff, Elisabeth von Thadden, Hanne Mertens, Margarethe Ruthe, Sophie Scholl and all the many even less-known others were Cordelias who 'with best meaning . . . incurr'd the worst'. No statues have been raised to them and very few German streets or schools have been named after them. Outside the two Germanies they have remained almost completely unknown. Yet we Europeans both in East and West facing as we do the threat of yet another 'total war' in the name of self-defence, need, I believe, to resurrect these particular dead German women almost above all others. We need them to quicken in us something of their pity for all who are vulnerable, their fellowship with those labelled 'alien' and their refusal to do evil in the name of a specious good.

6 Marianne's Citizens? Women, the Republic and Universal Suffrage in France

Siân Reynolds

That Marianne should be the symbol of the French Republic is not merely an irony long ago noted by feminists: her inspiring figure actually masks the masculinity of the republican tradition and of republican discourse as it has survived into the late twentieth century. Republicanism as an ideal has recently experienced a striking revival in France, both among politicians and historians. The reasons are complex: they include the economic crisis and the problem of 'the exercise of power' by the socialist government after 1981 as well as a certain disaffection both from Marxism and from the inheritance of 1968. One of the most visible signs of the republican revival was the decision in 1985 by the socialist Minister of Education to re-introduce civic instruction to the school curriculum. Less obvious, but significant in its own way has been the number of publications in law, history and politics in which republicanism has been a central theme.[1] But whether in school textbook or historical work, the republican world remains remarkably male both in its points of reference and its vocabulary. It is above all with the way people write about the Republic that this essay is concerned.

French women did not exercise their political rights (to vote and stand for election at local or national level) until after the Second World War and even then they had not achieved all their civil rights under the Civil Code, particularly if they were married. That they were excluded from citizenship in the past everyone agrees, but it could be argued that this exclusion is itself still, in the 1980s, being excluded both from the republican tradition as politically revived and from the historiography of the Republic. Great days and anniversaries are much commemorated in France, but one recently passed in silence: no particular commemoration in 1985 marked the fortieth anniversary of the introduction of universal adult suffrage. Women had voted for the first time in the local elections of April 1945 and the parliamentary election of October 1945.

While in any history of women's rights in France, 1945 is often alluded to as the most significant date of the twentieth century, in most general histories of twentieth-century France, it appears almost in parenthesis if at all. It has thus acquired the paradoxical status of a 'fact' significant for women but not for men. The post-1970 women's movement in France has also tended to regard 1945 as a non-date for this very reason: the invariable reduction of feminism to the suffrage, and the related assumption that once women did have the vote that was the end of the story. Modern French feminism, particularly in its radical forms, sees itself as defined in part by rejecting the legitimacy of the 'democratic parliamentary republic', and has been profoundly uneasy in its relations with the state. All the more so when − as in the last ten years, especially under the socialist government − the state has sought to introduce reforms in women's rights, setting up a special ministry to do so. 1945 in this context does not seem a particularly sacred date.

Women's history too, since 1970, has similarly tended to avoid the suffrage question precisely because it seemed a straitjacket. Recently however feminists, including historians have been more inclined to regard political power as the focus of analysis and the logical area of development of feminist thought. What follows is intended as a contribution to that debate (cf. Delphy, 1984; Faure, 1985). Behind the construction of 1945 as a date for women but a non-date for the Republic, lies a perception of history and in particular of the relation of universal suffrage to the Republic which has become something of an orthodoxy by default. I shall first outline (in unavoidable brevity) the orthodox historiography of the Republic in so far as it concerns itself with women (which is not very much) then suggest some elements of a feminist critique of the tradition − the more necessary because it is clear from the language of some contemporary French historians that they sincerely think a reference to the 'sexism' of the past is sufficient to deal with such a critique.

The answer offered by French republican history to the obvious question 'why were women not citizens before 1945?' has to be deduced to some extent from what it does not say, since it so rarely addresses the question. But it is possible to construct a set of arguments generally regarded as an acceptable explanation (an explanation, that is, from the point of view of the contemporary historian who does recognise that there is a case to answer).[2]

Abbreviating ruthlessly then, the argument would run as follows. The revolutionaries of 1789 gave France and the world the Declaration of the Rights of Man and the Citizen; and in 1792, the French Republic embodied certain ideals of citizenship. But civic rights were not extended to women, although it is usually accepted that women were by no means inactive politically during the Revolution. The question was never seriously discussed by the assemblies: but it can certainly be agreed that it would have been extraordinary, even in those extraordinary times, if women had been enfranchised.

When the Republic was briefly restored in 1848, the restricted franchise of the Restoration was abolished and the vote extended to all adult men. Here the argument runs straight into a question of terminology which is still significant today in France (as it is not in Britain for instance). It is commonplace to find the electoral qualification of the Second Republic — that is, one had to be over 21 and male — described as 'universal suffrage'. While some limits were very shortly to be imposed on male suffrage, 1848 is usually celebrated as the point at which 'Republic' and 'universal suffrage' became identified with each other (although it is doubtful whether any other means of disenfranchising 50 per cent of adults — the lower 50 per cent in terms of income for instance — would be described by historians or anyone else as 'universal' suffrage). As it was, however, the granting of the vote to large numbers of male peasants, although in principle 'progressive', inspired many republicans with the fear (justified as it turned out) that it would be used against them. Predictions about *how* men would vote were not in the event ever to restrict male suffrage in future. But, from now on, the history of why women did not get the vote becomes in part a history of how they would use it. Already in 1848, women who did campaign for the suffrage were being told, as Michelet told his audience at the Sorbonne in 1850, that giving women the vote would mean 'giving thousands of votes to the priests' (Albistur *et al.,* 1978, I, p. 310).

But it was under the Third Republic (1870 – 1940) that the clerical argument was to reach its peak. It could hardly now be argued by republicans that France would be ahead of her time by enfranchising women, since in the period up to 1914 a number of countries, very few of them republics, admitted women to at least part-citizenship (Hause and Kenney, 1984, p. 19). Instead, republican politicians, and historians ever since, have argued that clerical influence over women would be translated at the ballot box into a vote for clerical (that is reactionary and anti-republican) parties, at a time when the Republic was believed, with some reason, to be seriously under threat. Though not apparently a firm enough calculation to win parties of the right from their conviction that a woman's place was out of politics, this was certainly steadfastly believed by the powerful anticlerical radical party which dominated parliamentary coalitions both before and after 1914. It was not however the only available argument. Historians have also pointed out that there was no mass suffragist movement in France. No woman threw herself under the hooves of the President's horse at Chantilly, and the feminist movement that did exist is usually described as a tiny minority of middle-class intellectuals. French women it appeared, did not want the vote.

For the socialist parties of the early Third Republic, the question was a more difficult one. They all had a commitment in theory to equal rights for women. But among those, both men and women, to whom the class struggle was the priority, the woman question was regarded as a distraction from the class revolution; it would be solved afterwards. Meanwhile those socialists who were becoming more firmly integrated into the parliamentary republic were becoming susceptible to the argument that the women's vote would benefit parties of the right. Again the clerical issue was invoked: since all men already had the vote there could be no class divide as such about giving women the vote (as there was in Britain for instance, where property qualifications meant that there were still men who could not vote before 1918). But fierce anticlericalism was a powerful force among French socialists both before and after the First World War. Opposition to women's suffrage was not so much openly voiced on the left as secretly felt.[3]

During the inter-war period, there is a clear enough consensus that the major obstacle had become the Senate or upper house. The lower house, the *Chambre des députés*, passed by a large majority a Bill enfranchising women (at about the same time that women were being granted political rights in Britain and Germany). But the Bill was shelved and eventually defeated by Senate — a process which was to be repeated several times during the 1920s and 1930s. The Senate opposition was a mixture of traditional conservatism on the right and anticlericalism on the part of the radical party. It is often suggested that the *députés* could safely vote in favour, secure in the knowledge that the Senate would always vote against. The parliamentary left was certainly still divided on the issue: only the Communist Party (formed in 1920 and with few *députés* before 1936) was consistently in favour (without ever making it a priority); the socialists were in favour in theory but still had misgivings in practice; and the radicals remained firmly against. Republican historiography has on the whole embraced retrospectively the thesis of the non-communist left — sometimes expressed as the suggestion that if women had had the vote in 1936 the Popular Front would not have come to power (evidence from Spain to the contrary notwithstanding). It is further usually remarked that the suffragist movement was fairly quiescent between the wars.

Having explained, by a series of arguments which are thus only semi-apologetic, why women did not get the vote, republican historiography has comparatively little to say about how and why they did. Few of the questions raised in the various Resistance councils, among the Free French or the provisional government in Algiers during the Second World War are as difficult to find out about as the decision to grant women the vote. The texts themselves are clear enough. As early as 1942 (though this is rarely mentioned) General de Gaulle declared: 'Once the enemy is driven from our land, all French men and women (*tous les hommes et toutes les femmes de chez nous*) will elect a National Assembly which in the full exercise of its sovereignty will determine the country's destiny.' The ordinance of 21 April 1944 approved by the consultative assembly in Algiers, outlining arrangements for the government of France after the Liberation, contains as its Article 17: 'Women will vote and be eligible in the same way as men.'[4]

Few of the memoirs of those concerned and few of the secondary works give any details of the debate surrounding the decision. We do know that the final wording of Article 17 was at the insistence of communist representatives, and that there was even at this late date, fierce opposition from some radicals, one speaker using almost exactly Michelet's words of 1850. We also know from a recent study of the drafting of the political programmes of the Resistance, that it was again because of opposition from the radical party that the provision for women's suffrage was specifically *omitted* from the important 1944 Programme of the *Conseil National de la Resistance* (the internal Resistance forum in France itself) (Andrieu, 1984, p. 152). Despite this omission, the programme refers to the future 'establishment of democracy by the . . . *restoration* of universal suffrage' (my italics). At Algiers, however, the radicals were outvoted, and French women were at last enabled to vote.[5]

Perhaps more significant though than the muffled circumstances surrounding the decision, are the reasons given for it, both at the time and retrospectively. There is near unanimity on this from all historians including those with a strong commitment to women' rights. The reason most often cited is the 'courageous behaviour of women during the Resistance' (cf. for instance, Renard, 1965, p. 23). The notion that women had somehow 'earned' the vote is crucial and it was not new in 1944: war-work by women in the First World War is often cited for the wave of enfranchisement in 1919. It is perfectly true of course that there were many brave women in the French Resistance. Their individual records are well known although a satisfactory overall account has yet to be written. But it is evident that while emotionally comprehensible and sincerely put forward, this argument will not do as a logical explanation, if only because it was difficult to claim, even (or perhaps especially) in the highly-charged atmosphere of the Liberation, that all or indeed most women had been in the

Resistance. But it remains the orthodox 'respectable' explanation, with the implicit corollary that women were *not* granted the vote in recognition of some inalienable right, still less as a response to any demand for it from women themselves.[6]

* * * * *

From this rather schematic, but not, I hope, unfair outline of the republican orthodoxy, I would like to pick out one or two points for comment before going further. From the place they are accorded in mainstream history, neither the decree of 21 April 1944 nor the first votes in 1945 are regarded as major changes to the Republic. They are referred to as 'giving women the vote', rather than 'the institution of universal suffrage'. An anomaly (which had persisted for reasons not entirely unworthy it is suggested) was being rectified; citizenship was being extended to a previously excluded group. For women, it is assumed, the decision was unequivocally a good thing: admission at last to the city. What is not suggested is that the city was receiving anything of value, let alone half its long-vaunted claim to universalism. If anything, rather the reverse: before long since early studies of post-war voting showed women abstaining more often than men, they were being chided for 'poor citizenship'. All in all however, it seemed that their admission to the city had not changed anything very much. With the last of these statements feminists have tended to agree (Bouchardeau, 1977, p. 64).

Partly for this reason, partly because of the wish to escape the suffrage issue, many writers on women's history in the French context have given more attention to other areas of life (the family, employment, war work, the economy, education).[7] When historians have addressed the questions of power, the state and suffrage, they have tended to do one of two things: either to look at the women's movement in a broader perspective than the suffrage campaign; or to redefine power as traceable in informal structures as much as in formal institutions or politics. As an example of the first approach, it has been pointed out that the women's movement devoted much energy to civil rights as well as civic ones (because of the peculiar restrictions of the Civil Code) and to other issues, such as pacifism. The view that French feminism was a narrowly bourgeois movement has been to some extent challenged and attention drawn to working-class and socialist feminism, and to the modest origins of many activists. Research has also indicated that mainstream feminism both before and after the First World War was more active than it is generally assumed (Picq, 1984; Fraisse, 1984; Hause and Kenney, 1984). As an example of the second approach, Michelle Perrot's work has been outstanding, in her exploration for example of the working-class housewife as both actor and rebel, manager of the budget and bonny fighter, rather than invariably downtrodden and neglected (Perrot, 1979, 1984). Bonnie Smith's arresting study of the Catholic wives of mill-owners in northern France (1981) depicts the alternative world in which they immured themselves. Michelle Perrot, in Chapter 3 of this book, points out however that charting women's territory alone may have its own dangers, serving to bolster up the 'separate sphere' arguments of traditional history and leading for instance, to neglect of political power in the conventional sense. Her essay discusses the ways in which women's 'alternative power' was constructed and perceived, in France and in other countries during the nineteenth century. The present chapter is intended to complement hers by looking at the way political power was constructed without women in France after 1789.

The point is not so much to argue that the republican orthodoxy is 'wrong': most people, myself included, have tended to accept that it contains at least elements of a convincing explanation. But it is perhaps possible to ask whether it has got in the way of looking at the same history from a different and more feminist perspective. This might start from Mary Wollstonecraft's observation that both men and women are in some way damaged by the domination of one over the other. What the French republican tradition has never acknowledged is that the Republic was as flawed by its exclusion of women as it would have been by its exclusion (say) of working-class men. The latter, if they had not been enfranchised in 1848, would never have been invisible in the same way women are in the unthinking discourse on universal suffrage. But there is more to it than this. Women were not left out of the Republic by some sort of oversight. On the contrary, the Republic was in many ways created and forged into a myth against them, not merely without them. In a necessarily very brief outline of this argument, what follows will concentrate on three points of reference: the creation of the Jacobin Republic after 1792; the republican tradition as it solidified in the late nineteenth century under the Third Republic; and the way many historians and political scientists write about women in a political context today.

* * * * *

1789 did not bring a Republic to France; it was the failure of constitutional monarchy with the king's flight to Varennes which precipitated the declaration of the Republic in 1792 and the drafting of a republican constitution the following year. What is most relevant to our question is the extent to which, at this phase of the revolution, members of the assemblies went back to reading their Montesquieu and Rousseau, and also to renewed interest in the models of antiquity, particularly Rome and Sparta. Interpreting the influence of the Enlightenment or of antiquity on the French Revolution is fraught with risks, but it does seem that on the question of women and citizenship at least some general points can be made.

In the minds of many revolutionaries, women were associated with weakness, corruption, frailty and specifically with the court and the *ancien régime*, as Mary Wollstonecraft pointed out (cf. Chapter 1). Indeed under the *ancien régime*, certain privileged women of all three estates took part in the preliminary voting for the Estates General of 1789 (Hause and Kenney, 1984, p. 3). At court they were associated with the 'occult power' traditionally exercised by the king's consort, favourites or female relatives. In short they stood for everything that was the opposite of republican virtue. Neither Montesquieu nor Rousseau were as crudely misogynist as they are sometimes assumed to be, but they certainly provide encyclopedic reference for women as capricious, indiscreet, petty and above all weak.[8] The index entry for 'women' in *L'Esprit des Lois* (1748) in the Pléiade edition runs to several columns, hardly any of the references favourable. It could be argued that Rousseau's much publicised views on women draw on the same tradition: his solution in his political writing to the frightening power of Eve, frail and corrupting, amounts to an attempt to contain and imprison the threat she represented by turning her (ideally) into a Spartan mother.

The source for almost everything eighteenth-century (or indeed twentieth-century) readers knew about Sparta was Plutarch's *Life of Lycurgus,* which Rousseau heard at his father's knee and which was read by virtually all French schoolboys and a few girls (such as Manon Phlipon, later Madame Roland). The two points many readers remembered concerning women were first that young girls shared all physical exercise with boys and danced naked at gymnastic displays; and second that since Sparta was a military society where men served for long periods in the army, Spartan matrons ran the household. Remembered out of context, these contributed to the view of Sparta as a licentious society where women held great power. But this was to misread Plutarch, and both Rousseau and the Jacobin Saint-Just (who admired Sparta this side of idolatry) correctly drew the inference intended by Plutarch that the education of girls was designed specifically to produce healthy bodies capable of bearing strong children (preferably boys who would fight for the fatherland, an image which had particular relevance to the beleaguered French Republic of the Year II). 'Spartan mother' paintings depicting a stern matron instructing her son with the famous words 'Come back with your shield or on it', appeared in the Salons of the 1790s (Rawson, 1969, p. 286) It was the role of the Spartan mother to indoctrinate her children with virtue. She was not a citizen, but she was the chief source of civic education.

This is the image behind Rousseau's famous reference to women in the 'Dedication to the Citizens of Geneva' which precedes his *Discourse on the Origins of Inequality* (1755):

I must not forget that precious half of the Republic, which makes the happiness of the other; and whose sweetness and prudence preserve its tranquility and virtue. Amiable and virtuous daughters of Geneva, it will always be the lot of your sex to govern ours. Happy are we so long as your chaste influence, solely exercised within the limits of conjugal union, is exerted only for the glory of the State and the happiness of the public. It was thus that the female sex commanded at Sparta . . . It is your task to perpetuate, by your insinuating influence and your innocent and amiable rule, a respect for the laws of the State and harmony among the citizens. . . It is your task . . . to correct . . . those extravagances which our young people pick up in other countries whence they bring home hardly anything besides . . . a ridiculous manner acquired among loose women. (Rousseau, 1973 edn., pp. 36-7).

When Rousseau calls women 'the precious half of the Republic', he means the half without citizenship. In the terminology of the *Social Contract,* women are 'subjects' not 'citizens'.[9] Thus Eve can be recuperated and recruited as a transmitter of republican virtue, without being called upon to exercise political rights in person.

Neither Rousseau nor Montesquieu left women out of their writings as irrelevant: on the contrary, they feared and in a way respected them as a potentially destructive force. Antiquity provided a model of corrective training in the shape of the Spartan (or Roman) matron. While these views came to be shared by many of the men who made the French Revolution, it is worth pointing out that it *was* possible for men of the eighteenth century to think otherwise, to regard women not as Eve, Marie Antoinette, the Virgin Mary or the Spartan mother, but as human beings with rights. Condorcet, the philosopher and mathematician who was also a member of the revolutionary assemblies, voiced this opinion in his article 'On admitting women to the city', arguing on quite classic individualist grounds that women should be granted citizenship on the same terms as men. It was a thought, in other words, perfectly thinkable in the 1790s:

The rights of men derive entirely from their status as sentient beings, capable of acquiring moral ideas and reasoning about those ideas. So women having the same qualities necessarily have the same rights. Either no individual of the human race has any real rights, or all have the same. And one who votes against the rights of another, whatever their religion, colour or sex, has by so doing abjured his own.[10]

Condorcet's feminism as well as that of women feminists of the time was marginal and has no place in the tradition which sees the Republic as having been forged in the heat of battle, symbolised by the citizen-army that fought at Valmy. Women themselves entered into the patriotic role of the Spartan mother, giving both their ardour and their children to the revolution. Effectively, the Republic was built on a set of principles which wrote women out of the small share of public life they had previously been allotted and firmly back into private life (principles endorsed by Napoleon I, the republican general who as Emperor personally supervised the drafting of the Civil Code). The sinful female body was to become a virtuous republican body, bearing sons who would be soldier-citizens. (French women could confer citizenship on their sons by bearing them and on their foreign husbands by marriage). When in 1793, the Jacobin Chaumette closed down the women's political clubs, he said, 'the sans-culotte had a right to expect his wife to run the home while he attended public meetings: hers was the care of the family, this was the full extent of her *civic* duties' (Hufton, 1971, p. 102, my italics).

If one accepts that the Republic was constructed as much against women as without them, the development into a major issue of the clerical question in the nineteenth century can be seen as a development and consolidation of male republicanism rather than as something specific to the religious quarrels of the Third Republic (as contemporaries seem to have believed). There were certainly reasons to connect women with religion. We know (Hufton, 1971; Sutherland, 1985) that women were prominent in the religious reaction of the later 1790s. And it is certainly the case that before the 1850s, the education of girls in France was almost entirely in the hands of the Catholic authorities, mostly religious orders – as indeed was that of many boys in rural areas. By the time the embryonic feminist movement was gaining strength around 1900, the clerical/anticlerical division was at its height, exacerbated by the Dreyfus affair. But not even the fiercest republicans seriously suggested depriving churchgoers of their vote. It was because women had originally been excluded from the Republic that it was easy to convert an argument about rights into an argument about the putative result of giving women the vote.

It is not easy to discover hard facts about religious observance in nineteenth-century France. Twentieth-century surveys undoubtedly show that church attendance is higher, by a significant margin, among women overall than among men overall, and that the earlier the figures the greater the gap.

Anyone who has been inside a French church will know that the congregation has a majority of women, often elderly, and the same was true in the nineteenth century. But that is not the same thing as saying that most women attend church. Already in the last century, church attendance was falling fast, and there was a considerable difference between many industrial areas and big cities, where the working class was virtually dechristianised with neither men nor women attending church regularly, and certain rural areas (Brittany for instance) where both men and women were devout Catholics. To have suggested disenfranchising Brittany on such grounds would of course have been quite unthinkable as an infringement of republican indivisibility and 'universality', but the continued exclusion of women on rather less clear evidence posed no problem. Unverified hypotheses about women and the strength of their religious convictions as a sex, and about the links between religious observance and voting behaviour were complemented in positivist thought by biological arguments, as Michelle Perrot pointed out in an earlier chapter.

Hypothesis for hypothesis, it is arguable that republican politicians, who were mostly middle-class town-dwellers, were generalising from their own experience. In the urban bourgeoisie, it was not uncommon for a husband to be free-thinking and anticlerical, while his wife, with at least his tacit consent, went to church and supervised the religious upbringing of the children. The case of the socialist Jean Jaurès (censured by his party for allowing his daughter to take communion) is typical. Indeed, some of his colleagues urged him to dictate to his wife over religion. Behind the claim that women would vote as their confessors told them to lay an unvoiced fear that they would *not* vote as their husbands told them to.

Despite the nuances introduced by recent scholarship (e.g. McMillan, 1981 b), the clerical/anticlerical debate is usually presented starkly in French republican historiography as being between obscurantism, reaction and superstition on one hand and progress, justice and freedom on the other. Neither participant could recognise any of its own values on the other side. But without holding any brief for the French Catholic hierarchy, it might be argued that in one respect at least, the

Republic's universalism was less that that of the Church. When the Republic said 'universal suffrage' it meant 'unisexual suffrage', a term coined by French feminists (Hause and Kenney, 1984). When it said fraternity, it really meant brotherhood. The citizens of its heavenly city were all male.

In the Church on the other hand, where admittedly in the Middle Ages there had been debates about whether women had souls, the debate had at least been resolved in women's favour. It would be absurd of course to argue that women had anything much in the way of power and influence in a Church of which the hierarchy was and is male, and with a theology that powerfully reinforced sexual subordination. But at least all souls whether male or female were capable of salvation; women as much as men could be elevated to beatitude or sainthood; in short, all human beings 'capable of acquiring moral ideas' in Condorcet's words, whatever the shape of their bodies, were acceptable in the eyes of the Church and could aspire to fulfilment within it. Indeed this was precisely the ambition of a great number of French women, whose education as we have noted was within clerical schools and convents. Historians have increasingly pointed out in recent years how the work of women's religious orders, educational or charitable, and of lay organisations connected with the Church, provided many women with an outlet for energies denied a place in republican public life and gave them an opportunity, however limited in scope, to exert some initiative and leadership (cf. Smith, 1981; Bouchardeau, 1977; Langlois, 1985).

For the Republic, while regarding the Church's emphasis on 'the family' as a unit as reactionary, nevertheless saw women as best suited to the domestic sphere. In 1904 it celebrated with some pomp the centenary of the Civil Code, which enshrined many clauses depriving married women of a whole range of individual civil rights and which was being fiercely challenged by the feminists of the day (Hause and Kenney, 1984, pp. 75 ff). Even when the Republic tried to win women away from the Church, it did so with the intention that they should act as Rousseau had exhorted the women of Geneva to do. Behind the provisions for girls' education in the Jules Ferry laws of the 1880s, which undoubtedly brought durable benefits for French women, lay the aim not of making women citizens, but of making them the major repositories of republican values for the benefit of their sons. Like the Spartan mothers, they would act as a transmission belt for values that excluded themselves. When a reporter attended a prizegiving at a state girls' school in the 1880s, he professed admiration of both the physical and the moral superiority of the pupils compared to the girls in the Church school down the road:

How clear it is that the young girls whom Madam H. is preparing for the struggle of life will one day be valiant citizens (*de vaillantes citoyennes*) who will be able to bring up their children in respect for justice and hatred of prejudice. (Ozouf, 1963, p. 108)

We are not far from Rousseau's vision of Sparta here.

One could pursue the Spartan parallel even further in the post-1918 period, when concern for the birth-rate produced an official discourse directed at encouraging women to have large families, while still refusing them rights within the city. The rhetoric too of the various republican 'catechisms' produced during the Third Republic, has a Spartan, military quality.[11] The origins of the Republic thus seem to have combined with the clerical/anticlerical debate to consolidate women's position as subjects not citizens and to confine them within the family unit under a Republic which asked many things of women (taxes and children to name but two) but offered little or nothing in return. That by comparison the Church did not seem to be an entirely negative pole has increasingly been suggested by historians. Hause and Kenney (1984) have stressed the importance of the Catholic feminist movement, and a full discussion of the contradictions and convergences of clerical and anticlerical positions on the issue of women's rights is provided by McMillan's very well documented article (1981 b).

What the republican orthodoxy tends to do, when discussing this period, is to mask the extent to which republicans used the clerical threat (which was by no means imaginary) to bolster a long-standing, inherited view of the Republic in which women had a clearly-defined role. The result is to validate retrospectively the universalist discourse of the Republic (about democracy, the people, universal suffrage), while retrospectively invalidating (as sectional) the Church's universalist discourse (about human souls and salvation). Women are either absent from the picture, or are viewed as powerless objects of the debate. That they may have good reason to oppose the Republic, that in many cases they sought alternative channels for political energies, or even that they may have been torn between the republican values they received in school and their exclusion from political rights, are questions which do not therefore have to be confronted.

That the traditional version of the story tends to excuse rather than explore the Republic's unwillingness to admit women, may help to explain the survival of a universalist republican language which sometimes seems to be unaware of its masculinist assumptions. The men of the Third Republic were after all the prisoners of a cultural tradition of great strength, and French feminism, though no doubt underestimated by historians, was not in a position to make much impact on that tradition. Less explicable is the failure of present-day writers, especially in France, to absorb the findings of what is by now a large body of literature in women's/ feminist history into their analysis of the Republic. Sometimes (Nicolet, 1982) it is still a matter simply of silence. But other writers pay lip-service to modern feminism in a way that suggests that they have accepted its premises. Thus they include blanket condemnations of the past as 'sexist' (something the present presumably is not) within an analysis of the past in much the same terms as before.

Let two examples stand for the rest. Maurice Agulhon, an otherwise admirable historian, is guilty of this practice in his fascinating book on Marianne as a symbol of the Republic. He remarks that the nineteenth century, 'which we would call phallocratic', was a period 'marked by extreme inequality of the sexes' (Agulhon, 1981, p. 185). Yet throughout the book there is hardly any reference to the difficult paradox that real women were excluded from the Republic whose imagery was so overwhelmingly female, and the term 'universal suffrage' is used for the system introduced in 1848 without batting an eyelid (ibid., p. 161). Similarly, J.G.A. Pocock in *The Machiavellian Moment* (1975) writing of republican theory in an earlier period, (not only in France) after 450 pages with no

mention of women, has a single reference to a woman —
significantly as the capricious buyer of a dress which may
create work for commerce — in a context where the debate is
precisely about commerce versus republican virtue. Again the
writer feels obliged to pay lip-service to feminism by
commenting that the example illustrates the 'rather prominent
sexism found in Augustan social criticism' (p. 465). In other
words, writing an important and respected book on republican
theory in which this is virtually the only reference to women
cannot be remotely construed as 'sexism', prominent or
otherwise. Such writers — and the examples are deliberately
chosen from eminent historians whose work I would not wish
unduly to disparage — while adopting a sort of post-feminist
discourse, do not seem to recognise that the omission of gender
from their discussion of the Republic is itself a problem.

If the problem for historians describing the Republic before
1945 is a failure to register the masculinity of their own
perspective, the tendency of political scientists writing since
1945 has been to categorise women as unworthy of the
Republic. In the voting studies of the 1950s, much was made of
the higher abstention rates shown by women: having been told
all their lives that they were not supposed to vote, women were
now being criticised if they chose not to. A note of disapproval
(since most French political scientists are of the centre-left)
crept into commentaries on the higher proportions of women
voters for religious or right-wing parties. Slightly conflicting
with this finding was another which indicated that married
couples often voted for the same party — a finding writers
sometimes liked to interpret as evidence that women voted as
they were bidden by their husbands.

In more recent years, a more sophisticated 'revisionist'
account takes the form of excusing these forms of electoral
behaviour on the grounds that the generation under
observation in the first twenty years or so after 1945 contained
an unusually high proportion of elderly women who either
never acquired the habit of voting (not having done so before
the war) or who like men of their own generation, voted more
often for the right than for the left. This is the starting point for
the recent very thorough study by Janine Mossuz-Lavau and
Mariette Sineau (1983) of the political attitudes of women in

France today. From a middle-of-the-road feminist position, they accept the analysis of their predecessors: their concern however is to show that 'women have changed' since 1945, using as a major criterion paid employment outside the home and concluding that there is every indication that Frenchwomen who now make up over 40 per cent of the active population, take more interest in politics and vote in roughly the same proportions as men for parties of left or right.[12]

The point at issue here is not so much to support or deny the empirical findings of political scientists as to question the assumption behind all the studies, however sympathetic to women's rights their authors may be, and however scrupulous about interpreting the results, that somehow women are 'at fault' in abstaining from voting for instance; that they are — or were — 'poor citizens' in Alain Duhamel's words; and that at best this behaviour can be excused by finding that other factors besides sex are 'to blame'. Women have been only too ready to admit that they have felt inadequate in the political arena. But political scientists are no more inclined than historians to contemplate the possibility that the republic was imperfect and in a very profound sense invalid when it was created and sustained without women.

So it is understandable that radical feminists in France have simply ignored the Republic, despite the formal admission of women, as irrelevant and illegitimate. But this is not a satisfactory position to maintain over time. The first step towards a different stance must surely be a less triumphalist historiography of the Republic and more explicit exposure of it as single-sexed until 1945. That is not of course to suggest that it there was a problem then 1945 resolved it. The occulting of 1945 as a republican landmark, and the survival intact of the republican legend makes 1945 part of the problem rather than its resolution. It serves only to make it more invisible. As Anne Stevens's analysis of women's share of political power in contemporary Europe shows (Chapter 7), France comes off no better than countries without a republican tradition. Part of the explanation is surely that women could hardly feel other than alienated from the male political world whose rule had been devised expressly to disqualify them. It is significant that there were more women in the French Assembly in 1945 than there have been at any time since: the Resistance generation was used to playing by the emergency rules of wartime. As in times of revolution, women were more likely to participate than when the traditional political culture reasserted itself.

Feminist history should have a part to play in opening up this blind abcess. There are signs (cf. Faure, 1985; Fraisse, 1983, 1984) that this is beginning to happen. But in France more than in Britain and America, the language of 'la grande histoire' and the discourse of everyday politics remain extremely resistant to what must surely be the aim of feminist history – to force a revaluation of the past as a whole, not just women's past. It is true that since 1974 there has been a ministry responsible for the improvement of women's rights and status in France. Although feminists may be divided in their attitudes towards it, it has a list of impressive concrete achievements to its credit, especially when viewed from across the Channel. But significantly, it is in the political arena that the ministry has made least impact: its plans for introducing a quota of women candidates in elections were quashed by the Constitutional Council and in 1985, the minister herself was moved to protest at the shabby treatment of women in the distribution of winnable seats within her own party in the run-up to the 1986 election. [13]

Among the various explanations suggested for this, vague accusations of 'sexism' seem the least adequate, or at any rate the least susceptible of analysis. More satisfactory would be an explanation in terms of the continued masculinity, well into the 1980s, of the republican tradition, as most people perceive it. A good illustration was provided by a survey published in December 1984 by *Le Nouvel Observateur*, a left-wing Parisian weekly which is a reliable guide to fashionable sentiment. To mark the new prominence of republicanism, it asked a series of questions reminiscent of the republican catechisms of the nineteenth century ('Would you be prepared to fight for the Republic?')[14] When they were asked which of a select list of living politicians were 'good republicans', those questioned evidently found this a difficult label to apply to the only woman on the list, former Health Minister, Simone Veil. She received only 4 per cent of mentions, although she might be assumed to be at least as attached to republican values as

Raymond Barre (the former prime minister who, like herself, was not a career politician, but who received 33 per cent of mentions) if understandably scoring less than President Mitterrand (44 per cent). Since Simone Veil was at the time a very *popular* politician as measured by straight 'approval' opinion polls, it is simply as if 'republican' did not seem the right word to apply to her as a woman. This impression was reinforced by the accompanying statements from public figures about what the Republic meant to them. Madame Veil (again the only woman asked) gave a noticeably less clearly defined list of republican symbols than her seven male colleagues for whom republicanism was firmly rooted (whatever their politics) in two periods above all: the Jacobin Republic and the early years of the Third Republic. Valmy, the Marseillaise and the *école Jules Ferry* received several mentions. The reply of the socialist Minister of Education, Jean-Pierre Chévènement, is particularly striking:

My republican ideal is the school (i.e. the *école Jules Ferry*). It is the crucible of the Republic. It arouses the intelligence, gives access to knowledge, sharpens the critical spirit, in short it shapes the *free men and citizens* (*les hommes libres et les citoyens*) of whom the Republic has most need (my italics)

For him — and one suspects for many French people, including women — the symbolic apparatus of the Republic is thus one from which women are strikingly absent, yet the absence is rarely remarked. Similarly, and with even less justification, the minister's view of the primary school appeared from all the literature surrounding the 1985 reforms, to be dominated by the classic figure of *le maître,* the schoolmaster, the *instituteur* of the Third Republic. This, in an education system where 100 per cent of nursery school teachers and 62 per cent of primary school teachers are women (so that quotas have recently been introduced to protect the 'mixity' of the profession). The schoolmistress of today is almost as absent in republican discourse as the non-voting women of the past. Since women do not have a republican past, it is not surprising if they find it difficult to construct a republican present in terms of participating in a world built to exclude them (not to mention more material obstacles). Liberty on the barricades is from time to time reproduced as Marianne on French postage stamps and bank notes. Just as she is usually assumed by art historians, as Marcia Pointon argues in Chapter 2, to be an allegory or a figure representing the proletariat, without noticing the sexual power at the heart of Delacroix's painting, so the Republic she often symbolises is seen as a universal or sometimes as a class triumph, not as a system in which sexual power, that of men over women, has been enshrined.

7 Women, Politics and Government in Contemporary Britain, France and Germany

Anne Stevens

'Where power is, women are not.' When she coined this phrase Helga Nowotny was considering the historical record of women's access to positions recognised as powerful, and referring specifically to Austria[1] (Nowotny, 1981, p. 147). In an academic context the strength of her observation was starkly demonstrated by a photograph that appeared in *The Times* on 28 September 1984. Described as exclusive and unusual, the photograph was the group portrait of the Committee of Vice-Chancellors and Principals of United Kingdom Universities — a long, dark, double row of soberly suited men with not one woman amongst them. This picture of the power structures of the academic world is supported by a consideration of one not untypical British university[2] in which 48 per cent of the students are women. Only 1 of the 3 pro-vice-chancellors, 2 of the 53 professors and 6 of the 95 readers are women.

The picture that emerges so sharply from the academic world is confirmed by observation of other areas where power is. One of these is traditional political activity. In the general election of 1983 in West Germany, 51 of the 520 successful candidates were women, who thus constitute 9.8 per cent of the membership of the Bundestag, in which women had occupied 8.3 per cent of the seats in the previous session. The 'Green' party is present in the Bundestag for the first time, and 10 of their 27 members are women, as are 3 of the 35 Liberals, 21 of the 202 Socialist members, and 17 of the 256 Christian Democrats. In France in the general election of 1986, 33 of the 577 successful candidates were women, thus they form 5.5 per cent of the membership of the National Assembly. This is an increase in numbers but a decline in the proportion of women

123

in a larger Assembly elected by a new proportional representation system. In 1981 28 of the 491 members were women. In 1986 the largest group of women were in the Socialist Party (20 out of 199 members). In the British general election of 1983 there were 189 women candidates, 38 Conservatives, 77 Labour party candidates, and 74 candidates for the Liberal and Social Democratic Party alliance. Twenty-three candidates were successful, 13 Conservatives and 10 Labour party candidates. Women make up 3.5 per cent of the membership of the House of Commons.[3] Mrs Thatcher is the only woman in the British Cabinet; two of the 27 ministers of state and one of the 39 parliamentary secretaries are women. The French cabinet before March 1986 contained three women.[4] There were another three women amongst the 24 junior ministers. One woman was belatedly included in the French cabinet appointed immediately after the 1986 election.

At the top levels of the Civil Service the situation is not dissimilar. On 1 December 1984, there were 155 heads of French diplomatic missions of whom four were women. Of the 203 people holding the rank of Prefect[5] one was a woman. There were 166 *directeurs d'administration centrale* (heads of divisions within ministries). Seven of them were women, and in the rank immediately below there were only 46 women out of 456 officials. The three administrative *grands corps* – the élite of the French Civil Service – contained, on that date, 782 members: 44 of them were women (France, Fonction Publique, 1985, p. 142).

In Britain the figures are slightly less favourable to women. On 1 January 1984, there were 40 Permanent Secretaries (Civil Service heads of ministries) none of them women; and 136 Deputy Secretaries, five of them women. One rank below – that is, at Under-Secretary level – there were 482 men and 23 women (The Cabinet Office, 1984). The five Deputy Secretaries included two doctors who are deputy chief medical officers of health in the Department of Health and Social Security. One of the other three was promoted during 1984.[6]

In West Germany the proportion of women in the *Höherer Dienst* for which a university degree is the normal entry requirement was, in 1980, 20 per cent. However, if graduate teachers are excluded, the proportion reduces to 11 per cent.

Enfranchising women – granting them full *droit de cité* – is not the end of the story nor does it solve the 'woman question'. One response to the situation outlined above is to repudiate the terms in which it has been described and to argue that the position of women is but one symptom of a class-dominated and oppressive society which must be rejected and struggled against as a whole. Another response – that of some feminists – is that women not only are not, but should not be, present in the male-oriented institutions of a fundamentally patriarchal social organisation. The role of women, such feminists aver, is to create and operate new and different structures which are genuinely relevant to women's concerns.

In this chapter, however, I wish to analyse women's place within political and governmental institutions in Western Europe from a point of view that assumes that acceptance of the existing framework does not preclude the possibility of change and that such analysis may provide valuable insights into both the nature of the institutions and the place of women within them. From such a perspective there are two not entirely incompatible ways of looking at the position outlined above. One is to say that given the passage of time and the extent of progress in various directions since women were admitted to full civic status, it really is rather shocking and disappointing how little they have achieved – often with the underlying implication that women are somehow to blame for this. They may be characterised as apathetic or complacent; they may be thought unwilling or unable to play the political game properly. The other way of looking at the situation, as Stacey and Price point out (1981, pp. 1-2) is to say that since simply giving women the vote or admitting them to the Civil Service did nothing in itself to change the economic, social and cultural environment of Western European capitalism as it had developed over a century and more, it is surprising, and much to the credit of many women, how much *has* been achieved in a hostile world.

In an attempt to cast some light upon the position of women today, and to develop the two approaches described above, the remainder of this essay considers four aspects of women's relationship to power. The first aspect is some of the historical background to women's admission to Parliament and the Civil

Service. The second aspect is some of the factors that condition women's role within these areas. It seems necessary to consider, thirdly, the nature of power. What is this resource of which women seem to have so little? Finally and very briefly, the conclusion addresses the question of whether and why it should matter that women are or are not in positions of power, and what is the nature of their claim to such positions.

HISTORICAL BACKGROUND: HOW DID WOMEN REACH 'POWERFUL' POSITIONS?

Women entered the Civil Service in both Britain and France initially not because they seemed to have talents and abilities which could not be ignored − there was no bureaucratic equivalent of Elizabeth Garrett Anderson or Sophia Jex Blake in medicine or of Philippa Fawcett 'classed above the senior wrangler'[7] − but for simple and − the word is harsh but so were the circumstances − exploitative reasons. First, women were cheap. In Britain, women began in the telegraph service of the Post Office from the early 1870s. As the Playfair Commission noted in 1875, 'women are well qualified for clerical work of a less important character and are satisfied with a lower rate of pay than expected by men similarly employed' (quoted Humphreys, 1958, p. 32). In France, from the 1870s, some women were appointed as temporary auxiliary clerks without fixed posts or possibilities of promotion (Thuillier, 1982, pp. 602-3). In the postal administration, especially the telegraph services, rapid expansion went alongside a desire to reduce costs, so women, whose cost was half that of men, were increasingly employed, some five thousand being taken on in the three years after 1892 (Davisse, 1983, p. 17). Female typists came later to France than to Britain; by 1892 seven British government departments were employing them (Humphreys, 1958, p. 32) but in France they were first recruited, for the Ministry of Trade, in 1901 (Thuillier, 1982, p. 605).

By 1914 in Britain the Post Office was still the government department that employed much the largest number of women civil servants. They were, however, employed on a separate establishment from the men, and, although they could be promoted to supervisory positions within their own hierarchy, could not move outside it. They were segregated in other ways too. My grandmother worked in the Post Office Savings Bank in Kensington before she was married, around 1910. The girls were not allowed out of the building during their lunch hour but were permitted to get some fresh air on the flat roof. My grandfather, then a junior clerk in the Ministry of Agriculture, told me that he used, during his lunch hour, to travel from Whitehall to Kensington to walk in the road below and wave up to his future wife on the roof. The women were paid on separate, lower scales and were obliged to resign on marriage.

In both Britain and France, the very few higher-grade Civil Service posts that were open to women in the nineteenth century were as inspectors. Women were appointed to the inspectorate of welfare establishments in France from the late 1840s and to the equivalent body, the Poor Law Inspectorate, in Britain from 1873. Women Labour Department and factory inspectors were first appointed in both countries in 1892-93 (Thuillier, 1982, p. 605; Evans, 1934). In Britain, such inspectors were subject to the marriage bar, but otherwise were recruited and worked under the same conditions as the men – except that they received only half the male salary. In France, the women were not subject to the marriage bar (indeed, in 1913 the author of an article on opportunities for women noted maternity leave as one of the advantages of Civil Service employment) and were relatively better paid.

In both countries there was resistance to the possibility of admitting women to senior posts. Among the reasons adduced in France for this were, in the 1900s, female incapacity: in 1902, 'women do not seem to show the qualities of initiative, reasoning and judgment which such employment requires' (quoted Thuillier, 1982, p. 604); and in 1907, 'Even groups of women prefer to be supervised by a man who will meddle less' (quoted Thuillier and Tulard, 1984, p. 73). In 1908 the administrative court (the *Conseil d'Etat*) ruled that a woman could not compete for senior posts because she could not meet the necessary condition of having fulfilled military obligations (Thuillier, 1982, p. 608).[8] Textbooks on constitutional law added that women could not normally be admitted to official positions since, not having the vote, they were not in the possession of full civic rights (Bécane-Pascaud, 1974, p. 8).

In both countries, the First World War was the second major factor in the entry of women into the Civil Service. 'There was a great influx of women into the service' (Parris, 1973, p. 145) in both countries. In France this, combined with the need to provide for the widows and dependants of war victims, brought about equal pay in 1919 and encouraged the opening up of more senior posts to women. By 1926 two women were assistant heads of branches, one in the Ministry of Labour and one in the Ministry of Merchant Shipping. There were hesitations, however. The Ministry of War was particularly concerned when it became apparent that women would soon be likely to be promoted into posts where they would have military men under their control, and in 1934 banned them from such posts. There was no controversy over the express exclusion of women from the (unimplemented) plans made up under the Popular Front government of 1936 to set up a new and more open recruitment and training system for top officials. In 1945 Michel Debré[9] decided that the new post-war system should admit women. He faced hostility from the most senior officials and said 'Had it been voted on (amongst them) my proposition would have been lost' (Debré, 1978, p. XXII). However, Debré was in a position to refuse the representatives of the administration a vote, and when it came to the debate in the Provisional Assembly the change slipped through unnoticed.

In Britain too women took their places at senior levels only very slowly. In 1933 (Evans, 1934) there were only some 20 women in the administrative class of the Civil Service; the entry competitions were open to them but in 1931, 1932 and 1933 not one woman was successful. There were in 1933 only three women officials on salaries of over £1000 a year.[10] In the 1950s and 1960s the women compensated very slightly for this slow start by producing, in Dame Evelyn Sharp and Dame Mary Smieton, formidable and very senior officials. They were unmarried. Indeed all the four women to reach the grade of Permanent Secretary have been unmarried or divorced and childless. Between the wars 'women civil servants showed relatively little interest in the removal of the marriage bar. For many of them the bar to marriage lay not in the Treasury regulations but in the War Office records. The husbands they might have married had died in battle. It could even be argued that the exclusion of married women helped the career chances of spinsters' (Parris, 1973, p. 145). The bar was abolished in 1946. Equal pay took longer; it was achieved in 1955.

Women have been, perhaps, rather more prominent as politicians than as officials, but the figures quoted at the beginning of this chapter suggest that they have in general been no better represented as members of parliament. In Britain the first woman to be elected as a member of parliament was Countess Marckiewicz, a Sinn Feiner who did not take her seat. A striking feature of the early women members of the House of Commons was the extent of 'male equivalence' (Currell, 1974, pp. 58, 63, 167-172).[11] Indeed male equivalence seems to have been perhaps the leading motivation for seeking election. As Eleanor Rathbone noted 'scarcely any of those who helped to open the door of Parliament succeeded in walking in: very few even tried' (Rathbone, 1936, quoted Currell, 1974, p. 59). Women who enter politics as male equivalents may be highly effective in their own right. As Stacey and Price (1981, p. 94) remark, however, 'they were carrying over in modified form the old tradition of women standing in for the men of their families . . . . This was a far cry from the individual rights of women.'

In France the phenomenon of male equivalence was much less marked, if only because of the circumstances in which women first sat in a parliamentary Assembly. Among the 248 members of the Provisional Assembly of 1944-45 were twelve women, appointed by the Resistance organisations to which they belonged. In the first elections in which women voted, in 1945, 40 women were amongst the 630 successful candidates (Renard, 1965, pp. 24, 72). In subsequent elections, under electoral systems which changed in 1951 and 1958, the number of women diminished sharply.

In looking at the ways in which women have reached the positions which they now occupy, a number of factors have emerged about the environment with which they have had to contend. The argument that emerges from my description of women's entry into the spheres with which I am concerned is that if women have only with great difficulty achieved leading positions in those areas, it is because men have not recognised them as having any *intrinsic* claim upon such positions. They were not admitted in recognition of equality or merit or rights. They were admitted for reasons chiefly of economy and convenience, with some pressure from the very special conditions of war and the aftermath of war. Such motives provide no basis for claims to senior and powerful positions. The next section of this chapter develops some of these conclusions and also considers other aspects of the social environment within which women have sought powerful positions.

THE SOCIAL ENVIRONMENT

The feeling that women's main claim to advancement may be their cheapness and convenience has by no means disappeared. Lord Gowrie, then the British Minister for the Civil Service, said in March 1985 that he thought that opportunities for women at the top of the Civil Service were improving because, since the government had held back the pay of top civil servants to well below what was being offered in the City and in industry, the really senior men were, and would continue to be, deserting the service in droves for more lucrative pastures elsewhere. Women, less financially demanding, would thus be able to reach the top (Wheatcroft, 1985, p. 50). Only when a profession has become devalued, it might be said, do women find much of a place in it.[12]

The working environment within which women found themselves was frequently fairly hostile. Cheap women might well, and not without reason, be seen as threatening to men. In France in the 1890s, a Civil Service journal commented that the male personnel saw in the advent of women a competition which they regarded as almost *déloyale* — 'the weaker sex, having fewer needs than the stronger, can be satisfied with a lower remuneration' (*L'Echo des Ministères*, quoted Thuillier, 1982, p. 603). In Germany in the 1870s, the conditions of women working in the telegraph service were worsened as men sought to limit competition from them (Riemer and Fout,

1980, p. 40). In Britain some of the early Civil Service clerical unions were formed by men anxious, amongst other things, about the deterioration of conditions that might result from the advent of women (Humphreys, 1958, pp. 34-35). In the political sphere women MPs have experienced problems with the male-dominated 'club' atmosphere of legislatures — to be patronised may also be a disguised form of hostility.

There are other aspects of the social environment that make the achievement of high position in these fields difficult. Many of these have been summarised by Cynthia Fuchs Epstein (Epstein, 1981) and by Vicky Randall (1982) and I am much indebted to both for what follows.

Vicky Randall points out (p. 85) that some American studies of why so few women enter politics have suggested that the socialisation of women has led them to fear social disapproval if they take on the degree of independent and vigorous activism required in an aspirant to a political career. Women rely, it is suggested, upon the esteem of others and may be unwilling to pay the psychological costs engendered by the assumption of a role that may be 'marginal' or 'deviant' in relation to women as a whole. As Rosemarie Nave-Herz has pointed out (1973, p. 194, 197; see also Vallance, 1979, p. 13) it is those aspects of personality which are regarded as particularly required in leaders which are most in contrast with those by which society causes women to define their own identities. An inevitable and painful tension results. This factor, however, seems to me less inportant than a second element of the social environment which Vicky Randall calls 'situational constraints'.

The most important of these situational constraints is children. Of the 27 British women MPs elected in 1974 only two had children under the age of ten. In 1979 Fogarty, Allen and Walters repeated an earlier survey of top women civil servants and reported 'it would seem that the observation made of the women civil servants in 1968, namely that the responsibilities of family life take the ultimate competitive edge off performance continues to hold in their later career' (Fogarty, Allen and Walters, 1981, p. 60). 'The energy expended in creating a network of help and making it work did lead a substantial minority of the older women . . . to wonder whether, in the end, full-time work had been worth it' (ibid, p. 60). Others said that if it was planned that way from the beginning a *small* family was not incompatible with a successful career, but it was essential to maintain a professional approach to the organisation of both office and home life.

The problem of children is a rather specialised form of the much larger problem of the 'double shift' (see Epstein, 1981, p. 12). Countless women echo the cry of Ellen Wilkinson, one of the early women Labour MPs 'Oh! for a wife' (Summerskill, 1967, p. 139, quoted Currell, 1974, p. 16). The double shift continues to have profound effects upon the lives of working women, and not least upon the third environmental factor relevant to this discussion: eligibility for office, especially political office.

Political activity and participation correlates strongly with employment outside the home (Mossuz-Lavau and Sineau, 1983, pp. 222-6). Success in the type of political activity which results in elective office demands more than just employment, however. In the first place it may demand of a woman effectively a *triple* shift − home, employment, political activity. This is more than many women can contemplate or achieve.[13] Secondly, eligibility for political office may depend not merely on participation and employment but on a specific type of employment. Those who are to be successful candidates need the attributes which are looked for in such people. These may well include higher education and membership of a suitable profession. A disproportionate number of British MPs are company directors, lawyers, journalists, trade union officials; all professions in which women have not been well represented. In France many *députés* come from within the higher levels of the public services, where again women are largely absent, and in West Germany most senior officials and many politicians are lawyers, but in 1971 only 15 per cent of law students were women (Sanzone, 1981, p. 37). The political system places upon women aspirants a double demand; that they acquire the not readily available attributes deemed necessary to its recruits, and that they face a triple shift.

The fourth environmental factor that affects the situation of women is what I call 'presumptions of competence'. In the elective political field this is simply the question whether voters will have less faith in a woman candidate. Will they not vote for her? It is very difficult to disentangle the effect of the candidate's sex from all the other variables that affect electoral outcome. Elizabeth Vallance and Jill Hills (Vallance, 1979, p. 20; Hills, 1981, p. 22) have both concluded that in Britain the effect is marginal. The problem is thus shown to be not that women *are* less effective as candidates, but that those who select the candidates *think* that they will be.

In the Civil Service there is also a problem about presumptions of competence. A woman has, it seems, to be demonstrably better than a man to reach the same point. 'There may', a Civil Service observer said of the early stages of a high-flying administrative career, 'be truth in the contention that women have to prove clearly that they are successful, whereas the men are assumed to be successful until they definitely demonstrate that they are failures' (Fogarty, Allen and Walters, 1981, p. 44). Later in their careers too, women may suffer from presumptions – not necessarily about their competence but about their willingness to undertake and their interest in the crucial and demanding posts that mark people out for promotion. Elizabeth Brimelow pointed out that promotion in the British Civil Service is highly dependent upon the report of one's superior, who is required to assess one's suitability for promotion. 'And', she says, 'it requires a certain effort of imagination. You have to *see* the officer in the higher grade'. If there are few if any women in that grade alongside whom to picture the subordinate that effort may be very difficult and in the end potential is estimated on 'the conventional view of a woman's career pattern' (Brimelow, 1981, p. 329).

In France the promotion system is less important than the choice, very often a very personal choice, by ministers, perhaps influenced by one or two key officials, of people to fill the most vital posts. Ministers come and go and may have little time or opportunity to assess a wider field of choice. There must be a great temptation to opt for the candidate (usually male) who can particularly easily be visualised in any specific post.

There are also the hazards that women face from other women. Anne Mueller[14] has said she is worried about the sexism of women in the British Civil Service who tend to be very hard in making judgements of other women (Wheatcroft, 1985, p. 48). Such 'sexism' may not be just the product of a desire to avoid competition or maintain some exclusive status but rather of the environment within which women find themselves. All men are not judged on the performance of any one or of a considerable minority of their number, yet, as a top business woman explained 'I have a reputation for being harder on the women at (recruitment) boards than the men are. But if she fails, all women suffer' (Fogarty, Allen and Walters 1981, p. 101).

WOMEN AND THE NATURE OF POWER

This chapter has been concerned with women's position in relation to certain formal institutional manifestations of power. Many of the arguments and considerations advanced in respect of legislatures and administrations apply, however, equally to other bodies that are often described as powerful — the trade unions or the judiciary, for example. This section is concerned with the nature of power that is manifested in such institutions and how women relate to it.

The study of politics has since Aristotle been concerned with the nature and distribution of power. The central debates of the discipline focus around the implications of power, its possession and distribution. The Weberian definition of power regards it as the possession of the monopoly of the legitimate use of force within defined spatial limits. Power may be said, it is argued, to reside in the ability to constrain or oblige someone to act in a specific way. The ability legitimately to constrain is a characteristic, usually, of the state, whose legitimacy is acquired, and whose power is expressed, through a set of institutional arrangements which provide mechanisms for the resolution of conflicts. It is in relation to these public manifestations of power that its nature and distribution are frequently analysed, and it is with some of these formal manifestations that the preceding sections of this chapter have been concerned.

Four observations may be made about the relationship of women to formal manifestations of public power. First, this is the type of power to which the remark that opened this chapter (about the absence of women from the places of power) referred. Women, for the reasons considered above, are very little present in the groups and institutions where public institutional power is evident. Secondly, individuals may have a symbolic or representational function in relation to this power. This can prove a problem for women. There is a gap between Marianne as the symbolic representation of the republic in France and women's actual place within the republic.[15] Where the state's executive power *is* physically represented by an individual – an ambassador, a prefect – many men, but some women too, seem to have difficulty in accepting a woman as its personification. This was certainly one of the reasons behind the very slow acceptance of women in the prefectoral corps in France,[16] and in diplomatic corps. When Suzy Borel was successful in the entry competition to the French Foreign Office in May 1930, the prime minister would not consider admitting her: 'He could not allow that a woman should publicly represent her country' (Thuillier, 1983, p. 23).

Thirdly, women do, however, have representational roles in their capacity as wives. Consideration of these throws an intriguing light upon the place of women in the public sphere, especially when the effects of role reversal are considered. Why does Denis Thatcher fulfil so well part, but not quite all, of the role of 'Prime Minister's wife'? Why is the role of 'lady mayoress' almost invariably given to the sister or daughter of a woman mayor and not to her husband? In some cases such roles carry considerable hierarchical power within a limited area. The extent to which a head of mission's wife in a diplomatic post can constrain has been well described (Callan, 1975, pp. 91, 94) and, once experienced, is not forgotten. Finally, women who are not formally present in these institutional manifestations may nevertheless be powerful within them. Vicky Randall (1982, p. 83) cites Eva Peron and Rosalyn Carter, also Mme Ceausescu and, but chiefly as a warning, Jiang Qing. In the 1970s in Britain and France, Marcia Williams (Lady Falkender) and Marie-France Garaud were often taken to exemplify the power that a woman who is formally in a fairly subordinate position can wield.

Definitions of public power based on formal arrangements

may, however, themselves be inadequate. Power, it is suggested, may consist not merely in selecting and imposing certain courses of action, but in preventing other courses of action even being considered. The power to keep things off the agenda may be as important as the power to get things done. The argument may be advanced further, to suggest that power in society may be so entrenched that this is done quite unconsciously. In relation to women this proposition might be demonstrated by showing that the rules of the political game operate to keep women's issues at a low place on the political agenda. Women are then described as apathetic or incapable in politics because they do not accord a high level of salience to other issues which do indeed seem to them less pressing. The way that power is currently entrenched requires the characterisation of the major concerns of many women as trivial, irrelevant or irrational.

It is sometimes argued that to talk of women as being powerless is to ignore the existence of another phenomenon — the existence of a private domain of family relationships and kin networks within which women can and do operate in a distinctive and not necessarily powerless way. Both Cynthia Fuchs Epstein, who talks of 'alternative opportunity structures' (1981, pp. 10-11) and Margaret Stacey and Marion Price (1981, pp. 106, 173) argue that women may be powerful when they can use their private power bases as resources in the public domain. Male equivalence would be one example of this; another would be the possibility of moving on from experience in fields such as social welfare to a broader political sphere. The effects of the development of modern methods of both administration and industrial production, which divorced the running of public affairs from the running of households and industrial production from domestic production, reduced the possibility of movement between the public and private domains. As such movement became relatively more difficult, Stacey and Price seem to argue, so women's potential for the exercise of public power was diminished.

I am uneasy about the implication found in some arguments of this sort that the existence of a private sphere in which they can experience some autonomy provides women with a good measure of compensation for their exclusion from the public sphere. It seems to me to be precisely the limitations of a separate private domain that engenders the type of power that Mary Wollstonecraft castigated so vividly and forcibly as feminine – though by no means confined to women – and very corrupting.[17]

It may well be that the boundaries between public and private have become more rigid over the last two centuries.[18] It may have become more difficult for a woman to cross them, even in the capacity of a male equivalent. Interestingly, as some of the cultural and social restraints have recently lessened, some of the situational restraints have increased. Stacey and Price (1981, p. 74) point out that the feminists of the last century were not too concerned with the problems of the double shift. They were mostly middle-class and could rely on their servants for housework and childcare. Women's role in the public sphere even before the process of modernisation does not seem to me to have involved any clear recognition of their status as persons possessing merits and rights. Rather women's access to their public domain depended and still largely depends upon their acting like men, and their power when they have any derives from fulfilling what are normally male roles in a male kind of way.

WOULD WOMEN MAKE A DIFFERENCE?

Women, operating in the public sphere, may be obliged to operate as if they were men. Indeed, a study of women in top jobs in West Germany has concluded that:

once a women has reached a high occupational status, the experience of being a woman does not seem to be important to her political interests. That successful women hold the dominant values of the male elite also indicates that, if there are different cultural orientations of men and women, they are completly submerged, at least as far as politics is concerned, by structural factors (Streek, Bock-Rosenthal and Haase, 1981, p. 166)

Is it sensible to assume that women would 'naturally' act differently? If there were more of them in powerful positions would they feel free to 'be themselves'? And if there were enough of them would this produce a specifically female effect in terms of outcomes? Any consideration of such questions is bound to be speculative.

These questions are particularly difficult to answer because they raise problems about when and where and how people acquire the values that they bring to any particular activity. For instance the debates about democratising recruitment to the higher civil service, and about what is called representative bureaucracy (Subramaniam, 1967) tend to have underlying them the assumption that people carry with them into their professional lives the values of their childhood milieu. Vincent Wright deals forcibly with this point as it refers to the French civil service:

social and educational pressures may be offset by professional pressures . . . (senior French civil servants) are distributed amongst the *corps*, each of which has its own particular rites and norms and prejudices . . . . Furthermore, even if it were possible to extrapolate from an analysis of social educational and professional background to the construction of a syndrome of shared beliefs, it would still be necessary to demonstrate that shared beliefs lead to shared behaviour. There may be no relation between the two, because top civil servants, like members of every other group, differ in courage, ambition, assiduity and a whole range of other personal characteristics. (1983, p. 117)

Gender might be just another variable, no more, if no less, important than whether an MP is a back-bencher or a minister, or whether a civil servant works in the Treasury or the Department of Health and Social Security.

Bearing in mind all these provisos about the difficulty of deducing anything from people's backgrounds, it may nevertheless be possible to consider whether women bring to powerful positions any special characteristics. It is sometimes suggested that they are particularly conscientious, both as officials and politicians. It is also said that they are less corruptible than men. Vicky Randall (1982, p. 80) cites the South American country in which women tended to be given the key posts in the finance and personnel sectors; and the appointment of a woman to head the parliamentary enquiry into the P2 masonic lodge in Italy may have stemmed from similar motives. Vicky Randall concluded, on the basis of a number of studies, that while women politicians might have different styles from men, and some were not averse to exploiting popular ideas of womanhood in their public image — the image of the good housekeeper, for example — they did not overall behave very differently from men. Judith Evans (1985, p. 625) also effectively demolishes some of the claims made about female attitudes and characteristics in political behaviour. She points out that such evidence as is available suggests that major distinct differences between the political attitudes and behaviour of men and women do not exist, and such differences as are detectable are tending to disappear, especially between younger men and women.

Women today probably make very little difference to the exercise of the functions of powerful positions. It is harder to speculate what differences might arise were they much more massively present in these positions. Judith Evans is surely right to suggest that their increasing adoption of key roles will entail enormous changes in what she calls the structure, customs and mores of society and polity. There is nothing in the historical record to suggest that the advent of women to positions of power can occur without such changes.[19] The process, moreover, seems likely to be reciprocal. Changes will have to be both the cause and the consequence of the advent of women.

The claim of women to key positions does not, for me, rest upon the desirability of such changes. It does not rest upon claims to superiority, nor upon any idea that women would manage the executive functions of the state better than do men. Any such idea could only be speculation. Women's claims rest rather upon those assertions which were implicitly swept aside in the early years of their recruitment to modern politics and bureaucracy. These claims are very similar to those advanced by the proponents of some theories of democracy (Evans, 1985, p. 626; Pateman, 1983, 1970, chs II and III). Such theorists hold that the characteristic and virtue of any system that can properly be called democratic lies in its ability to educate and develop the personality of every individual and to instil in them a sense of personal efficacy. Women's claims must be based on the assertion that there is at least a *prima facie* case that women possess intelligence, talents and abilities that make them fully human, but which they are prevented, by multiple constraints, from exercising properly. There is a reason to believe that women could both contribute far more than at present to the good conduct of the affairs of the state and at the same time be afforded occasions which they do not now enjoy to develop and utilise their talents. Those who, consciously or unconsciously, cause or support constraints upon this, need to explain how it can be that a society that denies itself the benefit of the talents, achievements, abilities and intelligence of half its members is not thereby truly a society of deprivation, impoverished and unjust.[20]

ACKNOWLEDGEMENT

For their help and advice I am grateful to Siân Reynolds, Handley Stevens, and especially to Professor Rosemarie Nave-Herz, as well as to the members of faculty and students who both gave and attended the lectures upon which this book is based.

8 Revolting Women: Subversion and its Media representation in West Germany and Britain

Ulrike Hanna Meinhof

This chapter explores the media representation of two groups of women. One, the West German women of the so-called Baader-Meinhof group, a group of left-wing intellectuals who went underground in May 1970 to form the terrorist organisation RAF (*Rote Armee Fraktion*); the other, the women of Greenham Common, a peace organisation of women only, who since 1981 have been camping outside the American cruise missile base near Newbury in protest against the nuclear weapons housed there.

In the first section I shall argue that whereas initially in West Germany the right-wing press presented the Red Army Faction as a typical though extreme form of left politics, the later stages of reporting both in Germany and England seized on the fact that a number of its leading members were women as a central theme. As the image of the woman terrorist became increasingly powerful, it lost all connection with socio-political reality and became a transhistorical, transcultural myth in the Barthian sense (Barthes, 1957). In the first section, I explore the creation and composition of this myth in all its contradictory features of irrationality and deviancy. In the second part, I shall argue that the constituent elements of the myth of the violent woman, the woman terrorist, are invoked against a group involved in very different, dissident but non-violent activities, the Greenham women. Through an analysis of popular press reporting of the Greenham women I aim to demonstrate how paradoxical notions of sexual, social and political deviancy can help to validate repressive state actions.

PART 1: ESTABLISHING A MYTH

Let me begin with an influential male voice: Melvin J. Lasky, editor of the long-established journal *Encounter,* evokes the famous Delacroix painting to describe the activities of five subversive women in an article entitled 'Lady on the Barricades':

I. Margit
The day I arrived in Munich from what I fancifully think of as Rousseau's Geneva the trial had just begun of a sunny young kindergarten teacher who, with the help of two teenagers, armed with pistols and automatic weapons, had robbed a local bank of some fifty thousand marks. Why had she done it? Surely not for herself and her accomplices: that would be reprehensible bourgeois greed. It was for the children. All, perhaps, for Emile: for the hope of a good and innocent life, divorced — if need be, by force and violence — from the impurities of a corrupted society.
It could be that women are more susceptible than men to the peculiar seductiveness of this call, or at least appear to offer a more moving symbolism for those who would be led by this kindly light. Mother Earth herself, or one of her daughters, seems to be calling. Her full right breast exposed, as in Delacroix, Marianne angrily climbs on to the barricades.
For 30-year-old Margit Czenki the barricade happened to be the cashier's grille in the Bavarian Hypotheken- und Wechselbank. Although the job was done with dispatch and no one was hurt . . . it was only a matter of weeks before the gang was tracked down and picked up. Margit, innocent of society's encumbrances to the last, was arrested in the cellar flat of one of the other boys, quite naked ('nackt wie Gott sie schuf', as Oberkriminalrat Schmidt pedantically reported, before listing the details of her Walther pistol and the rest of the arsenal).[1]

This is the opening paragraph of Lasky's sarcastic account of five women who were involved in subversive actions of one kind or another. The West Germans Margit Czenki and Beate Sturm, the American Diana Oughton, Teresa Hayter from England — all four women of the 1960s and 1970s — are aligned with Théroigne de Mericourt of eighteenth-century France. Under the heading recalled insistently throughout the article, 'the lady on the barricades', they emerge across different times, countries and political motivations. There is nothing new either about the artistic allusion or about the use of allegory, as Marcia Pointon convincingly shows in Chapter 2 of this book.[2] Other writers on the subject of 'women and violence'[3] also produce resonant titles full of puns, allusions, literary quotations: 'Deadlier than the Male' (*Times*) 'Terror scene: Group Portrait with Ladies' (*Spiegel*) 'Daughters of the Gun' (*Observer Magazine*)[4]. But is there more to this collocation of gender and violence than the rhetoric of journalists struggling to explain the phenomenon of some women having become terrorists? Roland Barthes in his famous study *Mythologies* provides us with an intriguing paradigm for our analysis. To him a myth is neither concept, idea nor object, but a system of communication, a message. It is 'not defined by the object of its message, but by the way it utters this message' (Barthes, 1973, p. 109). It is a 'type of speech chosen by history' not one which evolved 'from the "nature" of things . . . Mythical speech is made of material which has already been worked on so as to make it suitable for communication' (*ibid.*, p. 110).

The question which the first section of this chapter will attempt to answer is whether we can trace the beginning, the development and the eventual establishment of a new myth, which goes past a mere recording of the obvious historical fact that a high proportion of contemporary political violence is committed by women. Lasky's article is one of the first examples I am aware of which runs together accounts of various divergent subversive actions under the connecting principle of gender. The women, whom Lasky usually calls by their first names, have no detail of their appearance and clothes omitted. Margit (Czenki), 'a smiling blue-jeaned blonde', is found naked by the police (p. 17). Théroigne (de Mericourt) was originally 'a happy and busy Paris courtesan' with a 'pleasant little singing voice' (p. 22). But according to Lasky she later adds to the confusion about whether all the women of 6 October 1789 were really women or men in disguise, because she is 'riding hard like a man on a dragoon's horse as the Versailles massacre took place' (p. 23).

We see here some of the ingredients of the myth in the making: (1) the young girl image: lovely innocent looks which deliberately disguise the terrorist goals; (2) the prostitute, the promiscuous or lesbian image: corrupt women who exploit their sexuality; (3) the Amazon image: of women who are not really women. These multiple threats from their gender are recorded but kept at bay throughout the article by Lasky's mixed tone of paternal condescension, sarcasm and disgust, which reduces both the motives behind the actions and their outcome to the inefficient and self-destructive behaviour of naughty daughters who never managed to grow up. There is no serious analysis of causes or motivations, as typical samples from the article show: Margit is said to have exchanged her love for dear little Jesus for Marx and Marighella because she was 'blinded by a brilliant light' (p. 19). Her belief in the 'socialization of the means of production and distribution' Lasky describes as a 'sound formula from her new catechism' (p. 19).

Juxtaposed with this picture of intellectual and ideological confusion and political ineffectiveness is the image of the world in harmony from which the girls come and against which they so stupidly and ungratefully revolt. Again Lasky's tone is sarcastic. 'Teresa (Hayter) was a disadvantaged child. What to others came naturally, she had to do the hard way' (p. 28). The disadvantage Lasky ironically refers to is that she had a happy childhood with liberal, well-meaning parents who had neither sold out 'to the bitch-goddess success nor cheered Hitler in their youth'. Not that the latter explains anything either, because according to Lasky the American 'kids' and the German 'Jugend' only imagine they have a grievance. They are in his analysis only the spoiled youth of countries that never had it so good.

Lasky's bitterly sarcastic article of 1972 is interesting mainly for giving us a first hint of the myth in the making. His idea of accumulating five subversive women from different times and places under the title of the lady on the barricades is not yet informed by a fully developed concept of the woman terrorist. By writing about them consecutively with a section devoted to each, he differentiates their life-style, family, and intellectual background, seriousness of crime, etc. The reference to the woman revolutionary seems to be more of a narrative ploy, an ironic pun. The fact that they are women mostly inspires the way Lasky writes rather than what he finds by way of structural comparison or contrast. Connecting the five sections of the article and the accounts of the five women is Lasky's tone of paternal condescension, intellectual derision, sarcasm about their ineffectiveness. What is interesting for us here, is how the elements of the consecutive narration about five individuals converge in the later myth of the woman terrorist with all the contradictory features present at the same time.

But let us examine first the initial reporting in West Germany itself. Early accounts in the West German press of what is generally referred to in the media as either the Baader-Meinhof group, Baader-Meinhof gang or Red Army Faction, did not in any way foreground the gender of several of the activists. From the time in April 1970 when Ulrike Marie Meinhof, a well-known political journalist, together with two other women helped Andreas Baader to escape from a prison sentence, up to the arrest of the so-called hard core in 1972, the conspiratorial group was perceived as a typical if more violent version of misguided left-wing activity. In particular the right-wing press, spear-headed by Axel Springer's empire from the tabloid *Bild* to his most serious newspaper *Welt* was more interested in saying that here was the true face of left intellectualism than in stressing gender explanations. The Baader-Meinhof underground activities, which by then included several bank raids and the shooting of a guard and a policeman but not yet any of the spectacular kidnappings, hijacking, and murders, were aligned with anything from moderate to extreme left-wing politics. This reached its climax in January 1972 as a result of a famous article by Heinrich Böll in the German magazine *Spiegel* in which he accused the Springer press of fascist practices in its treatment of the fugitive Baader-Meinhof members.

Böll's article is in itself of less interest or importance than the reaction it provoked: the unprecedented concerted attack by the Springer press and other right-wing papers on Böll himself and anybody else, who could be seen as an ally: the association of left-wing writers, professors, lawyers, politicians, journalists, students with terrorism as supposed sympathisers, supporters and helpers.[5] This is not to say that gender was not commented upon. The fact that some of the members of Baader-Meinhof as well as some of the vast circle of alleged sympathisers were women was naturally commented upon as part of the general reporting. Through the stereotypical association of women with children this occasionally led to some rather vague allegations. An article in the women's magazine *Praline* about psychologist Monika Seifert, for example, suggested that the anti-authoritarian education of children she had previously advocated on a TV programme provided the breeding-ground for future terrorists. But this only shows that gender associations functioned as the beginning of an associative chain which linked up anything remotely connected to the left with violence, so that Monika Seifert herself yielded another instance of the typical set of left-wing establishment figures, together with her father, the sociologist Alexander Mitscherlich, and other famous professionals.[6] Gender in those earlier accounts was not a constitutive characteristic, rather it was subsumed under the wide wing of left politics.

By June 1972 the entire hard core of Baader-Meinhof was arrested, after a series of bombings and shoot-outs which caused casualties amongst policemen, soldiers, and some civilians as well as among the terrorists themselves. Since then, several new generations of terrorists have emerged in West Germany whose increasing brutality makes journalists almost nostalgic in their reports of the 'first generation', none of whose leading members is alive today. It was only in relation to these later generations of terrorists – still misleadingly referred to as Baader-Meinhof terrorists – that gender became the focus of attention. Once the woman terrorist was established as a category, it acted as an analytic filter for both the present and the past.

By 1977 the category is firmly established. The magazine *Spiegel* prints on its cover an outline photograph of a woman terrorist (Susanne Albrecht) with a gun and the RAF insignia plus the title 'Women and Violence' (Frauen und Gewalt'). The lead story, several commentaries and interviews inside are devoted to this topic under highly suggestive titles such as 'Subversive Women: "Something Irrational"': or 'The activists live in complete incest'.[7]

In the analysis of the women terrorists we find several familiar features: the stress on their good looks, their charm, their youth, their good homes, their bourgeois upbringing, as counterpoints to their ugly deeds. However, these are now no longer consecutive descriptions of different women but, as the title suggests, are now subsumed under the associative chain of woman–irrationality–violence. Dualities are established which rest on varying assumptions of natural womanhood on the one hand and moral perversity on the other. The deviant woman is shown to share enough in appearance with the natural woman to make her doubly deceptive and dangerous. What is stressed is the paradoxical relationship between the two. This tension finds expression at all levels of the discourse from the choice of lexical items up to the conceptual categories. It is difficult to transpose the flavour of some of the word creations into English since their appeal is as much achieved by alliteration and other stylistic means as by the actual referential content.

Also, typically for *Spiegel* language, some of the word creations mix English with German. However, here are some examples. The women are said to be 'female supermen', they are 'man enough to act decisively', they are 'gangster babies' turned into 'gangster ladies'. They carry flowers and cosmetic bags but only to disguise their murderous intentions and their guns. Violent death comes thus 'in the shape of a young girl': girls have fallen from their traditional roles and their crimes don't fit a gender which is called 'in English "the fair sex"', the beautiful, the decent, the bright'.[8] The *Observer Magazine* later that year lists like an incantation their first names: 'Gudrun, Ingrid, Margit, Angela, Ilse, Hanna, . . . Gabriele, Astrid, Angelika, Verena, Sigrid, Susanne' – musing that 'the names are often incongruously beautiful . . . and cling like a last vestige of the bourgeois world to young women who were christened with a very different future in mind'.[9]

More important than these juxtapositions in the descriptions of their names and looks, or even their personalities and activities, is however the accumulation of motives. This is where the myth really takes off, bringing together a jumble of commonsensical (or perhaps rather nonsensical) notions from the vast store of theoretical discourses of our times. We find series of vulgarised psychoanalytical concepts, inverted Oedipal relationships, sexual dependencies and frustrations combined with an interest in family background, class and religion. What is surprising, though, is not the pseudo-psychoanalytic discourse as such. It is the sheer breathtaking contradictoriness of the accounts, not just from one article to the next, but sometimes within the same piece of journalism.

The explanations fit broadly into four categories: sexual neurosis: women's liberation: bourgeois background: and Oedipal girl – father relationship. Paradoxically, not only is each category partly undoing the other as explanatory system, but within each category the various causalities are also contradictory. The 'psychoanalytic' explanation which links the sexually disturbed with the politically violent comprises at least two different combinations: on the one hand, the women are said to be politically, sexually and emotionally dependent on the man, putting for example the two leading women, Meinhof and Ensslin, under the spell of Baader's psycho-terror: but they are also said to be sexually triumphant by making use of the gun, seen as the classical symbol of manliness. It is equally unclear whether sexual neurosis causes political activities or whether the political activities cause sexual neurosis. This confusion is echoed by the paradoxes relating the women's actions to women's liberation. There is the macho image of women who want to be like men, modelling themselves on male values of control, efficiency, lack of emotions, determination, and male notions of crime – guns rather than poison. There is equally the super-macho image of women wanting and managing to surpass men in these male values. *Spiegel* writes that Arab guerrillas found Gudrun Ensslin 'really militant', but Andreas Baader 'a coward'.[10] But in contrast to the macho image, the expression of female superiority is also said to be a result of the women's superior intelligence and their stronger personalities.

This confusion produces two sets of explanations in relation to their bourgeois background: they are sensitised to injustice, feeling guilty about their wealth and privileges, but equally they are spoiled, ungrateful brats who won't accept how good a life they are having. There is a special metonymic delight in some of the details which are quoted again and again. Susanne Albrecht is forever quoted as saying, that she was fed up stuffing herself with caviar. The *Times* article, not having properly researched the caviar syndrome turns her however into 'a lover of parties and good caviar'.[11] Family background is either quoted as having fostered an exaggerated social conscience or, on the other hand, a lack of ordinary human social feelings. The same double-bind informs the reporting of the girl – father relationships. An undigested childhood and youth, with fathers who are either the 'Hitlers' or those who opposed them, means the women were either emulating super-fathers or wanting to destroy them. A *Spiegel* commentary in a slight reshuffle of the Oedipal complex even suggests that the reason Susanne Albrecht didn't kill her father but instead tried to kidnap his friend was that this is the more effective patricide: by killing the friend you hit the father more.[12]

Having been offered such a wide range of conflicting explanations at once, one may well feel sympathetic towards one or the other, thinking that perhaps there is a grain of truth in some of this.[13] But when dealing with myth it is not the truth value of one or another element of the whole phenomenon which is in question. What is at stake is the package, the myth, which acts as a kind of filter to past events. Even seemingly historical accounts of who did what, why, and when, take on a totally ahistorical quality. Once we have dissected the myth, there is nothing left. If you look at the accounts just summarised, they do seem to have notions of history, of class, and gender conflicts in them. There are even titles of books such as Jillian Becker's *Hitler's Children* (1978) but apart from some crude analogies between left and right fascism, her analysis mainly dissolves into the same kind of amateur psychology as the journals employ. Typical for the myth of the woman terrorist is the collapse of history, class and gender into the neurotic conflicts of individual women. The reasons for the initial politicisation, the increasing criminalisation, the historical, social and ideological changes occuring inside a society under pressure of this kind, the spirals of action and reaction between state power and its attackers, between police and fugitive – all these features of a socio-historical analysis appear at most as a kind of nebulous background to the myth.[14] That is because the separation of the purposes of terrorist activities from the acts of terror themselves – by suppressing the former and exaggerating the latter – is the essential ingredient of the myth. Only by allowing the myth to float free of the socio-political moment of its conception can the various components of the myth be kept together. How else would it be possible to have a headline 'Deadlier than the Male' with a picture of six women from four countries in a serious newspaper such as the *Times*? The caption reads: 'The ferocious line-up of notorious women terrorists: Gudrun Ensslin, Patty Hearst, Ulrike Meinhof, Marion Price, Dolours Price, Leila Khaled.'[15] Like a jig-saw puzzle we are supposed to fit together the profile of the transcultural, non-historical, non-political phenomenon. Under the subtitle 'From well brought-up girls to female fanatics' we get a Patty Hearst ingredient for wealth, Ulrike Meinhof for her intellectual background, the Japanese Hiroko Nagata for extreme brutality, Susanne Albrecht for her deception, and so on. Because as Caroline Moorehead says in her article:

It isn't the presence of women amongst the terrorists that alarms people . . . it is their style . . .
   [This] particular ferocity and desperation of the female guerrilla . . . psychologists seem to suggest, stems from the need among many modern women to prove their equality to men, their ability not to do just well but better. 'There is nothing more calculated to make you equal than the gun' said one expert. Did Marcuse not praise sexual sadism as one of the forms of sexual freedom? Looked at in this way, the phenomenon is, in short, Women's Lib, distorted to an inappropriate, aberrant extreme.[16]

PART II: MYTH AND THRESHOLDS OF DISSENT

Let me now in the second part of this chapter draw some parallels which ought to come as a surprise to those of us who see terrorist activities and non-violent civil protest as the extreme opposites in the spectrum of political choices. I shall argue that the myth of the woman terrorist as a crossing-point of existing divergent discourses of our time can be and is invoked, consciously and unconsciously, in situations which − except for the fact that they include women − have as good as nothing in common with each other. I am referring to the way the peace campaigners at Greenham were written about by sections of the British popular press.

   What we need in order to understand an alignment of semantic and real life opposites, such as violent/non-violent activities, inside the same category, is a model such as the one developed by Stuart Hall and his collaborators at the Centre for Cultural Studies in Birmingham.

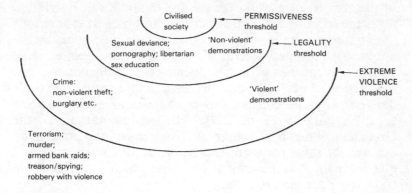

Reproduced, with permission, from:
Stuart Hall *et al., Policing the Crisis: Mugging, the State and Law and Order*
(Macmillan, London and Basingstoke, 1978, p. 226).

Hall's model assumes a consensus view of civilised society which while accepting plurality, denies structural dissent. When dissent does occur, it is placed outside the circle of civilised society in various forms of deviancy. There are three thresholds which determine the level of tolerance or intolerance with which the actions outside the central circle are perceived. The three thresholds as can be seen in the diagram are the permissiveness threshold beyond which moral disapproval is activated, the legality threshold, and the extreme violence threshold. 'The higher an event can be placed in the hierarchy of thresholds, the greater is its threat to the social order, and the tougher and more automatic is the coercive response' (Hall, 1978, p. 225). Associations between forms of deviancy, or in Hall's words, a resignification, can take two forms: convergence or escalation. For both phenomena we can find many instances in the Greenham women reporting. Convergence is the running together of 'undesirable' acts within the same threshold circle. Inside the same space, having passed beyond the acceptable but not yet entered the next circle of open illegality. Hall places, for example, sexual deviancy on one side and 'non-violent' demonstrations on the other. Convergence becomes then the conflation of these into one image. The description of the Greenham women as sexually deviant and the reinterpretation of their political protest in sexual terms are an obvious instance of the convergence of the sexual and the political. Escalation takes the form of association across thresholds. If elements of the convergent image can be related across thresholds by the apparent sharing of certain features, this can signal extreme violence, even when what is happening is actually non-violent. Any action of perfectly legal protest can thus seem potentially dangerous. Hall describes this mechanism as a 'signification spiral' (Hall, 1978, p. 223). The representation of the Greenham women as dangerous enemies of the state is an example of this process of escalation. Both convergence and escalation interact to criminalize dissent which in turn can help to justify state intervention.

Let us look at this in more detail. A very obvious slippage across the different thresholds occurred after the IRA bombing in Brighton, in 1984, in Mrs Thatcher's allusion to the need to fight all extremists in a society. Within the established Tory discourse, this linked striking miners, pickets, violent pickets, political extremists, and the IRA murderers in one associative chain. This slippage was reiterated by Norman Tebbit on his return to Parliament: 'Mr Tebbit said the Brighton bombing was not an isolated incident. It was part of an irrationality which had crept into politics and society, from groups who claimed that one issue was so important to them that they could indulge in civil disobedience, break the law or in the end murder to achieve their ends.'[17] No group which is perceived to be outside the threshold of consensus society can be sure of remaining within any of the boundaries of the thresholds.

Henry Porter in *Lies, Damned Lies* quotes the front page of the *Standard* of 20 December 1983: 'CND HOLDING HANDS WITH IRA – POLICE ANGER AS DEMOS TAKE MEN OFF BOMB WATCH DUTY', to show how the IRA bombing of Harrods was linked with the peace movement (Porter, 1984, p. 72). As I have shown in the first part, the early stages of Baader-Meinhof reporting similarly ranged across all the thresholds from student protest to urban terrorism before it concentrated into one single monolithic myth, that of the woman terrorist, who then, like the IRA here, became the focal point for the extreme end of the associations. Without sounding as ludicrous as the *Standard*'s comment, Tebbit's perception of protest makes essentially the same leap. The Greenham women thus become part of the 'irrationality' in politics, which is one of the important sign marks of the woman terrorist. Only through this associative path can the extraordinary reactions be explained which the Greenham women have experienced both from the right-wing press and the representatives of law and order, soldiers, police, politicians. Ulrike Meinhof was named by the German tabloid *Bild* as public enemy No. 1: the Greenham women, too, are the enemies who have to be defeated in battle.

The linguistic array of war and peace terminology in relation to the Greenham women is perhaps predictable given the popular press's delight with simple dualities. It is nevertheless worth illustrating to what extremes of linguistic association the war and peace rhetoric goes, in describing who is opposing whom and through which actions. 'The Women of Peace found themselves at war yesterday' writes the *Daily Star*,[18] while the *Sunday Telegraph* declares that 'peace-mongering and war-mongering are the two faces of the same coin, both of which are equally mindless and menacing, not to say obscene'.[19] According to the *Daily Express*, the 'so-called peace-women' are really 'at war'.[20] Their actions are also described as war-like. They 'batter at the fence as troops wait to repel them' (*Daily Express*),[21] they storm, they tear, whip horses with barbed wire, and knock policemen unconscious (*Daily Telegraph*),[22] they live in camps from which they have to be evicted. Several newspapers sent their own women reporters as 'undercover girls' in 'undercover operations' to the camp, to spy on their sources of illegal money and secret affiliations with other enemies like Moscow, or the Workers' Revolutionary Party, and so on.[23] Their evictions are thus not seen as actions against civilians but as war-like manoeuvres. The *Daily Express* had a huge headline: 'E-Day at Greenham'[24] − E = eviction − describing the day of defeat in their 'Battle of Survival'.[25]

The climax of this war-like rhetoric to date was the reporting in the *Daily Express* of the eviction in February 1985 of 150 demonstrators (both men and women in this case) from the Cruise missile site in Molesworth, Cambridgeshire: 'Heseltine's army routes Cruise protesters' in a 'spectacular

Army swoop' which 'made secure Britain's next Cruise missile base'. 'The battle of Molesworth' was the result of a 'secret invasion' to which the Defence Minister, Michael Heseltine, dressed in a combat jacket, came to survey 'the scene of his triumph' (*Daily Express*).[26] The similarity of such scenes with what happened in West Germany during the search for the fugitive Baader/Meinhof members did not escape the notice of Labour spokesman Denzil Davies, who is quoted in the *Guardian* as saying that 'the people who were evicted (were) pacifist Quakers not Baader/Meinhof terrorists',[27] though his words seem to imply that military operations on such a vast scale were justified against the West German terrorists. About 3000 soldiers and police moving in against 150 protesting citizens in Molesworth might be described as almost ludicrous over-reaction. One might also wish to argue that in the first stages of the Baader/Meinhof pursuit, the West German police over-reacted (and thus helped to escalate the threat which the group initially constituted).

If the myth of the woman terrorist acts as a focus for the escalation of the representation of Greenham women as potentially extremely violent people, it also provides an interesting parallel for convergence. This has to do with the undeniable fact that in both cases we are dealing with women. In contrast to the escalation move, which takes the known and feared violence of one group and grafts it onto the other, convergence works at the constitutive level: what we have to look at is how the element of womanhood is structured into the discourse. In the previous section I showed the association of woman—irrationality—terrorist: here we can see the link woman – irrationality – political protest. The clash of discourses analysed in the previous section is equally in action here, focusing as before on various notions of deviancy in connection with gender and sexuality. But whereas in the myth of the woman terrorist the conflicting discourses were eventually collapsed into one paradoxical myth, the Greenham women are simply divided up into different images of deviancy, which at the same time signal their division amongst themselves and their menacing unity.

The series of five articles by Sarah Bond, the 'undercover girl' of the *Daily Express* mentioned before, contains all these elements. First, the sexually and socially deviant: lesbians, drug-takers, bad mothers, general misfits. Secondly, the dangerous fool: the housewife who is not intelligent enough to see that she is used by others, the protester, who means well but does wrong. Thirdly, the militant revolutionary: the real powers behing the scene who are misguiding and manipulating the others for their own evil ends. The following extracts from the series of articles in the *Daily Express* give examples of these three categories.

Under the heading 'Squabbling women at war', Sarah Bond writes:

The day the police and bailiffs arrived, the peace camp was already breaking up anyway – racked by internal feuding.

The lesbians, flaunting their sexuality, fell out with the 'straights'. The scruffs, revelling in the rubbish, quarrelled with the women who longed to clean the place up . . .

Cynicism, acrimony over camp money, a divide between the lesbians and heterosexuals, and between the man-haters and man-likers gnawed at the Greenham core . . .[28]

Another sample of the same the next day:

Half the women I lived among at Greenham were lesbians, striding the camp with their butch haircuts, boots and boiler-suits.

They flaunt their sexuality, boast about it, joke about it. And some take a delight in proclaiming their loathing of men . . .

A lot of women 'go gay' after arriving at the camp. With no men around they turn to each other in comfort.

Other lesbians masquerade as peace women and go to Greenham just for sex because it is one of the few places where they can be open about it.[29]

A further extract from a front page:

The frontline troops of Greenham's peace women are being used as pawns in an orchestrated campaign to destroy Britain's nuclear defences.

I can reveal this today after sharing the squalor of their camps and penetrating the secrets of the cynical organisation behind the Greenham phenomenon.

I discovered that while the hungry shivering 'sisters' endure shantytown misery, a bank account backing them stands at a healthy £17,000.

And hardly any of the real leaders of the movement were to be seen bedding down in the mud for the sake of their cause. Throughout it all, the money for the propaganda machine keeps rolling in . . . The cash comes from left-wing councils, the Workers Revolutionary Party, trades unions . . .[30]

As a final extract from the same issue, this time written by a male journalist, there is the head-line 'Exposed: Gang of Four who pull the string', above the photographs of four women.[31]

A few days previously the *Daily Express* described a 'dramatic, secret meeting' of Tony Benn with the Greenham women, at which 'he presented the women with an astonishing three-point plan'. This secret three-point plan under the headline: 'EXCLUSIVE: THE EXPRESS EXPOSES SECRET PLAN OF LABOUR'S BOGEYMAN' turned out to be an alleged conspiracy between Tony Benn and the Greenham women: (1) to set up a peace camp outside the Defence Ministry, (2) to set up camp vigils at military bases across the country, (3) to 'picket Fleet Street with facts and figures about nuclear war and about the women's arrest and "harassment"'.[32]

These proposals are distinctly less dramatic than the headline: perhaps even *Express* readers may occasionally feel an urge to 'picket Fleet Street with facts and figures'. Undoubtedly the real purpose of the article was achieved: to give the sense of a conspiracy between the paper's favourite target Tony Benn and the Greenham women. The continuous insinuation that there is a secret leadership of the Greenham women inside the Common and subversive radical forces outside, certainly conflicts with all the accounts by the women themselves, as well as those of liberal papers like the *Guardian* and documentaries such as the study by Caroline Blackwell *On the Perimeter* (1984). But that is not the point at issue here. Any peace movement is open to the charge of harbouring subversive outside elements. What distinguishes the Greenham women from other protest movements is precisely the absence of leadership, a feature they share with other *women's* movements, as distinct from mixed movements like CND. Paul Brown in the *Guardian* describes under the headline 'Leaderless peace movement keeps law at arm's length'[33] the frustration felt by policemen and journalists alike at not being able to single out leading personalities to interview (or for that matter arrest).

When we study the responses to the Greenham women by the right-wing press and the forces of law and order, we can classify them according to the two aspects of subversion distinguished in this analysis, the irrational woman and the woman terrorist. First the escalation of the picture of peaceful protest into one of potential violence and terrorism serves to justify the treatment of these women as potential revolutionaries with wide-spread conspiratorial connections. As such they are a menace and must be stopped. Secondly, the convergence of the element of female political protest with irrationality, sexual deviancy, neurosis, drug addiction, social irresponsibility, or just plain silliness, accounts for the highly divergent accounts of them in the popular press. Together the two elements explain the confused and contradictory treatment they elicit. So the Greenham women can be: (1) despised for being smelly, flea-ridden and dirty: (2) insulted as the equivalent of football hooligans – peace yobs, screaming harridans, or weird lesbians: (3) laughed at for their weakness: (4) pitied as poor pathetic figures in the mud who are caught unaware by the evicters as well as (5) feared and loathed for their brutality, perversion and violence. Responses such as the American soldiers' show of their bared back-sides from a passing bus, physical attacks on the women by local youth, and military-style mass evictions can thus be shown to be structurally related.

What I would like to do in the last section of this paper is briefly to look at an interesting argument which Renate Gunther puts in her analysis of press representations of Greenham Common which in part conflicts with my own (Gunther, forthcoming). She analysed the 1982/83 reporting and found an intriguing difference between the two years. Whereas in 1982 the representations of the women were diverse in kind, the 1983 reporting reduced this variety to one major image: the 'women as the enemy'. With the continuation of the protest into another year Gunther argues that 'individualizing and trivializing the Greenham women's commitment no longer makes sense'. Whereas in 1982, 'the police appeared as a collective force, opposed by a few hysterical women', in 1983, 'the participants in this "individuals v. the group scenario" are made to swap places. Now the individual man (a police officer) becomes the victim of an attack carried out by a group of (violent) women' (*ibid.*). So the women become criminals and the individual policeman the victim. Although my own analysis confirms most of Renate Gunther's findings I think her explanation of a chronological shift is only partially correct, especially if one includes the 1984 coverage which Gunther could not yet know about.

First, as I have explained, paradoxically the accounts of the women as individuals on the one hand and as a menacing group on the other run side by side, often shifting within the same article, as in the *Daily Express* story, or consecutively, as for example various articles in the *Daily Mail* show between December 1983 and April 1984. So whereas it is correct to say that the idea of the women as enemy comes more to the forefront in 1983, it is not replacing any of the other conflicting images. With the principles of convergence and escalation we can easily account for this double encoding.

Secondly, if we consider those articles where the 'violent women' image occured, along with the accompanying material of the newspapers of the days in question, we may find another intriguing explanation. The articles on which Renate Gunther bases her reversal idea all come from the same period, December 1983. They report a mass demonstration at Greenham Common where one policeman was hurt and many women were arrested. The demonstration coincided with the first showing to a mass audience of British TV viewers of the American film *The Day After*, which shows in a dramatised form some of the possible effects of a nuclear war. A British public shocked by a TV film about nuclear war on the one hand and mass demonstrations against nuclear bases on the other could easily create a solidarity between the two. The Minister of Defence, Michael Heseltine, was acutely aware of the risk. When asked to appear in a TV panel to discuss the film and his government's nuclear policy, he declined; but he reserved the unusual right for himself to deliver a statement, unopposed, as an introductory comment to the film.

A short analysis of the way these three events, the demonstration, the film, and Heseltine's introduction were reported by two of the papers we have been looking at, shows their intriguingly different strategies to achieve similar ends. First, the shock about the fictional nuclear holocaust was not to be turned into a disagreement with the government's nuclear policy. Secondly, the Greenham women's protest was not to appear as legitimate and representative of the feelings of the British public. The *Sun* used the most obvious strategy of all. It simply separated the events. This way it could indulge in all the horrors of the nuclear effects which it spread over a double page, pictures and all.[34] On a separate page it reported Heseltine's comments: 'Tarzan blasts "unfair" TV film',[35] and on yet another page it gave an unusually modest coverage of the Greenham demonstration, only one column, centring on the hurt policeman: 'Cop hurt in peace camp'.[36] The only connection was that the showing of the film was declared to be a 'coup for CND'.

In contrast, the *Daily Express* reported all events side by side emphasising three points: (1) the violence of the women against the troops underlined by two front-page pictures, one showing the unconscious policeman, the other soldiers behind a fence being 'attacked' by battering women: subtitle 'Faces of violence'; (2) the ordinary families' response to the TV film: nobody wants nuclear war and violence; (3) the 'vital message of the TV movie: the free world must never agree to abandon its nuclear defences.' This comes under the headline: 'Making sure the day after never dawns.'[37] This way the ordinary person's distress and fear of the holocaust is directly used to confirm the government's nuclear policy, whereas the Greenham women are aligned with those violent forces which might cause the disaster in the first place. The image of the women-as-enemy can thus be seen as necessarily foregrounded at those moments when the risk of a more widespread sympathy with them is considered to be high, giving way to other images when the risk is low. This may even include a gesture of sympathy for one or another individual. This way, the illusion of a pluralist approach is kept up, checking the impression of too much bias whilst keeping dissent firmly in its deviant outsider position.

At this point it may be necessary to insist that the analysis I have presented is focused on discourse strategies of texts. Deconstructing representations of different groups of women and showing the purposes which they can be made to serve does *not* imply a conspiratorial manufacturing of these images by a group of Machiavellian journalists. The difficult and important theoretical point is that we all produce and are part of the conflicting discourses of our time. Understanding this process just a fraction better is one of the reasons for writing this chapter.

Let me conclude with a short summary of the argument. Women's political actions from the non-violent oppositional civil disobedience up to the engagement in terrorist violence are mediated by representations of natural *vs.* unnatural womanhood on the one hand and ideas of political consensus and dissent on the other. Since these repose on the highly restrictive ideals of natural womanhood as well as those of political quiescence, it is clear that a challenge at any of these points may arouse public anxiety about all the others. Irrationality and hysteria presented both as causes and as effects of political activities are some of the controlling mechanisms for ideological representations in the media. These can lend support to restrictive measures by the state, just as conversely, state actions can inspire and reinforce the media presentations. The relationship is not a simple one, which is why I have attempted to explain it in detail by drawing on two such highly divergent groups of people as the ones discussed here.

When I began the research into historical and fictional representations of subversion of which this chapter forms one instance, I realised that this was not easily containable within any one academic discipline. Moving along different sections of the library I found to my amusement on the literary shelves one critic in *Critical Quarterly* accusing Heinrich Böll of falsifying events, because in his novel he did not make Katharina Blum into a terrorist (Rhys W. Williams, 1979, p. 49). Across the rows in the *Journal of Contemporary History* a historian despairs at political science for its attempts to analyse and understand terrorism, telling us that 'fiction holds more promise for the understanding of the terrorist phenomenon' (Walter Laqueur, 1977). Reading Heinrich Böll's novel *The Lost Honour of Katharina Blum* or seeing films like *Germany in Autumn* or the two Margarethe von Trotha films, *The Second Awakening of Christa Klages* and *German Sisters*, we might find it tempting to agree with Laqueur if only for the reason that good fiction knows of its fictionality, whereas the myth does not. But wherever we encounter the myth of the violent, sexually neurotic woman driven into politics by her irrationality, it must be broken open because it affects all women involved in political protest.

Notes

CHAPTER 1

1. In her *Vindication of the Rights of Woman,* Mary Wollstonecraft also applied this phrase to Rousseau, thus maintaining her allegation that despite Burke's enmity towards Rousseau, they both encouraged a feverish sensibility.
2. Cf. 'Why are we to love prejudices merely because they are prejudices (*Vide* Mr Burke)? A prejudice is a fond obstinate persuasion for which we can give no reason . . . vulgarly termed a woman's reason; for women sometimes declare that they love or believe certain things, *because* they love or believe them' (Wollstonecraft, *Vindication of the Rights of Woman,* 1975 edn, p. 216).
3. In her thought-provoking essay 'Wild Nights', Cora Kaplan (1983) rightly suggests that *Mansfield Park* reads in many places like a fictional reworking of *A Vindication* (of the Rights of Woman). Even more than Jane Austen's judgement on Mary Crawford, which Kaplan compares to Wollstonecraft's denunciation of hereditary aristocracy in that work, is this passage about colonial wives (in Wollstonecraft's *Vindication of the Rights of Men*) echoed in *Mansfield Park.* Those who search for political clues in Jane Austen beneath her seductive prose may find a less savage picture of the same thing in her portrayal of Lady Bertram in *Mansfield Park,* who sat long hours on her sofa, thinking perhaps more deeply about her pug dog than about her children, in a mansion supported by the slave labour of Sir Thomas Bertram's sugar plantations in the West Indies. The corruption within was observed by the moralist outsider, Fanny, who shared a surname with Burke's great enemy and Mary Wollstonecraft's great friend, Dr Price. In general, the exposure of Pride and Prejudice and the reunion of Sense and Sensibility are common themes of these two great women writers and gain in richness thereby.
4. 'Every woman adores a fascist,/ The boot in the face, the brute/ Brute heart of a brute like you' (Sylvia Plath, from 'Daddy' (1962), in *Collected Poems,* Faber & Faber, London, 1981, p. 223).
5. Without the constant help of the famously knowledgeable and kind staff of the London Library, I could not have written this chapter.

6. This quotation from Mary Wollstonecraft's letters has been taken from Richard Holmes's *Footsteps* (1985) which had not been published at the date of my lecture. I have used it for relevance and also as an occasion to express my pleasure to discover unexpectedly that Richard Holmes was simultaneously exploring revolutionary Paris tracing the steps of Mary Wollstonecraft with his customary sensitivity.

CHAPTER 2

1. The painting is on display in the Louvre.
2. *Lettres Intimes,* quoted Johnson (1981).
3. H. Toussaint (ed.), *'La Liberté guidant le peuple' de Delacroix,* catalogue, (Paris: Réunion des Musées Nationaux, 1982) points out that the artist's immediate source for the figure of Liberty were sketches from an episode in the Greek-Turkish war. Italo Calvino used the occasion of the 1982 exhibition for an essay entitled 'Un romanzo dentro un quadro', reprinted in Italo Calvino, *Collezione di Sabbia* (Garzanti, Milan, 1984).
4. There is a very full account of this imagery in N. Hadjinicolaou, ' "La Liberté guidant le peuple" de Delacroix devant son premier plan', *Actes de la Recherche en Sciences Sociales* (June 1979), pp. 3-26. See also Hadjinicolaou's comments in 'Disarming 1830: A Parisian Counter-Revolution', *Block,* 4 (1981), p. 13.
5. Melvin J. Lasky, 'Lady on the Barricades', (1) *Margit,* in *Encounter* (July 1972), p. 17. I am grateful to my colleague, Ulrike Hanna Meinhof, for drawing my attention to this passage, which she discusses in Chapter 8.
6. In view of the argument I shall develop here, it is worth mentioning that two other images of women are presented in Moffat's picture (all shadowy adjuncts to the male portraits): one is a stripper and the other a street-walker.
7. Marlborough Fine Art, 25 January-1 March 1985.
8. In contrast, Jean Victor Schnetz's massive painting *Combat de l'Hôtel de Ville, le 28 juillet 1830* (Salon, 1834), recently resurrected from the store of the Petit Palais, had little or no after-life. Significantly, while it is in many ways a striking image, the central figure is that of a heroic male who supports in his arms a dying boy.
9. Natalie Davis points out that sexual reversals, including the transformation of women into warriors, like other rites and ceremonies of reversal, are ultimately sources of order and stability in a hierarchical society. 'Women on Top: Symbolic sexual inversion and political disorder in early modern Europe', in Barbara A. Babcock (ed.) *The Reversible World* (1978).
10. It should be noted that a woman dressed thus was almost fully clothed and that many women, laundresses for instance, worked in their *jupons.*
11. Adhémar (1954) states that the story was invented to promote sales of the engraving after the picture.

12. It is now in the Louvre. The fullest art-historical discussions of how the allegory is constructed are to be found in G. H. Hamilton, 'The Iconographical Origins of Delacroix's Liberty', in *Studies in Art and Literature for Bel da Costa Greene* (Princeton: Princeton University Press, 1984) and W. Hofmann, 'Sur la "Liberté" de Delacroix', *Gazette des Beaux-Arts* (September 1975).

13. *Journal des Artistes* (1831), quoted by Adhémar (1954).

14. See, notably, Ingres' *Joan of Arc* (Louvre), Wilkie's *The Defence of Saragossa* (Royal Collection, London), Goya's *What Courage* (*Desastros*), Karoly Kisafuldy (d. 1830), *A Magyar*. Fred Roe's painting relates to the Russian Revolution and was sold at Sotheby's Belgravia, on 12 December 1978.

15. Now lost but reproduced in Clark (1973).

16. D. Bellos, 'On Interpretation: Delacroix's *La Liberté*', unpublished paper (Edinburgh, 1982; to be included in Bellos, *Art, History and the Beholder*, forthcoming), p. 4.

17. Author's translation. Gustave Planche, as Adhémar points out (1954), argued that the picture's grey tone derived from the terrible dust of the struggle. The quotations come from Ambroise Tardieu and from an anonymous review in *La Tribune*. Hadjinicolaou gives an extremely detailed account of the pejorative comments of critics and points out how these have been suppressed by art historians. (1979, pp. 22-4).

18. The poem, 'La Curée' (the rush for spoils) was published in Barbier's *Iambes*. It is also quoted by Agulhon (1981), p. 40. Author's translation.

19. An interesting and perceptive critique of Agulhon is to be found in A. Rifkin, 'The Sex of French Politics', *Art History*, (September 1983).

20. The most interesting discussion of this subject (as well as a great deal of illustrative material inadequately documented) is to be found in K. Theweleit, *Mannerphantasien* (Frankfurt: Roter Stern, 1978).

21. S. Ringborn compares Delacroix's *Liberty* and Guérin's *Iris and Morpheus* in 'Guérin, Delacroix and "The Liberty"', *Burlington Magazine* (1968), pp. 270-4. It does seem extraordinary that these works can be compared for their formal similarities without their enormous differences in colour and handling being signalled.

22. See, for instance, Guérin's *Henri de Rochejequelin* (Salon, 1817), Municipal Museum, Cholet.

23. As in Bernard Debia's *L'Arbre de la Liberté*, Musée de Montauban, where a larger-than-life allegorical female presides over a *tableau vivant*.

24. The reference to Bicêtre is Auguste Jal's, quoted by Hadjinicolaou (1979), p. 23; Adhémar (1954) quotes Maxime du Camp's criticism of the picture when it was exhibited at the 1855 Exposition Universelle; 'Non, non, il n'y a rien de commun entre la vierge immortelle et féconde que nous adorons et cette drôlesse échappée de Saint-Lazare': ('No, no, there is nothing in common between the immortal and fecund virgin whom we adore and this hussy escaped from St. Lazare').

25. This cartoon is reproduced in Theweleit (1978), without any information regarding its context or location. Extensive enquiries have

so far failed to identify the language of the inscription: 'Prenki do Gure'.

26. Marina Warner alone has acknowledged the significance of this figure (p. 272) but failed to recognise how it functions.
27. Reproduced in J. Root, *Pictures of Women* (London and Boston: Pandora Press, 1984, p. 62).
28. J. L. E. Meissonier, *The Barricade rue de la Mortellerie* (Salon 1851), Louvre, Paris; E. Manet, *The Barricade*, (1871) lithograph.
29. C. Baudelaire, *Eugène Delacroix, His Life and Work,* ed. S. J. Freedberg (Garland, New York and London, 1979) p. 82.
30. Brussels, Musées Royaux des Beaux-Arts.
31. Musée des Beaux-Arts de Bordeaux. Nina M. Athanassoglou-Souyoudjoglou in *French Images from the Greek War of Independence 1821-1827: Art and Politics under the Restoration* (Ann Arbor: UMI, 1980) points out (p. 115) the connection between Delacroix's painting of *Greece* . . . and the 1825 French translation of 'Dithyrambe sur la Liberté' by the Greek poet Dionysios Solomos.

CHAPTER 3

1. These remarks have much in common with Marcel Bernos's article (1982) which is directly relevant to the subject treated here.
2. Albert Hirschman (1982) argues that throughout history and in particular since the sixteenth century, there have been alternating cycles when first public then private interests have predominated.
3. In her thesis, 'Sur la théorie du droit maternel. Discours anthropologique et discours socialiste', University of Paris-Dauphine, 1979.
4. 'La littérature antiféministe en France de 1871 à 1914', thesis, University of Paris-III, 1983.
5. According to a paper given by Elizabeth Fox-Genovese at the EHESS in Paris in 1982.
6. See Katherine Blunden (1982) on the withdrawal of women from the world of production and the construction of their role as wife, mother and consumer in Victorian England. Cf. also Anne Martin-Fugier (1983).
7. Georges Deherme (a disciple of Auguste Comte) who believed that the social was indeed women's territory, gave his book the title *Le Pouvoir social des femmes* (1912).
8. Cf. Christian Thibon, 'L'ordre villageois au XIXe siecle, le cas du pays de Sault (Aude)', paper given at a conference in France in December 1983 on public order in nineteenth-century Europe.
9. Lise Vanderwielen's autobiographical novel *Lise du plat pays* (1983), constructed on the model of the serial stories which were the author's chief reading matter, is a good twentieth-century example of the influence of reading on the imagination.
10. See Mayeur (1979) and Marie-Françoise Lévy (1984) on the '1867 crisis' in girls' education.

11. Michaud (1985) used Baudelaire's phrase as his title. The books by Maurice Agulhon (1981) and Claude Quiguer (1979) both present remarkable examples of the symbolic representation of the female figure.
12. Weininger's own book *Geschlecht und Charakter (Sex and Character),* which was published in Vienna in 1903, was a sort of breviary of anti-feminism for a whole generation.

CHAPTER 4

1. There are three main western biographies of Kollontai, by Clements (1979), Farnsworth (1980) and Porter (1980). The Soviet biography is by A. M. Itkina (1964, 2nd edn 1970). See bibliography for details.
2. See Broido (1978) and Engel (1983), as well as Engel's chapter in *Socialist Women* (ed. M. Boxer and J. Quartaert, 1978).
3. Quoted in J. Smith (1929, pp. 53-4). *Baba* was an insulting term for women.
4. See Edmondson (1984) and her article on Russian feminists in *Russian History* (1976). Cf. A.M. Kollontai, *Iz moei zhizni i raboty* (Moscow, 1974 edn, pp. 111-15).
5. On female radicalism, see Bobroff (1974, pp. 550-55). For figures see S. Smith, *Red Petrograd* (Cambridge University Press, Cambridge, 1983, p. 23) and V. Bonnell (ed.), *The Russian Worker* (University of California Press, Berkeley, 1983, pp. 17-18).
6. P. Sorokin, *Leaves from a Russian Diary* (Boston, 1950, p. 3).
7. V. Kaiurov in *Proletarskaia Revolutsiia,* no. 1 (13) 1923.
8. V. I. Lenin, *Sochineniia* (4th edn, Moscow, 1941-60, vol. 30, p. 25).
9. 'The Workers' Opposition', in Holt's selection (1977). See also Clements (1975).
10. Quoted in Stites (1978, p. 267). See also Kollontai, 'Communism and the Family', in Holt (1977, pp. 250-60); and A. M. Kollontai, *Izbrannye stat'i i rechi* (Moscow, 1972, p. 241).
11. E.g. Sabsovich. Cf. Farnsworth (1980, p. 155).
12. F. Halle, *Women in Soviet Russia* (Secker and Warburg, London, 1933, pp. 378-93).
13. Stumilin's estimate is in Lapidus (1978, pp. 75-6). See also Geiger (1968, p. 58) and Farnsworth (1980, p. 146).
14. Quoted in Stites (1978, p. 360). For an early critic of Kollontai, see P. Vinogradskaya, *Pamyatnye Vstrechi* (Moscow, 1972).
15. Cf. Farnsworth's chapter on the 1926 marriage law debate in Atkinson *et al* (1977, pp. 139-66). Quotation from Hayden (1976, p. 170).
16. Blekher (1979, p. 190); D. Dallin in Atkinson *et al* (1977, p. 394); cf. B. Kerblay *Modern Soviet Society* (Methuen, London, 1983, p. 136).
17. N. Baranskaya, 'Nedelia Kak Nedelia', *Novy Mir,* November 1969.
18. Itkina (1970, p. 208); Holt (1977, p. 25); see also A. M. Kollontai *Izbrannye stat'i i rechi* (1972) and *Iz moei zhizni i raboty* (1974). One rare example of a sympathetic treatment of her ideas on love, but not the family, is by V. Z. Rogovin in *Sotsial'nye issledovaniya,* no. 4 (1970).

CHAPTER 5

All translations from the German are by the author.

1. E.g. Grant, Mommsen, Reichardt and Wolf (1966) and Klessmann and Pingel (1980), mention not a single woman; A. J. Dulles (1947) and Peter Hoffmann (1977) mention only one woman in passing, and Löwenthal and von zur Muhlen (1982) mention just three women. The general study edited by R. Bridenthal *et al., When Biology became Destiny: Women in Weimar and Nazi Germany* (see Bibliography) did not become available in time to be consulted when this chapter was being written, but is clearly relevant.
2. E.g. Zorn and Meyer, (1974), Hanna Elling, (1981) and Vera Laska, (1983).
3. See Daniela Weiland, (1983), pp. 306-10.
4. See Bridenthal, (1973) and Mason (1976).
5. Helene Stöcker was a radical feminist, champion of the unmarried mother and her child, and a leading figure in War Resisters International.
6. For the feminist, pacifist life-work of Lida Gustava Heymann, see her memoirs, *Erlebtes-Erschautes,* (1977).
7. Dr Anita Augspurg was Germany's first woman lawyer.
8. Tim Mason (1976): 'In respect of its attitudes and policies towards women, National Socialism was the most repressive and reactionary of all modern political movements.'
9. E.g. Lina Haag, Luise Rinser and Sophie Scholl.
10. Gertrud von le Fort also wrote a very fine short story, *The Wife of Pilate,* first published in 1955, and translated in Herrmann and Spitz (1978) which can be read as a parable on the intercessor role of martyred women resisters in Nazi Germany.
11. See *Der lautlose Aufstand* (1974) p. 43 (Weisenborn, who himself had been a resister, is one of the very few male historians who fully acknowledges the part played in the German Resistance by women.)
12. See Elling, Zorn and Meyer, Haag, and Szepansky for the survivors' testimony.
13. For further details of the persecution of Jehovah's Witnesses see King (1979).
14. See *Die Zeit,* 27 December 1985, for numerous letters from German Jewish survivors testifying to the loyalty of their German Gentile women servants before 1939.
15. See Heinrich Fraenkel's chapter 'Kindness to Prisoners', in *The Other Germany* (1943), which quotes Nazi newspaper reports on the many German women given terms of imprisonment for the smallest acts of humanity; see also Anna Haag (1978, pp. 161-73).
16. All these women were connected to the Schulze-Boysen/Harnack group which did vital work warning the Soviet Union of Hitler's planned invasion of southern Russia.
17. The clearest account of German communist resistance and its

independence from Moscow is by Hermann Weber, in Löwenthal and von der Mühlen (1982).

18. The most detailed study of the Hamburg White Rose group of students is in Hochmuch and Meyer (1969).

19. See Inge Scholl (1970) and Hermann Vinke (1984). A German feature-film has recently been made of Sophie Scholl's life, and the University Square in Munich is named after her and her brother.

CHAPTER 6

1. The proposals put forward by the minister, Jean-Pierre Chévènement, were widely discussed in the French press in June and September 1985. See also the minister's collection of speeches, *Apprendre pour Entreprendre* (Livre de Poche, Paris, 1985). Claude Nicolet, himself the author of a study of republicanism (Nicolet, 1981) from which women are notably absent, was asked to prepare a report on civic instruction for the ministry in November 1984 (cf. *Le Débat*, no. 3, March 1985). For the revival in the history of republicanism see Pierre Nora (ed.) *Les Lieux de la Mémoire*, vol. 1, *La République* (Gallimard, Paris, 1984); Luc Ferry and A. Renart, *Philosophie Politique*, vol. 3, *Des Droits de l'Homme à l'Idée Républicaine* (PUF, Paris, 1985); and the renewal of interest in Alain, republican philosopher *par excellence*.

2. It should be said here that the 'republican orthodoxy' is a composite from general works published in France, where even comparatively recent works, such as the volumes of the *Nouvelle Histoire de la France contemporaine* (1970s) or the very recent book by J. Mayeur, *La Vie Politique sous la Troisième République* (Seuil, Paris, 1984) hardly mention women at all. A good example of the orthodoxy made explicit (in condensed and as it happens anticlerical form) is Lequin (1983, vol. 3, section on women's suffrage). Historians writing in English about France have been readier to incorporate material about women. While the older histories, such as those by Cobban and Brogan do not do so, Zeldin (1972) was something of a pioneer in his time by including a separate chapter, and J.F. McMillan's recent survey *Dreyfus to De Gaulle* (Arnold, London, 1985) devotes a number of pages to sexual inequality.

3. The relation of women to socialist politics in France has been well examined, in rather different ways, by Sowerwine (1982) and Hilden (1986).

4. Charles De Gaulle, *War Memoirs*, vol. I, *The Call to Honour*, trans. J. Griffin (Collins, London 1955, p. 430); and vol II, *Unity, Documents*, trans. J. Murchie and H. Erskine (Weidenfeld and Nicolson, London, 1959, p. 266). One of the less 'respectable' reasons sometimes given for the decision was that De Gaulle and the emergent Christian Democrat party (the MRP) politically close to him, expected to benefit from the women's vote. Women's political rights were for the first time ever firmly written into the Constitution of the Fourth Republic (1946).

5 The fullest first-person account of the Algiers debate known to me is F.

Grenier's chapter in *Les Femmes dans la Résistance* (1977). See Andrieu (1984, pp. 35, 76, 152) for details of the internal resistance debates as they related to women; Renard (1965) gives a general account.

6. Although it *was* specifically demanded in clandestine publications by women in the resistance (information for which I am grateful to my colleague Rod Kedward).

7. E.g. the writings of Yvonne Knibiehler; Segalen (1983); Verdier (1979); McMillan (1981 a) gives particular attention to women's employment during the First World War.

8. Space prevents more than the sketchiest reference to the 'Enlightenment debate on women'; for full discussion see Tomaselli (1985) and Faure (1985), both of which were published after the first draft of this chapter was written. Montesquieu was not of course a republican, but later republicans drew on his thought.

9. 'Those who are associated . . . take collectively the name of people and severally are called citizens as sharing in the sovereign authority, and subjects as being under the laws of the State', Rousseau, *Social Contract* (1973) edn, I, vi, p. 175).

10. Condorcet, 'On the Admission of Women to the City', in *Oeuvres de Condorcet* (1847 edn, vol. X, p. 122, my translation). Condorcet's high reputation during the Third Republic is discussed by Nicolet (1982) − but without any reference to Condorcet's feminism, On Mary Wollstonecraft's contacts with Condorcet, see Holmes (1985, p. 103).

11. Cf. for example Charles Renouvier (ed. M. Agulhon), *Manuel Républicain de l'Homme et du Citoyen, 1848* (Garnier, Paris, 1981); Professor John Renwick of Edinburgh University kindly let me see an anonymous *Catéchisme Républicain* of 1872 which he owns.

12. Their views are published in English in their contribution to Lovenduski and Hills (1981), which also summarises the earlier debate.

13. Cf. Christiane Chombeau's articles in *Le Monde* 8/9 December 1983; cf. articles in the *Sunday Times,* 1 December 1985, and the *Guardian,* 7 January 1986. For the number of women in the National Assembly after the March 1986 election, see Chapter 7 below.

14. 'Hourra pour la République', *Le Nouvel Observateur,* 7 December 1984.

CHAPTER 7

1. Marion Price and Margaret Stacey use Helga Nowotny's phrase to open their essential study of the question (Stacey and Price, 1981, p. 1).

2. The university is the University of Sussex. The figures relate to January 1985. See also the *Guardian,* 10 September 1985.

3. For all these figures and much other detailed information about the position of women, the European Community's regular publication *Women in Europe* is invaluable.

4. Georgina Dufoix, Edith Cresson and Huguette Bouchardeau. For both Britain and France, the information relates to January 1985.

5. The title 'Prefect' designates the members of a very senior rank in part of

the French Civil Service, many but by no means all of whom exercise the prestigious function of *Commissaire de la République* – the government's representative in each territorial division *(département)*.

6. She is Anne Mueller, who became Second Permanent Secretary in the Cabinet Office, in charge of the Office of Personnel and Management that runs the Civil Service.

7. In 1890, Philippa Fawcett achieved results in the mathematical tripos (final degree examination) at the University of Cambridge that were better than those of the best of the men (known as the senior wrangler). Since women were not admitted as members of the University of Cambridge until 1948, their results were issued separately.

8. Feminists at the time pointed out that men who were exempt from military service on medical grounds were not so excluded.

9. Michel Debré began his administrative career in the *Conseil d'Etat* in 1935, where he was associated with the Popular Front Government's proposals to reform Civil Service entry. In 1945, having been active in the Resistance and as the Provisional Government's representative in Angers he was appointed to head the Commission for Civil Service Reform. He later (1959) became the first Prime Minister of the Fifth Republic.

10. They were an Inspector in the Ministry of Education, a Special Officer in the Ministry of Health concerned with mental health, and an Assistant Secretary in the Scottish Home and Health Department (Evans 1934).

11. The first three women actually to take their seats fell into this category; Lady Astor replaced her husband who had succeeded to a peerage; Mrs Wintringham was elected to her seat within three weeks of her husband's death; and Mrs Hilton Philipson's husband had been barred from standing because of irregularities over election expenses. Similar examples occurred later, for instance in 1928-29 Mrs Runciman and Mrs Dalton held seats for fairly short periods in what appear to have been 'holding operations' until their husbands were available (Currell, 1974, pp. 58, 63).

12. 'The presence of women is directly related to the deficit in rewards; that is . . . we find that, where the proportion of women is higher, the deficit in rewards, as compared with those of men, increases' (Coser, 1981, p. 17). This phenomenon can clearly operate in several ways.

13. Two instances from personal knowledge illustrate the point. Two of the women candidates for the British Social Democratic Party at the 1983 general election found that they could not combine families and full-time employment with adoption as a prospective parliamentary candidate. One changed her senior research fellow contract with a university into a part-time contract, and the other gave up a senior school-teaching position for supply teaching. Neither was successful in the election, though both continue in this form of employment and nurse their constituencies. But many women cannot or will not make such decisions.

14. See above, note 6.

15. See Chapter 6.

16. The first woman sub-prefect was appointed in 1974, the first woman prefect in 1981.
17. See Chapter 1.
18. For a forceful critique of the concept of a division between a public, political sphere and a private, non-political sphere see Siltanen and Stanworth (1984, pp. 185-208).
19. The evidence from Eastern Europe, where women are alleged both to be much more widely present in top positions and to be still very tied to traditional household roles, does not seem to me to contradict this. It is far from clear that women have reached genuinely key positions, or that they will do so without changes (Sokolowska, 1981, p. 112). In the Hungarian local government elections of June 1985 in which two candidates contested every seat, women were, a senior local government official informed me, successful only where they were standing against another woman.
20. Joni Lovenduski's most recent book, *Women in European Politics: Contemporary Feminism and Public Policy* (Harvester, Brighton, 1986) which had not been published when this chapter was written, is an important reference for the questions discussed here.

CHAPTER 8

1. Melvin J. Lasky, 'Lady on the Barricades', *Encounter,* (July 1972, p. 17).
2. Marcia Pointon, 'Liberty on the Barricades', Chapter 2 in this volume.
3. *Spiegel,* 33 (1977) Title page (Frauen und Gewalt). Unless marked otherwise all translations from the German original are my own. If considered necessary, the German original will appear in brackets in the notes.
4. 'Deadlier than the male': compare with Kipling's poem, *The Female of the Species* (1911): 'For the female of the species is more deadly than the male'; 'Group portrait with ladies', Spiegel 33 (1977) p. 30: a pun on Heinrich Böll's novel *Gruppenbild mit Dame* (1971). This was not the first time that Böll's novel titles were used in connection with Baader/Meinhof activities. See for example the 1971 caricature by Hicks in the German newspaper *Welt* of a clown (= Heinrich Böll) carrying Ulrike Meinhof with a gun in her hand away from a shot policeman. Subtitle to the caricature: *Ansichten eines Clowns.* See Meinhof and Rach (1980, p. 32).
5. Some of the documents of the time were collected in the paperback by F. Grützbach (ed.) (1972) *Heinrich Böll, Freies Geleit für Ulrike Meinhof: Ein Artikel unde seine Folgen . . .*
6. *Praline,* 2; reprinted in F. Grützbach (1972, p. 151).
7. *Spiegel,* 33 (1977) p. 22 (Frauen im Untergrund: 'Etwas Irrationales'); *ibid.,* p. 28 (Die Täter leben in absoluter Inzucht).
8. *Spiegel,* 33 (1977), pp. 22 ff, quoting various sources.
9. *Observer Magazine* (11 December 1977), p. 34.
10. *Spiegel,* 33 (1977), p. 25.

11. *Times* (16 January 1985), p. 13.
12. Gerhard Mauz, 'Phänomen der Verzweiflung', in *Spiegel*, 33 (1977), p. 32.
13. My analysis is of representation and cannot attempt any historical account of the Baader/Meinhof group itself. It does not contain any stance either for or against their activities. At one time in West Germany one had to preamble any public statement about politics by declaring one's lack of sympathy with the group. To highlight the absurdity of this situation let me indulge in this personal anecdote. When I had the chance in 1977 to change my name on marriage but chose instead to keep it for obvious feminist reasons, I was sternly rebuked by a German official. His final suggestion was that if I wanted to keep that name it must imply that I was a secret sympathiser with Baader/Meinhof.
14. For an excellent account of the German situation, see Michael Horn (1982).
15. *Times* (16 January 1985), p. 13.
16. *Ibid.*
17. *Times* (19 December 1984), p. 1.
18. *Daily Star* (14 December 1982). Reprinted together with other similar quotations in A. Cook and G. Kirk (1983).
19. *Sunday Telegraph* (12 December 1982).
20. *Daily Express* (9 April 1984).
21. *Daily Express* (12 December 1983).
22. *Daily Telegraph* (12 December 1983).
23. See for example *Daily Express* (5-12 April 1984).
24. *Daily Express* (9 April 1984).
25. *Daily Express* (11 April 1984).
26. *Daily Express* (7 February 1985).
27. *Guardian* (7 February 1985).
28. *Daily Express* (9 April 1985).
29. *Daily Express* (10 April 1985).
30. *Daily Express* (9 April 1985, front page).
31. Ibid., p. 19.
32. *Daily Express* (5 April 1984).
33. *Guardian* (31 March 1983).
34. *Sun* (12 December 1983), pp. 14-15.
35. Ibid., p. 4.
36. Ibid., p. 2.
37. *Daily Express* (12 December 1983).

Bibliography of Works Cited

H. Adhémar, 'La Liberté sur les Barricades de Delacroix', *Gazette des Beaux-Arts* (1954).

Maurice Agulhon, *Marianne into Battle: republican imagery and symbolism in France 1789 – 1880,* trans. J. Lloyd (Cambridge University Press, Cambridge, 1981).

Maïté Albistur and Daniel Armogathe (eds), *Le Grief des femmes, anthologie de textes feminins du moyen âge à nos jours* (Editions Hier et Demain, Paris, 1978).

Sally Alexander, Anna Davin and Eve Hostettler, 'Labouring Women: a reply to Eric Hobsbawm', *History Workshop Journal,* 8 (1979).

Peter von Altmann, H. Brudigam, B. Mausbach-Bronberger and M. Oppenheimer (eds), *Der deutsche antifaschistische Widerstand* (Röderberg, Frankfurt, 1975 and 1984).

Claire Andrieu, *Le Programme commun de la résistance, des idées dans la guerre* (Editions de l'Erudit, Paris, 1984).

Anon., *Vindication of Burke's Reflections* (1791).

Shirley Ardener (ed.), *Perceiving Women* (J.M. Dent, London, 1975).

Dorothy Atkinson, Alexander Dallin and Gail Lapidus (eds), *Women in Russia* (Stanford University Press, 1977 and Harvester, Hassocks, 1978).

E. Ayoub, 'La Femme dans la fonction publique', *Droit Social,* 3 (March 1971).

Angelica Balabanova (Balabanoff), *Impressions of Lenin,* trans. I. Cesari (University of Michigan Press, Ann Arbor, 1964).

Angelica Balabanova, *My Life as Rebel* (Indiana University Press, 1973; originally published New York, 1938).

Roland Barthes, *Mythologies,* trans. A. Lavers (Granada, New York and London, 1973, selections from the French edition of the same title, 1957).

C. Baudelaire, *Eugène Delacroix: his life and work,* ed. S.J. Freedburg (Garland, New York and London, 1970).

G. Bécane-Pascaud, *Les Femmes dans la fonction publique* (Documentation française, Notes et Etudes documentaires, Nos 4056-77, Paris, 1974).

Jillian Becker, *Hitler's Children* (Granada, New York and London, 1978).

David Bellos, 'On Interpretation: Delacroix's *La Liberté'*, unpublished paper, Edinburgh, 1982 (to be included in David Bellos, *Art, History and the Beholder,* forthcoming).

Henri Bernard, *Histoire de la résistance européenne, la 'quatrième force' de la guerre 1939 – 45* (Gérard, Verviers, 1968).

Marcel Bernos, 'De l'influence salutaire ou pernicieuse de la femme dans la famille et la société', *Revue d'histoire moderne et contemporaine,* 29 (1982).

Caroline Blackwood, *On the Perimeter* (Flamingo, London, 1984).

Feiga Blekher, *The Soviet Woman in the Family and in Society,* trans. H. and R. Hardin (Kete, Jerusalem, distributed by Wiley, 1979).

Katherine Blunden, *Le Travail et la Vertu. Femmes au foyer: une mystification de la révolution industrielle* (Payot, Paris, 1982).

Anne Bobroff, 'The Bolsheviks and working women 1905-20', *Soviet Studies,* 26 (1974).

Heinrich Böll, *The Lost Honour of Katharina Blum,* trans. L. Vennewitz (McGraw-Hill, New York, 1976).

Heinrich Böll, *Group Portrait with Lady,* trans. L. Vennewitz (Secker and Warburg, London, 1973).

Huguette Bouchardeau, *Pas d'histoire les femmes* (Syros, Paris, 1977).

Huguette Bouchardeau, *Un Coin dans leur monde* (Syros, Paris, 1980).

James T. Boulton, *The Language of Politics in the Age of Wilkes and Burke* (Routledge and Kegan Paul, London, 1963).

Jeanne Bourin, *La Chambre des Dames* (Table Ronde, Paris, 1981).

Marilyn Boxer and J. Quataert (eds), *Socialist Women* (Elsevier, New York and Oxford, 1978).

Elisabeth Brandle-Zeile, *Frauen fur den Frieden* (DFG-VK, Stuttgart, 1983).

Renate Bridenthal, 'Beyond Kinder, Küche, Kirche, Weimar women at work', *Central European History,* 6 (1973).

Renate Bridenthal, Atina Grossman and Marion Kaplan (ed.), *When Biology Became Destiny: Women in Weimar and Nazi Germany* (Monthly Review Press, New York, 1984).

Elizabeth Brimelow, 'Women in the Civil Service', *Public Administration,* 59 (1981).

Vera Broido, *Apostles into Terrorists: women and the revolutionary* movement in the Russia of Alexander II (Viking, New York, 1977, and Temple Smith, London, 1978).

B. Brown and P. Adams, 'The Feminist Body and Feminist Politics', *m/f*, 3 (1979).

Norman Bryson, *Tradition and Desire* (Cambridge University Press, Cambridge, 1984).

Margarete Buber-Neumann, *Mistress to Kafka* (Secker and Warburg, London, 1966).

Edmund Burke, *A Philosophical Enquiry into the Origins of our Ideas of the Sublime and the Beautiful,* (1757).

Edmund Burke, *Reflections on the Revolution in France* (1790).

Cabinet Office, Personnel and managements office, *Civil Service Statistics* (HMSO, London, 1984).

H. Callan, 'The Premiss of Dedication, notes towards an ethnography of diplomats' wives', in S. Ardener (1975).

Bernice Carroll (ed.), *Liberating Women's History, Theoretical and Critical Essays* (University of Illinois Press, Urbana, Chicago and London, 1976).

Ulrich Cartarius, *Deutsche Widerstand, 1933 – 45* (Siedler, Berlin, 1984).

D. Cherry and G. Pollock, 'Woman as sign in Pre-Raphaelite literature; a study of the representation of Elizabeth Siddal', *Art History,* 7 (1984).

T. J. Clark, *The Absolute Bougeois: artists and politics in France 1848 – 51* (Thames and Hudson, London, 1973).

T.J. Clark, *The Painting of Modern Life: Paris in the art of Manet and his followers* (Thames and Hudson, London, 1985).

Barbara Clements, 'Emancipation through communism. The ideology of A.M. Kollontai', *Slavic Review,* 32 (1973).

Barbara Clements, 'Kollontai's contribution to the Workers' Opposition', *Russian History,* 2 (1975).

Barbara Clements, *Bolshevik Feminist: the life of Aleksandra Kollontai* (Indiana University Press, Bloomington, 1979).

Condorcet, J.N. de C., marquis of, *Oeuvres de Condorcet,* ed. A.C. O'Connor and M.F. Arago (Firmin Didot, Paris, 1847), vol. X.

Alice Cook and Gwyn Kirk, *Greenham Women Everywhere: dreams, ideas and actions from the Women's Peace Movement* (Pluto, London, 1983).

Michèle Coquillat, *Qui sont-elles? Les femmes d'influence et de pouvoir en France* (Mazarine, Paris, 1983).

R.L. Coser, 'Where have all the women gone? Like the sediment of a good wine, they have sunk to the bottom', in Epstein and Coser (1981).

Melville Currell, *Political Woman* (Croom Helm, London, 1974).

Anna Davin, in symposium 'What is Women's History', in *History Today* (July 1985).

Natalie Davis, 'Women on top, symbolic sexual inversion and political disorder in early modern Europe', in *The Reversible World, symbolic inversion in art and society,* ed. Barbara A. Babcock (Cornell University Press, Ithaca and London, 1978).

A.Davisse, *Les Femmes dans la fonction publique* (Documentation française, Collection des Rapports Officiels, Paris, 1983).

Michel Debré, 'Une grande reforme en 1945', in *La Politique de la fonction publique,* ed. M.C. Kessler, (FNSP, Paris, 1978).

Christine Delphy, 'Les Femmes et l'Etat', *Nouvelles Questions féministes* (1984).

Mary Douglas, *Purity and Danger, an analysis of the concept of pollution and taboo* (Ark, London and Boston, 1984).

Georges Duby, *The Knight, the Lady and the Priest, the making of modern marriage in medieval France,* trans. B. Bray (Pantheon, New York and Allen Lane, London, 1983).

Claire Duchen, *Feminism in France from May '68 to Mitterrand* (Routledge and Kegan Paul, London, 1986).

C. Dufrancatel *et al., L'Histoire sans qualités* (Galilée, Paris, 1979).

Allen W. Dulles, *Germany's Underground* (Macmillan, New York, 1947).

Linda Edmondson, 'Russian feminists and the first all-Russian Congress of Women', *Russian History,* 3 (1976).

Linda Edmondson, *Feminism in Russia 1900 – 1917* (Heinemann, London, 1984).

Ehrenbuch der Opfer von Berlin-Plotzensee (VVA, Berlin-Ost, 1974).

Hanna Elling, *Frauen im deutschen Widerstand* (Röderberg, Frankfurt, 1981).

Barbara Engel, *Mothers and Daughters: women of the intelligentsia in nineteenth-century Russia* (Cambridge University Press, Cambridge, 1983).

Cynthia F. Epstein, 'Women and elites, a cross-national perspective', in Epstein and Coser (1981).

C. F. Epstein and R. L. Coser (eds), *Access to Power: cross-national studies of women and elites* (Allen and Unwin, London, 1981).

D. Evans, *Women and the Civil Service, a history of the development of the employment of women in the civil service and a guide to present-day opportunities* (Pitman, London, 1934).

Judith Evans, 'Women and Politics, a reappraisal', *Political Studies,* 28, (1980).

Judith Evans, 'The Good Society: implications of a greater participation by women in public life', *Political Studies,* 32 (1984).

Richard Evans, *The Feminist Movement in Germany 1894 – 1933* (Sage, London and Beverly Hills, 1976).

Arlette Farge, *Vivre dans la rue à Paris au XVIIIe siècle* (Gallimard, Paris, 1979).

Beatrice Farnsworth, 'Bolshevism, the Women Question and Aleksandra Kollontai', *American Historical Review,* 81 (1976).

Beatrice Farnsworth, *Aleksandra Kollontai: socialism, feminism and the Bolshevik Revolution* (Stanford University Press, Stanford, 1980).

Christine Faure, *La Démocratie sans les femmes, essai sur le libéralisme en France* (PUF, Paris, 1985).

Les Femmes dans la Résistance, Colloque de l'UFF (Editions du Rocher, Paris, 1977).

Michael P. Fogarty, Isobel Allen and Patricia Walters, *Women in Top Jobs 1968-1979* (Heinemann, London, 1981).

M.P. Fogarty, R. and R. Rapoport, *Sex, Career and Family* (Allen and Unwin for PEP, London, 1971).

Michel Foucault, *The History of Sexuality,* I, *An Introduction,* trans. R. Hurley (Pantheon, New York and Penguin, Harmondsworth, 1978).

H. Fraenkel, *The Other Germany* (L. Drummond Ltd, London, 1942).

Geneviève Fraisse, 'Droit naturel et question de l'origine dans la pensée féministe au XIXe siècle', in *Stratégies des femmes* (Tierce, Paris, 1983).

Geneviève Fraisse, 'Singularité féministe: historiographie critique de l'histoire du féminisme en France' in *Une Histoire des femmes est-elle possible?,* ed. Michelle Perrot (Rivages, Marseilles, 1984).

France, Secrétariat d'Etat chargé de la Fonction Publique, *La Fonction publique de l'état en 1984* (Documentation française, Paris, 1984).

H.K. Geiger, *The Family in Soviet Russia* (Harvard University Press, Cambridge, Mass., 1968).

Rose Glickman, *Russian Women: workplace and society 1880 – 1914* (University of California Press, Berkeley, 1984).

William Godwin, *Memories of Mary Wollstonecraft* (Joseph Johnson, London, 1798; re-ed. by J. Middleton Murry, Constable, London, 1928 and by W. Clark Durant, New York, 1927).

Helmut Gollwitzer, Käthe Kuhn and Reinhold Schneider, *Dying we live: the final messages and records of the resisters,* trans. R.C. Kuhn (Collins, London, 1962).

Stephen Jay Gould, *The Mismeasure of Man* (Norton, New York, 1981).

Hermann Grant, H. Mommsen, H.J. Reichhardt and W. Ernst, *The German Resistance to Hitler* (Batsford, London, 1970).

Martin· Green, *The Von Richthofen Sisters: the triumphant and tragic modes of love* (Basic Books, New York, and Weidenfeld and Nicolson, London, 1974).

F. Grutzbach (ed.), *Heinrich Böll: Freies Geleit fur Ulrike Meinhof, ein Artikel und seine Folgen,* (Kiepenkeuer und Witsch, Köln, 1972).

R. Gunther, 'Women against "the Nation"': press representations of Greenham women', forthcoming article.

Anna Haag, *Das Gluck zu Leben* (Steinkopf, Stuttgart, 1978).

Lina Haag, *How Long the Night* (Gollancz, London, 1948).

N. Hadjinicolaou, 'La Liberté guidant le peuple de Delacroix devant son premier plan', *Actes de la recherche en sciences sociales,* no. 28 (1979).

N. Hadjinicolaou, 'Disarming 1830: a Parisian counter-revolution, *Block,* 4 (1981).

Stuart Hall *et al.,* *Policing the Crisis: mugging, the state and law and order* (Macmillan, London, 1978).

Fannina W. Halle, *Women in the Soviet East,* trans. M. Green (Secker and Warburg, London, 1938).

G.H. Hamilton, 'The iconographical origins of Delacroix's Liberty', in *Studies in Art and Literature for Bel da Costa Greene* (Princeton University Press, Princeton, 1984).

Carola Hansson and Karen Liden, *Moscow Women, Thirteen Interviews,* trans. G. Bothmer and G. and L. Blecher (Allison and Busby, London, 1984).

Steven Hause with Anne Kenney, *Women's Suffrage and Social Politics in the French Third Republic* (Princeton University Press, Princeton, 1984).

C.E. Hayden, 'Zhenotdel and the Bolshevik Party', *Russian History,* 3 (1976).

E. H.Herrmann and E. H. Spitz, *German Women Writers of the twentieth century* (Pergamon, Oxford and New York, 1978).

Florence Hervé and Renate Wisbar, *Leben Frei und in Frieden, Frauen gegen Faschismus* (Röderberg, Frankfurt, 1981).

L.G. Heymann, *Erlebtes-Erschautes* (Anton Hain, Meisenheim, 1977).

Patricia Hilden, *Working Women and Socialist Politics in France, 1880 – 1914, a regional study* (Oxford, Clarendon Press, 1986).

J. Hills, 'Britain', in Lovenduski and Hills (1981).

Albert Hirschman, *Shifting Involvements; private interest and public action* (Princeton University Press, Princeton, 1981 and Martin Robertson, London 1982).

Eric Hobsbawm, 'Man and Woman in Socialist Iconography', *History Workshop Journal,* no. 6 (Autumn 1978).

Ursel Hochmuth and Gertrud Meyer, *Streiflichter aus dem Hamburger Widerstand 1933-45* (Röderberg, Frankfurt, 1969).

Peter Hoffmann, *The History of the German Resistance, 1933-1945,* trans. R. Barry (MacDonald and Jane's, London, 1977).

W. Hofmann, 'Sur la Liberté de Delacroix', *Gazette des Beaux-Arts* (September 1975).

Richard Holmes, *Footsteps, adventures of a romantic biographer* (Hodder and Stoughton, London, 1985).

Alix Holt (ed.), *Selected Writings of Alexandra Kollontai,* translated from the Russian (Allison and Busby, London, 1977).

Magda Hoppstock-Huth, *Lida Gustava Heymann* (Internationale Frauenliga fur Frieden und Freiheit, Hamburg, 1948).

M. Horn, *Sozialpsychologie des Terrorismus* (Campus Verlag, Frankfurt and New York, 1982).

Olwen Hufton, 'Women in Revolution 1789 – 1796', *Past and Present,* no. 53 (1971).

B. Humphreys, *Clerical Unions in the Civil Service* (Blackwell and Mott, Oxford, 1958).

Ivan Illich, *Gender* (Marion Boyars, London and New York, 1983).

A. M. Itkina, *Revolyutsioner, Tribun, Diplomat: Stranitsy Zhizn Aleksandry Mikhailovny Kollontai* (Moscow, 1964; 2nd edn, 1970).

Lee Johnson, *The Paintings of Eugène Delacroix,* catalogue (Oxford University Press, Oxford, 1981).

L.J. Jordanova, 'The History of the Family', in Cambridge Women's Studies Group, *Women in Society, interdisciplinary essays* (Virago, London, 1981).

Cora Kaplan. 'Wild Nights (Pleasure/Sexuality/Feminism)' in *Formations of Pleasure* (Routledge and Kegan Paul, London, 1983).

Martha Kearns, *Käthe Kollwitz, Woman and Artist* (Feminist Press, New York, 1976).

Benedicta Maria Kempner, *Nonnen unter dem Hakerkreuz* (Naumann, Wurzburg, 1979).

Basile Kerblay, *Modern Soviet Society* (Methuen, London, 1983).

Christine E. King, 'Strategies for survival: an examination of the history of five Christian sects in Germany, 1933-45', in *Journal of Contemporary History,* 14 (1979).

Christoph Klessman and Falk Pingel (eds), *Gegner des Nazional-sozialismus* (Campus, Frankfurt, 1980).

A.M. Kollontai, *Izbrannye stat'i i rechi* (Moscow, 1972).

A.M. Kollontai, *Iz moei zhizni i raboty* (Moscow, 1974). (See also Holt, 1977.)

Käthe Kollwitz, *Aus meinem Leben* (List, Munich, 1958).

Elisabeth Langgasser, *In Hiding,* in Herrmann and Spitz (1978).

Claude Langlois, *Le Catholicisme au féminin* (Editions du Cerf, Paris, 1985).

Gail Warshovsky Lapidus, *Women in Soviet Society: equality, development and social change* (University of California Press, Berkeley, 1978).

Walter Laqueur, 'Interpretations of terrorism: fact, fiction and political science', *Journal of Contemporary History,* 12 (1977).

Vera Laska (ed.), *Women in the Resistance and in the Holocaust* (Greenwood, Westport, 1983).

Melvin J. Lasky, 'Lady on the Barricades', *Encounter* (July 1972).

Annedore Leber, *Conscience in Revolt* (Valentine and Mitchell, London, 1957).

V.I. Lenin, *On the Emancipation of Women* (Moscow, n.d.).

Yves Lequin *et al., Histoire des Français, XIXe et XXe siecles,* vol. 3, *Les Citoyens et la démocratie* (A. Colin, Paris, 1983).

Jacques Le Rider, *Le Cas Otto Weininger: racines de l'antiféminisme et de l'antisémitisme* (PUF, Paris, 1982).

H.D. Leuner, *When Compassion was a Crime* (Wolff, London, 1978).

Marie-Françoise Levi, *De Mères en filles, l'education des Françaises 1850-1880* (Calmann Lévy, Paris, 1984).

Joni Lovenduski, *Women in European Politics: Contemporary Feminism and Public Policy* (Wheatsheaf, Brighton, 1986).

Joni Lovenduski and Jill Hills (eds), *The Politics of the Second Electorate, women and public participation* (Routledge and Kegan Paul, London and Boston, 1981).

Richard Löwenthal and Patrick von zur Muhlen (eds), *Widerstand und Verweigerung in Deutschland 1933 bis 1945* (Dietz, Berlin, 1982).

James F. McMillan, *Housewife or Harlot: the place of women in French Society 1870-1940* (Harvester, Brighton, 1981a).

James F. McMillan, 'Clericals, anticlericals and the women's movement in France under the Third Republic', *Historical Journal,* 24, 2, (1981b).

Tatyana Mamonova (ed.), *Women and Russia: feminist writings from the Soviet Union,* trans. R. Park and C. Fitzpatrick (Blackwell, Oxford, 1984).

Anne Martin-Fugier, *La Bourgeoise: la femme au temps de Paul Bourget* (Grasset, Paris, 1983).

Tim Mason, 'Women in Germany, 1925 – 1940', *History Workshop Journal,* nos. 1 and 2 (1976).

Françoise Mayeur, *L'Enseignement secondaire des jeunes filles sous la Troisième République* (FNSP, Paris, 1977).

Françoise Mayeur, *L'Education des filles en France au XIXe siècle* (Hachette, Paris, 1979).

U.H. Meinhof and R. Rach, *Textlupe: Die verlorene Ehre der Katharina Blum* (Harrap/Nelson, London, 1981).

Gertrud Meyer, *Nacht über Hamburg* (Röderberg, Frankfurt, 1971).

Stéphane Michaud, *Muse et Madone: visages de la femme, de la Révolution française aux apparitions de Lourdes* (Seuil, Paris, 1985).

Andrée Michel, *Activité professionnelle de la femme et vie conjugale* (CRNS, Paris, 1974).

Jules Michelet, *Histoire de la Révolution française,* (Gallimard, Pléiade, 1939, 2 vols.)

Thérèse Moreau, *Le Sang de l'histoire: Michelet, l'histoire et l'idée de la femme au XIXe siècle* (Flammarion, Paris, 1982).

J. Mossuz-Lavau and M. Sineau, *Enquête sur les femmes et la politique en France* (PUF, Paris, 1983).

J. Mossuz-Lavau and M. Sineau, 'France', trans. A. Batiot, in Lovenduski and Hills (1981).

Marie Mullaney, *Revolutionary Women: gender and the socialist revolutionary role* (Praeger, New York, 1983).

Rosemarie Nave-Herz, 'Die Frau im Zwiespalt der Normenorientierung', in *Recht der Jugend und des Bildungswesens,* 21, Jahrgang, Heft 7 (1973).

Claude Nicolet, *L'Idée républicaine en France 1789-1924* (Gallimard, Paris, 1982).

Pierre Nora (ed.), *Les Lieux de la Mémoire,* vol. I, *La République* (Gallimard, Paris, 1984).

Helga Nowotny, 'Women in Public Life in Austria', in Epstein and Coser (1981).

Mona Ozouf, *L'Ecole, l'église, la république, 1870 – 1914* (Seuil, Paris, 1963 and Cana, Paris, 1982).

H. Parris, *Staff Relations in the Civil Service: fifty years of Whitleyism* (Allen and Unwin for RIPA, London, 1973).

Carole Pateman, *Participation and Democratic Theory* (Cambridge University Press, Cambridge, 1970).

Carole Pateman, 'Feminism and democracy', in G. Duncan (ed.), *Democratic Theory and Practice* (Cambridge University Press, Cambridge, 1983).

Régine Pernoud, *La Femme au temps des cathédrales* (Stock, Paris, 1984).

Michelle Perrot, 'La femme populaire rebelle', in Dufrancatel *et al.* (1979).

Michelle Perrot, 'La ménagère dans l'espace parisien au XIe siècle', *Annales de la recherche urbaine* (Autumn 1980).

Michelle Perrot (ed.), *Une Histoire des femmes est-elle possible?* (Rivages, Marseilles, 1984).

Françoise Picq, 'Qu'est-ce que le féminisme bourgeois?', in *Stratégies des femmes* (Tierce, Paris, 1984).

Cathy Porter, *Alexandra Kollontai, a biography* (Virago, London, 1980).

Henry Porter, *Lies, Damned Lies and some Exclusives* (Chatto and Windus, London, 1984).

Claude Quiguer, *Femmes et machines de 1900, lecture d'une obsession modern style* (Klincksieck, Paris, 1979).

Vicky Randall, *Women and Politics* (Macmillan, London, 1982).

Elizabeth Rawson, *The Spartan Tradition in European Thought* (Clarendon Press, Oxford, 1969).

Marie-Thérèse Renard, *La Participation des femmes à la vie politique* (Editions Ouvrières, Paris, 1965).

Margherita Rendel, *Women, Power and Political Systems* (Croom Helm, London, 1981).

E. S. Riemer and J. C. Fout, (eds), *European Women: a documentary history 1789 – 1945* (Schocken Books, New York and Harvester, Brighton, 1980).

A. Rifkin, 'The sex of French politics', *Art History* (September 1983).

S. Ringborn, 'Guérin, Delacroix and "The Liberty"', *Burlington Magazine* (1968).

Susan Rogers, 'Female forms of power and the myth of male dominance', *American Ethnologist,* vol. 2 (November 1975).

Susan Rogers, 'Rules of order, the generation of female/male relationships in two rural French communities', paper given to American Anthropological Association, November 1977.

J. Root, *Pictures of Women* (Pandora Press, London and Boston, 1984).

Margaret A. Rose, *Marx's Lost Aesthetic* (Cambridge University Press, Cambridge, 1984).

Jean-Jacques Rousseau, *The Social Contract and Discourses,* trans. G. D. H. Cole (Everyman edition, Dent, London, 1973).

Pierre Samuel, *Amazones, Guerrières et Gaillardes* (Editions Complexe, Brussels, 1975).

D. E. Sanzone, 'Women in Politics, a study of political leadership in the UK, France and the Federal Republic of Germany', in Epstein and Coser (1981).

Rudolf Schlesinger (ed.), *Changing Attitudes in Soviet Russia: The Family* (Routledge and Kegan Paul, London, 1949).

Inge Scholl, *Students against Tyranny* (Wesleyan Union Press, Connecticut, 1970).

Martine Segalen, *Love and Power in the Peasant Family,* trans. S. Matthews (Blackwell, Oxford, 1983).

Richard Sennett, *The Fall of Public Man* (Knopf, New York and Cambridge University Press, Cambridge, 1977).

J. Siltanen and M. Stanworth, 'The politics of private woman and public man', in J. Siltanen and M. Stanworth, *Women and the Public Sphere* (Hutchinson, London, 1984).

Bonnie Smith, *Ladies of the Leisure Class, the bourgeoises of northern France in the nineteenth century* (Princeton University Press, Princeton, 1981).

Jessica Smith, *Women in Soviet Russia* (Vanguard Press, New York, 1929).

M. Sokolowska, 'Women in decision-making elites: the case of Poland', in Epstein and Coser (1981).

Charles Sowerwine, *Sisters or Citizens, women and socialism in France since 1876* (Cambridge University Press, Cambridge, 1982).

M. Stacey and M. Price, *Women and Power* (Athlone Press, London, 1981).

L. Steinberg, *The Sexuality of Christ in Renaissance Art and in Modern Oblivion* (Pantheon, New York, 1983).

Richard Stites, *The Women's Liberation Movement in Russia* (Princeton University Press, Princeton, 1978).

John Strachey, *The Strangled Cry* (Bodley Head, London, 1962).

Stratégies des femmes (Editions Tierce, Paris, 1984).

S. Streek, E. Bock-Rosenthal and C. Haase, 'Political attitudes of women in high status occupations in West Germany', in Epstein and Coser (1981).

V. Subramaniam, 'Representative bureaucracy: a reassessment', *American Political Science Review*, 61 (1967).

Donald Sutherland, *France 1789 – 1815, Revolution and Counter-Revolution* (Fontana, London, 1985).

Gerda Szepansky, *Frauen Leisten Widerstand 1933 – 1945* (Fischer, Frankfurt, 1983).

K. Theweleit, *Mannerphantasien* (Roter Stern, Frankfurt, 1983).

G. Thuillier, 'La Révolution féminine des bureaux 1900 – 1940', I and II, *Revue administrative*, nos. 210 and 211 (Nov.-Dec. 1982, Jan. 1983).

G. Thuillier and J. Tulard, *Histoire de l'administration française* (PUF, coll. Que sais-je? Paris, 1984).

Claire Tomalin, *The Life and Death of Mary Wollstonecraft* (Weidenfeld and Nicolson, London, 1974).

Sylvana Tomaselli, 'The Enlightenment debate on women', *History Workshop Journal*, no. 20 (1985).

H. Toussaint (ed.), *'La Liberté guidant le peuple' de Delacroix*, catalogue (Réunion des Musées Nationaux, Paris, 1982).

L. Trotsky, *Problems of Everyday Life and Other Writings* (Monad Press, New York, 1973).

E. Vallance, *Women in the House* (Athlone Press, London, 1979).

Yvonne Verdier, *Façons de dire et façons de faire: la laveuse, la couturière, la cuisinière* (Gallimard, Paris, 1979).

Herman Vinke, *The Short Life of Sophie Scholl,* trans. H. Pachter (Harper and Row, New York, 1984).

Marina Warner, *Monuments and Maidens* (Weidenfeld and Nicolson, London, 1985).

Daniela Weiland, *Geschichte der Frauen Emanzipation: Deutschland und Osterreich* (Econ, Dusseldorf, 1983).

Gunther Weisenborn, *Der lautlose Aufstand* (Röderberg, Frankfurt, 1974).

P. Wheatcroft, 'Women in charge', *Working Woman* (March 1985).

Rosalind Williams, *Dream Worlds: mass consumption in the late nineteenth century* (University of California Press, Berkeley and Los Angeles, 1982).

R. W. Williams, 'Heinrich Böll and the Katharina Blum debate', *Critical Quarterly,* 21 (1979).

Christa Wolf, *A Model Childhood* (Farrar Strauss, New York, 1980).

Lore Wolf, *One Life Is Not Enough* (People's Publications, Newcastle upon Tyne, 1982).

Mary Wollstonecraft, *Thoughts on the Education of Daughters, with Reflections on Female Conduct in the more important Duties of life* (Joseph Johnson, London, 1787).

Mary Wollstonecraft, *Mary. A Fiction* (Joseph Johnson, London 1788) and ed. James Kinsky and Gary Kelly (Oxford University Press, Oxford and New York, 1976 and 1980).

Mary Wollstonecraft, *A Vindication of the Rights of Men in a Letter to the Right Honourable Edmund Burke occasioned by His Reflections on the Revolution in France* (2nd edn, Joseph Johnson, London, 1790).

Mary Wollstonecraft, *A Vindication of the Rights of Woman with Strictures on Political and Moral Subjects* (Joseph Johnson, London, 1792); ed. Miriam Cramnick (Pelican Books, Harmondsworth, 1975); ed. Carol Parker (New York, 1976).

Mary Wollstonecraft, *An Historical and Moral View of the Origin and of the Progress of the French Revolution* (Joseph Johnson, London, 1794).

Mary Wollstonecraft, *The Wrongs of Woman or Maria. A Fragment,* in *Posthumous Works,* Vols I & II, ed. W. Godwin and G.G. and J. Robinson (Joseph Johnson, London, 1798); edited (together with *Mary*) by James Kinsky and Gary Kelly (Oxford University Press, Oxford and New York, 1976 and 1980).

Virginia Woolf, *The Common Reader* (Hogarth Press, London, 1925 and Harcourt Brace Jovanovich, New York, 1925).

Virginia Woolf, *Women and Writing,* ed. Michèle Barrett (Women's

Press, London, 1979).

Vincent Wright, *The Government and Politics of France* (Hutchinson, 2nd edn, London, 1983).

Theodore Zeldin, *France 1848 – 1945* (Oxford University Press, Oxford, 1972 – 73).

Klara Zetkin, *Reminiscences of Lenin* (Modern Books, London, 1929).

Gerda Zorn and Gertrud Meyer, *Frauen gegen Hitler* (Röderberg, Frankfurt, 1974).

Index of Proper Names